Natural Wonders

EXPLORE AMERICA

Natural Wonders

Reader's Digest

THE READER'S DIGEST ASSOCIATION, INC.
Pleasantville, New York / Montreal

NATURAL WONDERS was created and produced by ST. REMY MULTIMEDIA INC.

STAFF FOR NATURAL WONDERS
Series Editor: Elizabeth Cameron
Art Director: Solange Laberge
Editor: Elizabeth Warrington Lewis
Assistant Editor: Neale McDevitt
Photo Researchers: Geneviève Monette, Linda Castle
Cartography: Hélène Dion, David Widgington
Designer: Anne-Marie Lemay
Research Editor: Robert B. Ronald
Contributing Researcher: Olga Dzatko
Researcher: Jennifer Meltzer
Copy Editor: Judy Yelon
Index: Linda Cordella Cournoyer
System Coordinator: Éric Beaulieu
Technical Support: Mathieu Raymond-Beaubien, Jean Sirois
Scanner Operators: Martin Francoeur, Sara Grynspan

ST. REMY STAFF
PRESIDENT, CHIEF EXECUTIVE OFFICER: Fernand Lecoq
PRESIDENT, CHIEF OPERATING OFFICER: Pierre Léveillé
VICE PRESIDENT, FINANCE: Natalie Watanabe
MANAGING EDITOR: Carolyn Jackson
MANAGING ART DIRECTOR: Diane Denoncourt
PRODUCTION MANAGER: Michelle Turbide

Writers: Christine Colasurdo—Mount St. Helens
Michael Collier/Rose Houk—Death Valley
David Dunbar—El Yunque
Lori Erickson—Mammoth Cave
Kim Heacox—Glacier Bay
Jim Henderson—Big Thicket National Preserve; Niagara Falls
Steven Krolak—Hells Canyon; The Great Basin
Rick Marsi—The Great Wass Archipelago

Contributing Writers: Adriana Barton, Maxine Cutler, Brian Polan

Address any comments about *Natural Wonders*
to U.S. Editor, General Books, c/o Customer Service,
Reader's Digest, Pleasantville, NY 10570

READER'S DIGEST STAFF
Editor: Kathryn Bonomi
Art Editor: Eleanor Kostyk
Assistant Production Supervisor: Mike Gallo
Editorial Assistant: Mary Jo McLean

READER'S DIGEST GENERAL BOOKS
Editor-in-Chief, Books and Home
Entertainment: Barbara J. Morgan
Editor, U.S. General Books: David Palmer
Executive Editor: Gayla Visalli
Art Director: Joel Musler

Opening photographs
Cover: Capitol Reef National Park, Utah
Back Cover: Campobello Island, New Brunswick
Page 2: Glacier Bay National Park and Preserve, Alaska
Page 5: Bar Island, Maine

Library of Congress Cataloging in Publication Data

Natural wonders.
        p.   cm.—(Explore America)
    Includes index.
    ISBN 0-89577-904-8
    1. United States—Tours. 2. Natural areas—United States—
Guidebooks.   3. National parks and preserves—United States—
Guidebooks.   4. Natural history—United States—Guidebooks.
I. Reader's Digest Association. II. Series.
    E158.N33   1997
    917.304'929—dc20   96-38845

CONTENTS

THE GREAT WASS ARCHIPELAGO ▪ *MAINE* 8

NIAGARA FALLS ▪ *NEW YORK* 18

EL YUNQUE ▪ *PUERTO RICO* 28

MAMMOTH CAVE ▪ *KENTUCKY* 38

BIG THICKET NATIONAL PRESERVE ▪ *TEXAS* 48

DEATH VALLEY ▪ *CALIFORNIA* 58

THE GREAT BASIN ▪ *UTAH* 70

HELLS CANYON ▪ *OREGON, IDAHO* 82

MOUNT ST. HELENS ▪ *WASHINGTON* 94

GLACIER BAY ▪ *ALASKA* 106

GAZETTEER: *Traveler's Guide to Natural Wonders* 118

INDEX 142

CREDITS AND ACKNOWLEDGMENTS 144

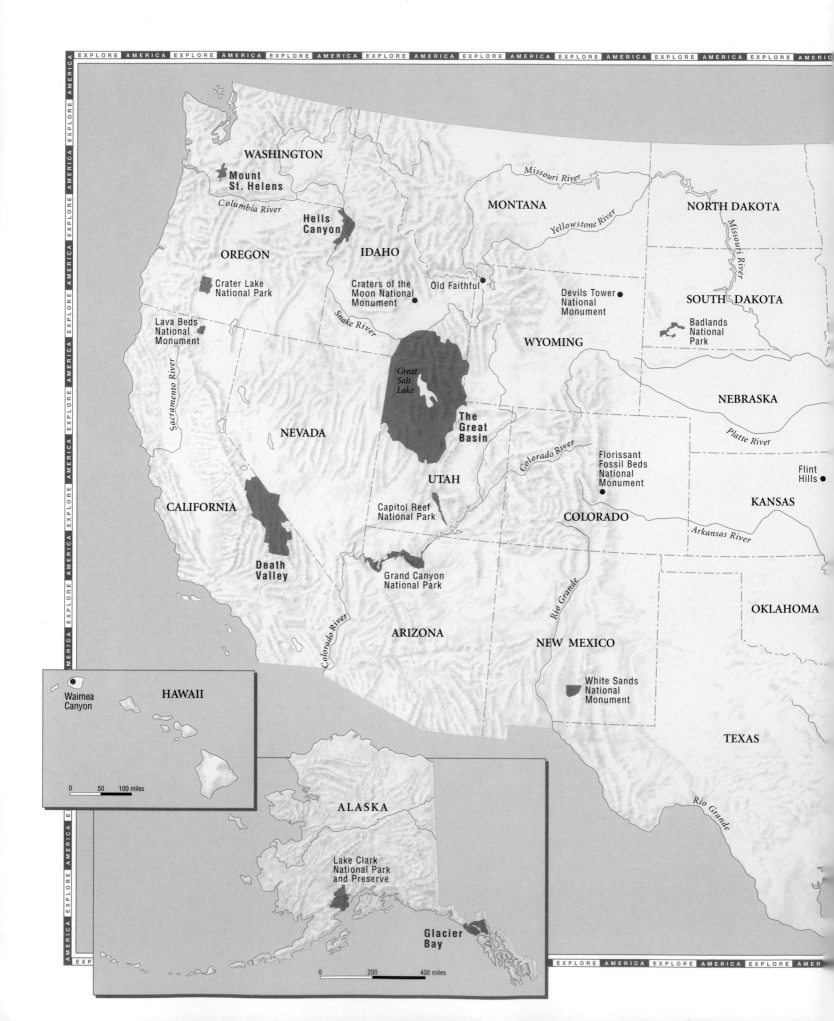

WASHINGTON

Mount
St. Helens

Columbia River

MONTANA

Missouri River

NORTH DAKOTA

Hells
Canyon

OREGON

IDAHO

Yellowstone River

Missouri River

Crater Lake
National Park

Craters of the
Moon National
Monument

Old Faithful

Devils Tower
National
Monument

SOUTH DAKOTA

Lava Beds
National
Monument

Snake River

Badlands
National
Park

WYOMING

Sacramento River

Great
Salt
Lake

The
Great
Basin

NEBRASKA

NEVADA

Platte River

Colorado River

Florissant
Fossil Beds
National
Monument

Flint
Hills

UTAH

KANSAS

CALIFORNIA

Capitol Reef
National Park

COLORADO

Arkansas River

Grand Canyon
National Park

Death
Valley

Colorado River

Rio Grande

OKLAHOMA

ARIZONA

NEW MEXICO

White Sands
National
Monument

TEXAS

Rio Grande

Waimea
Canyon

HAWAII

0   50   100 miles

ALASKA

Lake Clark
National Park
and Preserve

Glacier
Bay

0   200   400 miles

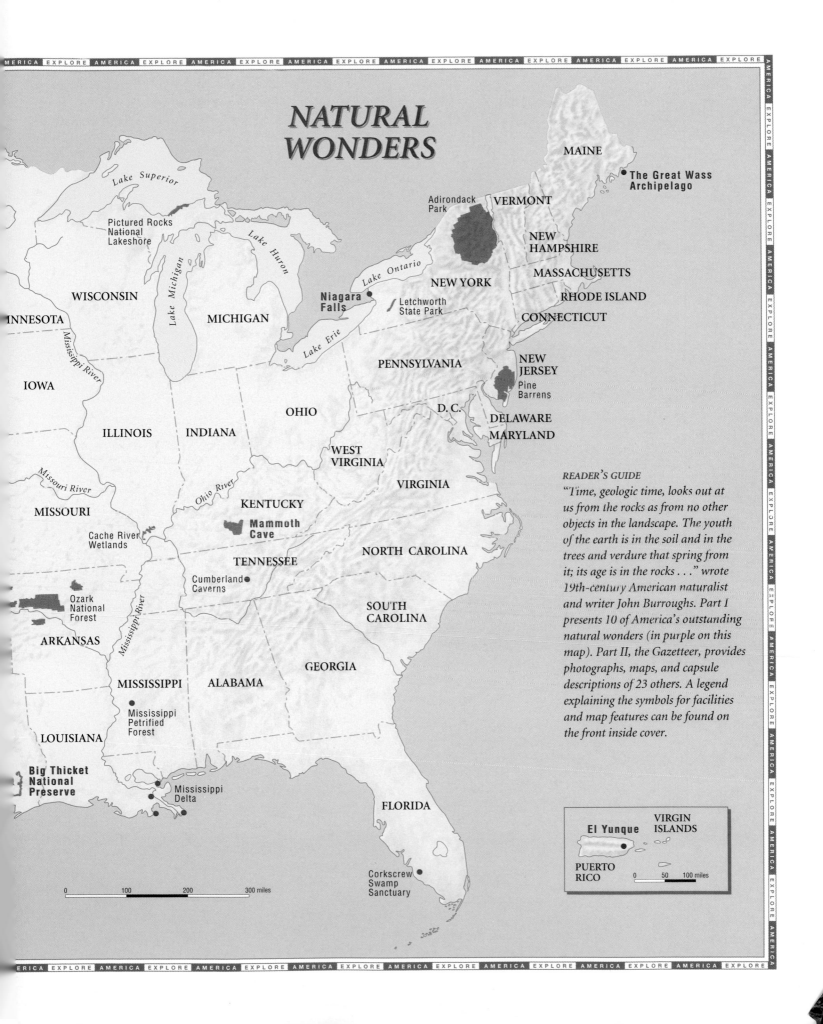

THE GREAT WASS ARCHIPELAGO

Jutting into the ocean off the coast of Maine, these islands are known for their robust yet fragile beauty.

Scoured by wind, drenched with rain, and enshrouded in dank coastal fog, the Great Wass Archipelago—a group of islands off the coast of Maine—thrives in a climate buffeted by the salt and the sea. The nearly two dozen islands are clumped like a handful of maritime marbles off the coastal village of Jonesport, where lobster traps heaped on the docks outnumber the fishermen who work them. Each island is unique. Some, such as Great Wass and Head Harbor, are several miles long; others are no more than several acres of hardscrabble. High, rolling landscapes topped by dense forests of spruce and fir are poised next to islands dominated by lowland bog or barren domes of cracked granite that thrust starkly out of the cobalt blue sea.

This is a hard land, where people go when they have grown weary of their secure and civilized ways. Here, amid the gnarled jack pines that cling stubbornly to granite boulders is a strange and

resilient landscape where the wind-whipped sting of the sea awakens a sense of reverence for nature in its wild, unruly state.

The Great Wass Archipelago was created 380 to 420 million years ago when molten magma, bubbling deep within the earth's core, oozed toward the surface and crystallized into igneous rock formations. Chiseled away by time and the elements, the surrounding rock eroded, leaving behind granite outcroppings called plutons. The composition of plutons varies depending on where they are formed. However, granite samples taken from the various islands of the Great Wass are similar in composition, suggesting that at one time the archipelago may have been a single large island.

Part of the archipelago's unique character stems from the fact that it is situated where the waters of the Gulf of Maine collide with those of the Bay of Fundy. This confluence has created a microclimate that swaddles the archipelago in cool, moist air year-round and offers sanctuary from the extreme temperatures that affect the interior of Maine and other islands to the north and south. The archipelago's subarctic climate ensures that it is never hot in summer or cold in winter.

Where the cooler and more oxygenated water of the Bay of Fundy mixes with that of the Gulf of Maine, whose high tides and strong currents sweep rich nutrients from the ocean bottom to the surface, the sea is thick with plankton—the building block of the marine food-chain. While visitors can't see the microscopic plankton in the water that surrounds the archipelago, they certainly enjoy watching the high concentration of seals and whales drawn to this major feeding area.

UNCOMMON VEGETATION

The islands are home to vegetation that is uncommon not only to the state of Maine but to the United States as well. Jack pines, the most northerly of all pines, are at the southern edge of their range in these island enclaves. A sprawling 550-acre jack pine grove on Great Wass Island represents Maine's second-largest stand of these short-lived trees. Creeping across exposed bedrock like vine tendrils, the roots of the trees mold themselves to each granite contour and find footholds in the humus-filled cracks. The bonsai-shaped jack pines flourish in soil other trees find inhospitable, under climatic conditions too harsh for many temperate species.

Amateur botanists should also keep their eyes open for other plant species usually found in more northerly climates. Bogs and shorelines are dotted with delicate beach head iris, oysterleaf, bird's-eye primrose, and baked-apple berry plants—a relative of the raspberry whose golden berries can be used to make delicious jams and pies.

Relatively unknown to people outside the region, the unique environments of the Great Wass Archipelago caught the attention of an international conservation group called The Nature Conservancy, an agency dedicated to protecting the habitats of endangered plants and animals worldwide. Looking to shield the spectacular terrain from the encroachment of civilization, the Maine chapter of the conservancy began purchasing the islands in 1978. Today, the chapter owns six islands and helps protect the wild character of four others.

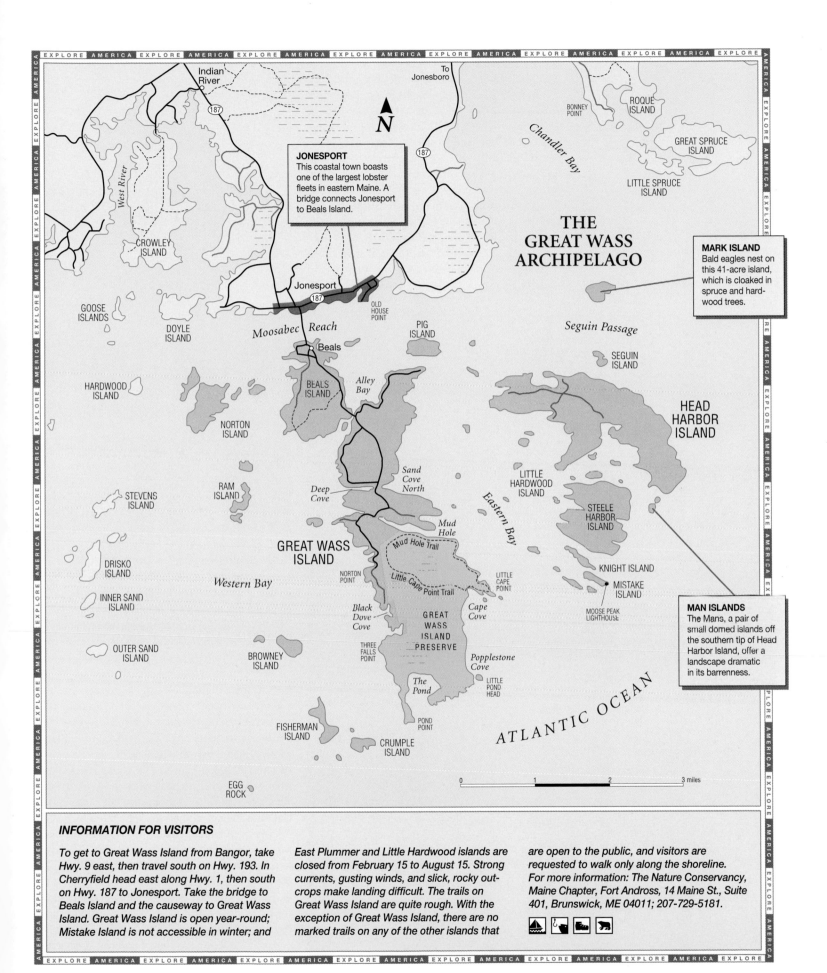

JONESPORT
This coastal town boasts one of the largest lobster fleets in eastern Maine. A bridge connects Jonesport to Beals Island.

THE GREAT WASS ARCHIPELAGO

MARK ISLAND
Bald eagles nest on this 41-acre island, which is cloaked in spruce and hardwood trees.

MAN ISLANDS
The Mans, a pair of small domed islands off the southern tip of Head Harbor Island, offer a landscape dramatic in its barrenness.

To Jonesboro

Chandler Bay

BONNEY POINT

ROQUE ISLAND

GREAT SPRUCE ISLAND

LITTLE SPRUCE ISLAND

Indian River

187

West River

CROWLEY ISLAND

GOOSE ISLANDS

DOYLE ISLAND

Jonesport

187

Moosabec Reach

Beals

OLD HOUSE POINT

PIG ISLAND

Seguin Passage

SEGUIN ISLAND

HARDWOOD ISLAND

BEALS ISLAND

Alley Bay

NORTON ISLAND

LITTLE HARDWOOD ISLAND

HEAD HARBOR ISLAND

STEELE HARBOR ISLAND

RAM ISLAND

STEVENS ISLAND

Sand Cove North

Deep Cove

Eastern Bay

Mud Hole

Mud Hole Trail

KNIGHT ISLAND

MISTAKE ISLAND

MOOSE PEAK LIGHTHOUSE

DRISKO ISLAND

GREAT WASS ISLAND

Western Bay

NORTON POINT

Little Cape Point Trail

LITTLE CAPE POINT

INNER SAND ISLAND

Black Dove Cove

THREE FALLS POINT

GREAT WASS ISLAND PRESERVE

Cape Cove

LITTLE POND HEAD

Popplestone Cove

OUTER SAND ISLAND

BROWNEY ISLAND

The Pond

POND POINT

ATLANTIC OCEAN

FISHERMAN ISLAND

CRUMPLE ISLAND

EGG ROCK

0   1   2   3 miles

INFORMATION FOR VISITORS

To get to Great Wass Island from Bangor, take Hwy. 9 east, then travel south on Hwy. 193. In Cherryfield head east along Hwy. 1, then south on Hwy. 187 to Jonesport. Take the bridge to Beals Island and the causeway to Great Wass Island. Great Wass Island is open year-round; Mistake Island is not accessible in winter; and East Plummer and Little Hardwood islands are closed from February 15 to August 15. Strong currents, gusting winds, and slick, rocky outcrops make landing difficult. The trails on Great Wass Island are quite rough. With the exception of Great Wass Island, there are no marked trails on any of the other islands that are open to the public, and visitors are requested to walk only along the shoreline. For more information: The Nature Conservancy, Maine Chapter, Fort Andross, 14 Maine St., Suite 401, Brunswick, ME 04011; 207-729-5181.

In order to preserve the special habitats of the archipelago, the conservancy recommends that travelers restrict their visits to Great Wass Island, which has several trails and a broad shoreline, and Mistake Island, which has a boardwalk trail that runs the length of the island and leads to a Coast Guard lighthouse. As even one careless step can cause severe damage to the terrain, visitors who keep to the trails, shoreline, and boardwalk will ensure that this fragile environment is protected for future generations.

Access to many of the islands is limited, and other islands are privately owned. Great Wass Island and the 1,540-acre Nature Conservancy Preserve

GUIDING LIGHT
The Moose Peak Lighthouse, below, a beacon of safety for wayward mariners, stands on Mistake Island.

that occupies most of its southern half, can be reached easily from the Maine coast by car. Each island is different in character. Knight Island is forested by stands of stunted spruce trees. Little Hardwood Island is the preferred nesting habitat for bald eagles, which can be seen perched on high treetops scanning the shoreline for food. Dome-shaped Crumple Island is nearly bare of vegetation, its fissured granite worn by time and crashing waves. Low-lying, almost treeless, Mistake Island features open heathland.

When motorists cross the bridge linking Beals to its neighbor island, Great Wass, the trappings of modern life fall away. The Great Wass Island Preserve is a pristine place, unmarred by human activity, where hikers tread on the needle-carpeted trails that wind through the preserve.

Visitors to Great Wass Island will quickly learn that the warning "prepare for the worst" could very well serve as the region's motto. Damp intemperate weather launches frequent assaults upon these rocky shores. Wind, saturated with salt spray, sometimes whips the rain sideways, blowing hats into the water and chilling lightly dressed explorers.

When the weather allows, however, spectacular days do dawn here. At such times, wafting breezes

COASTAL BOUNTY
Rows of wharves along Moosabec Reach, left, are cluttered with empty lobster traps to be used on the next day's shellfishing expeditions.

FOGGED IN
Herring gulls, above, take refuge on some offshore rocks as a thick fog moves in. The most common of all gull species, the herring gull is often seen cracking open clams by dropping them on rocks.

carry the sounds of waves slapping against the rocks into the heart of the island's spruce groves, and calm coastal waters reflect a pale blue sky.

On occasions such as these, visitors can meander through the fragrant stands of spruce and balsam that cover much of Great Wass Island. White birches glow like wispy ghosts in the center of the dark forests, and a soft carpet of sphagnum moss muffles hikers' footsteps and mutes the bright calls of chickadees that flit in the branches.

Massive granite boulders are strewn throughout the dense growths of spruce. Many of these serve as nurse rocks for tree seedlings that extend their roots into the rich layer of mosses and lichens, which collect on the rocks over time. In spring, beds of Canada mayflowers and bunchberries burst forth in bloom, adding their delicate white blossoms to an evergreen scene. Bubbling over gold-colored cobbles, a stream enters the soft, hushed world, its water stained the color of tea by tannin seeping from a bog just upstream. At high tide, the pink granite headlands on the island's ocean-facing shore are pummeled by windswept waves.

To fully appreciate the stark beauty of Great Wass Island's interior and coastal features, visitors should "walk the loop." This excursion begins with a two-mile hike on Little Cape Point Trail through mossy woods, past large open bogs, and along exposed bedrock ridges studded with tenacious jack pines.

The challenging trail climbs up to several open granite ledges where walkers are afforded expansive views of the bog. Called heaths by local residents, these treeless bogs originated thousands of years ago, when sphagnum moss began accumulating in basins left behind by retreating glaciers. Sphagnums are large mosses that absorb and retain water, giving the moss a spongy quality. However, unlike the sagging, or quaking, bogs that are common to the mainland, these dome-shaped depositories of acid and peaty soil are relatively firm under foot. Called coastal raised bogs because they bulge from the surrounding terrain, they are unique to the harsh marine environs of New Brunswick, Nova Scotia, and Maine. Low shrubs, cranberry and black crowberry bushes, and carnivorous sundew and pitcher plants grow on the heaths.

Mounting the rocky ledges, hikers weave through hundreds of jack pines whose shapes have been stunted and gnarled by the rigors of a harsh environment and constant marine exposure. Dipping quickly, the trail winds through a spruce stand so dense it blocks all but a few shafts of sunlight.

ROCKY BEACH
Huge granite boulders, their edges burnished by the relentless action of wind and water, line Cape Cove, above.

Pushing on toward the sea, travelers feel the tingle of a fine salt mist on their cheeks. Patches of white-capped ocean appear now and then through the trees as the trail heads toward the boulder-strewn shoreline. Then, just past a copse of stunted spruce trees, the trail opens up on the wild shore. At high tide the deep blue water, whipped into a froth by the gusting wind, fills Cape Cove to the brim. Looking like the backs of whales breaching the surface, huge granite boulders break through the water from the cove and across Eastern Bay.

LOW-TIDE TREASURES

From this vantage point, visitors are often treated to the sight of dozens of harbor seals basking on the rocky slabs. The seals' glossy oversized bodies shimmer in the sunlight as the surf thumps their rugged fortress.

On shore above the high-tide line, a rubble of loose cobbles makes walking a test of a hiker's balance. Worn smooth by the surf, the cobbles are littered with scattered mounds of mussel shells, once black and now dulled a pale purple, their pearly insides bleached bone white. Hardy beach peas tucked among the rocks display their showy pink blossoms. Sedum plants poke through the crannies of nearby boulders, their succulent, spiraling leaves topped with beautiful purplish blooms.

When the tide goes out, this shore will look radically different. Like a large tidal bathtub after its plug has been taken out, Cape Cove's rocky bottom will lie fully exposed, plastered with limp strands of rockweed and ribbons of kelp. Low tide at Cape Cove is a beachcomber's dream. Shallow tide pools, encircled by slippery heaps of seaweed, reveal secrets of a world between water and land. The mussels, small mollusks called periwinkles, and minuscule life forms that gather in these pools are evidence of the rich variety of marine life that lives here. Overhead, a bald eagle lifts off its tree perch, flaps over the high-tide line for a few hundred yards, then turns seaward on its wide, steady wings.

As the eagle soars from view, a lobster boat chugs closer. Roused from their siesta, a colony of seals slips into the ocean swell. They dive underwater, splashing their rear flippers, and remain submerged for a brief moment before popping back to the surface. Heads bobbing in the swirling water and swiveling like brown periscopes, the seals watch the boat go out to sea. As the boat passes, the seals ride the next wave back to their rocky sanctuary.

PROTECTED SPECIES

A cooing sound arises from the waters beyond the tide line, where a raft of common eider ducks has convened. These sturdy sea ducks with long, sloping bills are frequent visitors here. The females are russet brown and the males boast a striking combination of jet black, cream, and snow white, with a small patch of sea-green plumage on their heads. This convivial scene would have been quite different at the end of the 19th century, when eider nests were plundered for eggs and the ducks were shot for food. Under the onslaught, the region's resident eider population was decimated. By 1905 less than a dozen pairs of eiders still bred along the Maine coast, this bird's southernmost breeding location.

In 1918 the Migratory Bird Treaty Act was passed, which outlawed year-round hunting and pillaging of the eggs of migratory birds. As a protected species, eider ducks began to make a comeback in the Great Wass Archipelago. Now hundreds of eiders congregate off the islands each spring during mating season. Pointing its beak straight up to the sky, a male eider issues forth its courtship call. The low melodic moan possesses a humanlike quality that can carry great distances over water.

After taking in the sights and sounds of this secluded beach, hikers can continue on the loop's second leg: a one-and-a-half-mile walk north along the coast to a spot where a cairn marks the eastern end of another of the preserve's major walking paths—the Mud Hole Trail. Heading inland along the fjordlike shoreline of Mud Hole cove, visitors wind their way through a small stand of birch and hardwood where ospreys sometimes nest. On occasion an osprey can be seen soaring above its nest with a large fish clutched in its talons. Continuing westward, the trail penetrates an aromatic spruce forest patched with moss and lichen. Travelers complete the five-mile hike at a point near the preserve's parking area where the Mud Hole and Little Cape Point trails converge.

Making their way back to their cars, visitors can still hear the gentle whisper of the wind rippling through the trees. In the distance, the cry of an eider rides the low-flying fog that rolls in from the sea. The once-blue sky has grown overcast and threatening—as if to warn people not to tarry too long on this rocky enclave. For all its rugged beauty, the Great Wass Archipelago is surprisingly delicate and needs protection.

A ROCK AND A HARD PLACE
Delicate silverweed blossoms, left, push their way up through cracks in the rock at Black Duck Cove on Great Wass Island.

GIANT CREATURES OF THE DEEP
Two humpback whales, left, churn the ocean surface as they break through the waters off the coast of Maine.

NEARBY SITES & ATTRACTIONS

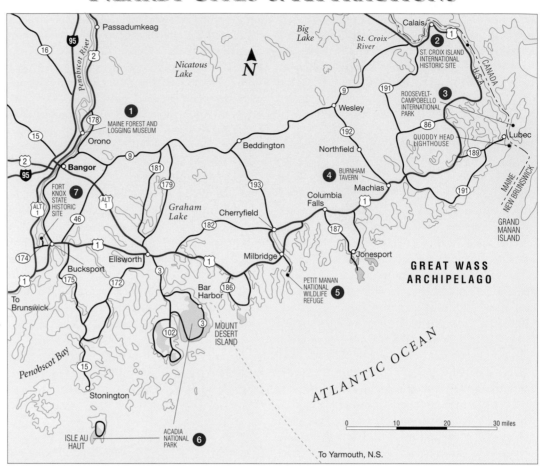

The 1770 Burnham Tavern, below, has maintained its rustic charm for more than two centuries. The original sign still hangs outside the tavern. It reads "Drink for the Thirsty. Food for the Hungry. Lodging for the Weary and Good Keeping for Horses."

1 MAINE FOREST AND LOGGING MUSEUM, MAINE

This 275-acre museum, located on the site of an 18th-century sawmill, is devoted to recounting the history of Maine's forest and logging heritage. The site is the outlet of Chemo Pond on Blackman Stream, where a water-powered sawmill was built and operated by a lawyer named Oliver Leonard in the 1790's. Leonard's Mills has been rebuilt in a village setting with a millpond, covered bridge, black-

smith's shop, early settler's barn, and log cabin. The complex also includes a steam-powered Lombard log hauler that was built around 1900 and is being reconditioned. A self-guided tour begins at the gate, passes through the village, and extends along nature trails through a mixed wood and mature softwood forest. Markers indicate each tree species' importance to the lumber industry. Demonstrations illustrate various aspects of logging, from life in a logging camp and the dangers of spring log drives to wood harvesting and forest management. The survey concludes with exhibits on today's lumber and paper industries. Located on the campus of the University of Maine in Orono on Hwy. 2.

2 ST. CROIX ISLAND INTERNATIONAL HISTORIC SITE, MAINE

St. Croix Island was the site of France's first attempt at colonization in North America. The island near the mouth of the St. Croix River was chosen in 1604 by the expedition leaders—Pierre de Gua, Sieur de Monts, and Samuel de Champlain—to be the site of a fur trading post. The 79 men who set up camp on St. Croix were ill-prepared for the harsh Maine winter, during which the outpost's supply of drinking water ran out, and scurvy killed half the men. In spring the colonists who had survived the terrible winter moved to mainland Port Royal. A lighthouse, built on the island in 1856 to guide ships into the

river, burned down in 1976. The island today looks much as it did when the first colonists arrived. The only evidence of human habitation is a plaque commemorating the 17th-century French settlement. The island is accessible by boat from Calais.

3 ROOSEVELT-CAMPOBELLO INTERNATIONAL PARK, NEW BRUNSWICK

It was on Campobello Island that Franklin Delano Roosevelt spent much of his happy youth and where, in 1921, he was stricken with polio. The international park was established in 1964 to honor the man who served as president for four terms through the Depression years and most of World War II. The 34-room Roosevelt Cottage contains Roosevelt's belongings, including his fishing rod and canes. Hiking trails and roads wind through the heavily wooded 2,800-acre park, leading visitors to rocky shores and serene coves. The East Quoddy Head Lighthouse, a prime spot for whale watching, is on the island but is not part of the park. The lighthouse can be reached by foot at low tide. Located on Campobello Island.

4 BURNHAM TAVERN, MAINE

When news of the outbreak of the Revolutionary War at Lexington and Concord reached Machias in 1775, the men of the settlement gathered at Burnham Tavern to discuss their stance. They met here again later and decided to erect the Liberty Pole on the village green as a symbol of their defiance to British rule. On another occasion at the tavern they made the plans that culminated in the capture of the Royal Navy ship, the *Margaretta,* on June 12, 1775—in what was the first naval engagement of the American Revolution. The tavern was privately owned until 1910 when it was given to the Daughters of the American Revolution. The tavern now houses collections that pertain to the Revolution, including weapons, clothing, and documents. Located on Free and Main streets in Machias.

5 PETIT MANAN NATIONAL WILDLIFE REFUGE, MAINE

Occupying a mainland peninsula and several offshore islands, this 3,335-acre refuge is the nesting ground for thousands of waterfowl. It is also a popular migration stop on the Atlantic Flyway. The refuge attracts a wide variety of bird species because of a diverse topography that includes blueberry and hay fields, spruce forests, bogs, and fresh- and saltwater marshes. Northern harriers, kestrels, and merlins are among the birds who stop in the refuge on their long migratory flights, and blackburnian and magnolia warblers are two of the many species that nest here. Colonies of sea birds, such as Atlantic puffins, roseate terns, and razorbills, take up residence along the shore, and peregrine falcons and eagles are frequently seen soaring overhead. The refuge is home to 5,000 sea ducks, and in the late summer as many as 15,000 eiders have been sighted here. Two trails wind through the refuge and offer spectacular views of the birds. A boardwalk links the islands to the mainland section. Located nine miles south of Millbridge off Hwy. 1.

6 ACADIA NATIONAL PARK, MAINE

This 35,000-acre park, the first national park established east of the Mississippi River, encompasses mainland Schoodic Peninsula and several offshore islands, including Mount Desert Island and Isle au Haut. Millions of visitors are drawn every summer to the park's long white sandy beaches, rocky shorelines, and crashing seas. The wooded interior of the park is accessible via old carriage roads. The roads were built under the direction of oil magnate John D. Rockefeller, who, along with George Dorr, led the way for the park's creation in 1919. The roads are used for cross-country skiing and snowshoeing in the winter, and are perfect for a summer hike. The Champlain and Cadillac mountains, which reach heights of only 1,530 feet, offer vistas of the surrounding landscape and sea. The summits are devoid of vegetation, providing an unobstructed view of Somes Sound, a deep fjord that slices through Mount Desert Island. The sound was created by glacial activity during the last ice age. The visitor center is located three miles north of Bar Harbor on Hwy. 3.

7 FORT KNOX STATE HISTORIC SITE, MAINE

Fort Knox was built at the mouth of the Penobscot River in the 1840's to protect the city of Bangor from British invasion during border disputes. Construction of the fort began in 1844 when the border of Maine and New Brunswick was a point of contention between the United States and Britain. Although the fort never saw military action, it was used to house Union troops during the Civil War and American troops during the Spanish-American War. Visitors can tour the parade ground, soldiers' quarters, powder magazines, batteries, and the bakery. On display are hotshot furnaces, and both 10- and 15-inch Rodman cannons. Located two miles west of Bucksport off Hwy. 174.

The rocky shore of Acadia National Park, left, shrouded in thick fog and buffeted by waves, epitomizes Maine's marine attractions.

A white-tailed deer in Petit Manan National Wildlife Refuge, above, stands poised to bound away at the slightest sound.

NIAGARA FALLS

Carved from the rock by thundering torrents of water, Niagara Falls is nature at its most sublime.

From the deck of the excursion boat *Maid of the Mist*, the distant sheets of cascading water are full of sound and fury. Like a thunderstorm, Niagara Falls menaces even from afar as it rumbles in all its unchecked fury.

Then, as the bow of the boat strains against the swift currents of Niagara Gorge, the falls draw nearer, seem to rise up, and suddenly appear even taller than they are—an illusion conjured, perhaps, by the collision of sensory signals. At peak tourist times, more than 100,000 cubic feet of water a second slide over the edge of the dolostone bed of the Niagara River and free fall 167 feet into a roiling abyss of spume, dragging wind and tumult along as well.

The boat motors past American Falls, whose descent has been shortened by caprock rubble deposited at its base over the course of centuries of erosion. This half of the double cataract was formed between 500 and 700 years ago as the falls—it was then a single flow—gnawed its way backward from the Niagara Escarpment and

INTERNATIONAL BORDER
Seen from the air, the Niagara River, above, splits into two falls: Horseshoe Falls on the Canadian side of the border and American Falls on the United States side, beyond Goat Island.

SHORTENED DESCENT
Overleaf: A view of the American Falls shows the pile of talus that has collected at the foot of the drop. Sometimes called the honeymoon capital of the world, the falls attract thousands of newlyweds each year.

spread across the Tonawanda plain. When it reached its present location, the less powerful eastern cataract was not strong enough to wash away the rocky debris, known as talus, that had collapsed and collected below.

Nosing past one-and-a-half-mile-long Goat Island, which separates the two cataracts, the boat's engines churn against the powerful pull of the rapids. Deftly maneuvering to the Canadian side, the vessel, wrapped in a shroud of vapor, settles into the foam surface of the pool with a thrust as heavy as iron. The boat then pivots to stand face to face with what the poet Nathaniel Hawthorne called "an ocean tumbling down out of the sky."

	The raw, terrifying ferocity of
SPELL OF THE WATERS	nature asserts itself in full force in this remarkable place. The sweeping arc of the falls seems

to surround the boat, holding and repelling at the same time. A short distance downriver, the cloud of mist formed at the base of Horseshoe Falls climbs some 100 feet above the precipice, catches the sunlight, and spins it into rainbows. The spray drenches the slicker-clad passengers. Huge boulders line the shore, and the voice of the falls is a loud and ceaseless rumble. Here, as the boat rides low in the aerated rapids, unnerving thoughts take shape in the visitor's mind—of being swallowed up by the

INFORMATION FOR VISITORS

From Buffalo, take I-190 to Niagara Falls; from St. Catharines, Ontario, take the Queen Elizabeth Way. The closest major airport is Buffalo International; shuttle buses take visitors from the airport to the Niagara Falls area. U.S. citizens are not required to carry a passport or visa to cross into Canada but they are requested to show proof of citizenship, preferably a birth certificate. The Maid of the Mist Steamboat Co. Ltd. operates a small fleet of boats, which depart daily at 15- and 30-minute intervals from mid-May through October. Helicopter tours are offered by several companies, when the weather permits.
For more information: Niagara County Tourism, 139 Niagara St., Lockport, NY 14094-2713; 800-338-7890 (U.S. side); or Niagara Parks Commission, P.O. Box 150, Niagara Falls, Ontario L2E 6T2; 905-356-2241 (Canadian side).

INTO THE MIST
Slickered against the penetrating vapor, passengers aboard the Maid of the Mist, *above, approach an overarching rainbow.*

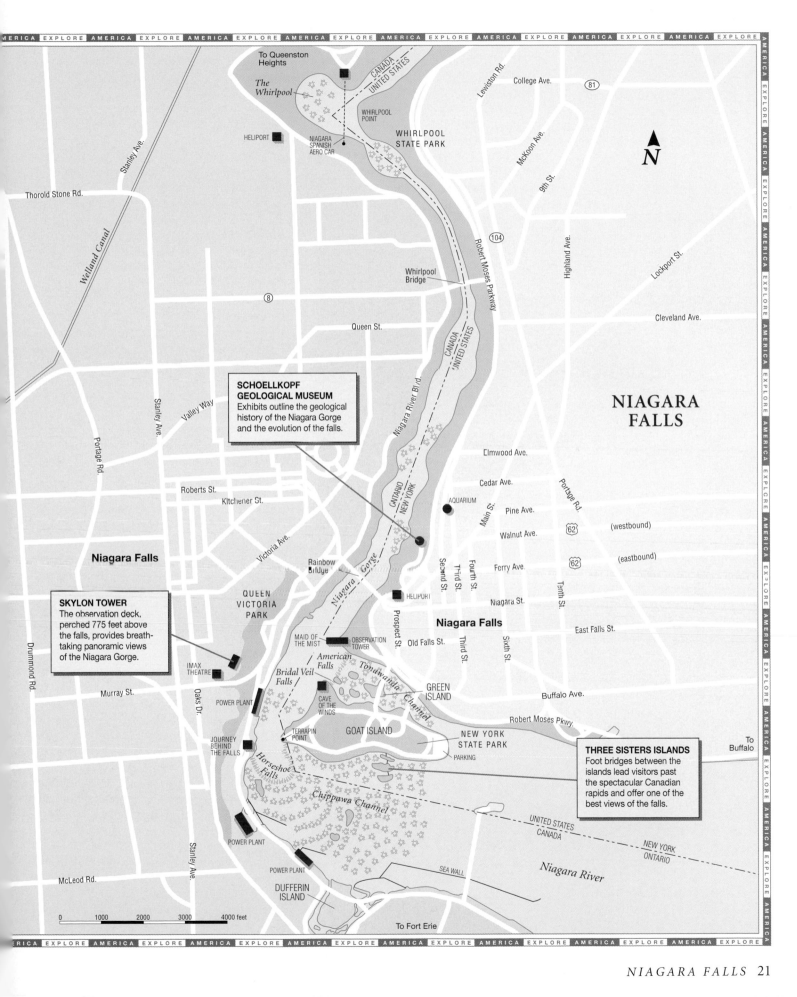

To Queenston Heights

The Whirlpool

HELIPORT

NIAGARA SPANISH AERO CAR

CANADA UNITED STATES

WHIRLPOOL POINT

WHIRLPOOL STATE PARK

Lewiston Rd.

College Ave.

81

9th St.

McKoon Ave.

Stanley Ave.

Thorold Stone Rd.

Welland Canal

104

Highland Ave.

Whirlpool Bridge

Robert Moses Parkway

Cleveland Ave.

Lockport St.

8

Queen St.

CANADA UNITED STATES

NIAGARA FALLS

SCHOELLKOPF GEOLOGICAL MUSEUM
Exhibits outline the geological history of the Niagara Gorge and the evolution of the falls.

Stanley Ave.

Valley Way

Portage Rd.

Roberts St.

Kitchener St.

Elmwood Ave.

Cedar Ave.

AQUARIUM

Main St.

Pine Ave.

Portage Rd.

62

(westbound)

Walnut Ave.

62

(eastbound)

Niagara Falls

Victoria Ave.

Rainbow Bridge

Niagara River Blvd.

ONTARIO NEW YORK

Niagara Gorge

Second St.

Third St.

Fourth St.

Ferry Ave.

Tenth St.

SKYLON TOWER
The observation deck, perched 775 feet above the falls, provides breath-taking panoramic views of the Niagara Gorge.

QUEEN VICTORIA PARK

Prospect St.

HELIPORT

Niagara St.

Niagara Falls

East Falls St.

MAID OF THE MIST

OBSERVATION TOWER

Old Falls St.

Third St.

Sixth St.

IMAX THEATRE

Drummond Rd.

Murray St.

Oaks Dr.

Bridal Veil Falls

American Falls

CAVE OF THE WINDS

Tonawanda Channel

GREEN ISLAND

POWER PLANT

JOURNEY BEHIND THE FALLS

Terrapin Point

GOAT ISLAND

NEW YORK STATE PARK

Buffalo Ave.

Robert Moses Pkwy.

THREE SISTERS ISLANDS
Foot bridges between the islands lead visitors past the spectacular Canadian rapids and offer one of the best views of the falls.

To Buffalo

Horseshoe Falls

PARKING

Stanley Ave.

Chippawa Channel

UNITED STATES CANADA

NEW YORK ONTARIO

McLeod Rd.

POWER PLANT

SEA WALL

Niagara River

POWER PLANT

DUFFERIN ISLAND

0 1000 2000 3000 4000 feet

To Fort Erie

DEEP RIVER

The deepest part of the Niagara River, 158 feet, occurs just below the falls at Whirlpool State Park, below. From here the river runs downstream through the Niagara Gorge for seven miles to the foot of the escarpment at Queenston.

swirling pool or crushed by the endless wall of falling water. But the unease is tinged with an inexplicable allure that draws people ever closer.

From earliest times, the falls have stirred something deep and primitive in the human heart, leading ancient tribes to worship them, and modern elegists to rhapsodize on their grandeur. The cascades are like a magnet, drawing people from around the world, and compelling them to gaze upon this truly majestic spectacle.

"I have seen the Falls, and am all rapture and amazement," extolled Irish poet Thomas Moore during his visit in 1804. "I felt as if approaching the very residence of the Deity. . . . Oh! Bring the atheist here and he cannot return an atheist! . . . It is impossible by pen or pencil to convey even a faint idea of their magnificence." Over the years many masters of pen and pencil have tried to circumscribe the falls, but Niagara always seems to exhaust their capacity for words.

TOURIST ATTRACTION

The first European to describe Niagara Falls was Father Louis Hennepin, a Belgian friar and explorer, who accompanied Sieur de La Salle during his expedition of 1678. Apparently under Niagara's spell, Hennepin reported the height of the falls at 600 feet, a three-and-a-half-fold exaggeration. But Hennepin viewed Niagara Falls when it carried the full spillage of four of the Great Lakes—200,000 cubic feet per second—explaining, perhaps, why it loomed so large in his imagination.

By 1815 word of Niagara Falls as a place of unparalleled magnificence was spreading. Artists' sketches and paintings of the falls were circulated throughout North America and Europe, whetting the appetite of curious adventurers. When the Erie Canal opened in 1825, it connected the Hudson River to Lake Erie and gave travelers easier access to the falls. By the mid-1800's hordes of visitors flocked to the region.

The powerful surge of the cataracts seemed to have a strange, hypnotic effect on people, causing them to approach the falls with a reverence usually reserved for shrines. It was as though they saw demons and angels dancing in the perpetual mist. In 1834, two years before her marriage to Calvin E. Stowe, American novelist Harriet Beecher paid a visit to the Niagara area. Her recollections of that encounter with the mesmerizing falls revealed her dark elation: "I felt as if I could have gone over with the waters; it would be so beautiful a death; there would be no fear in it. I felt the rock tremble under me with a sort of joy. I was so maddened that I could have gone too, if it had gone."

The name Niagara is derived from *Onguiaahre*, an Indian word that has been translated at various times as "throat," "the strait," or "thundering waters." Perhaps the falls are so seductive because they are an event as well as a place—the falls may be the closest mortals can stand to the naked might of nature and yet remain secure in the knowledge they will survive.

Wobbling on the deck of the *Maid of the Mist* as it rocks in the howling din is not so perilous after all. Boats have been snuggling up to Horseshoe

Falls for more than a century. Wooden walkways parallel the water's descent, and parks and greenbelts perch on the crests of the gorge.

VOICE OF MYSTERY Local lore claims that in the 19th century some visitors traveled all the way across the Atlantic Ocean to see the falls. Turning back in fear as the thunder of the waters intensified with their approach, the party left without ever beholding the spectacle.

Nathaniel Hawthorne, who visited Niagara Falls the same year as Harriet Beecher Stowe, suggests in his writings that he approached the falls with the eager anticipation of a child expecting a candy treat. He deliberately delayed the encounter, contemplating the waters from his hotel room window,

visualizing them over dinner, alternately ignoring them and cocking an ear to their resounding summons. At last, he answered the siren call.

"Oh that I had never heard of Niagara till I beheld it!" he later wrote. "Had its own mysterious voice been the first to warn me of its existence, then, indeed, I might have knelt down and worshiped. I climbed the precipice and threw myself on the earth, feeling that I was unworthy to look at the great falls, and careless about beholding them again. All that night . . . a rushing sound was heard, as if a great tempest was sweeping through the air. It mingled with my dreams, and made them full of storm and whirlwind. . . ."

What is it about this sublime geological phenomenon that has drawn pilgrims for centuries, fills them with dread and tingling anticipation,

UNDER THE RAINBOW
Rainbow Bridge, above, overlooks Niagara River at Goat Island's Bridal Veil Falls and the American Falls—a drop of 167 feet. The bridge spans the gorge between New York State and the Canadian province of Ontario.

AN ELDERLY MAID
Millions of visitors, including presidents, royalty, and movie stars, have observed the base of the falls from aboard the Maid of the Mist, *left. The boat began ferrying visitors past the falls in 1846.*

*THUNDERING WATERS
More than 600,000 cubic feet of
water crash over the crestline of
the falls every minute, as water
from Lake Erie flows 36 miles
to Lake Ontario, right.*

and sets them off on such lofty flights of fantasy? Why does Niagara Falls continue to be America's most exhilarating and, to many, spiritually uplifting natural wonder?

It is not, by any means, the nation's tallest waterfall. The cascades arise out of a short and unspectacular strait of water that can be called a river only by stretching the definition of the word. The walls of the gorge leading to the escarpment contain an astounding memoir of geological time, but they also exhibit distinct signs of extensive industrial development and commercial exploitation.

Though about half of the falls' natural flow has been diverted for the generation of hydroelectric power, it remains a glorious sight. Niagara is a living, breathing organism whose origins go back 12,000 years, to the last retreat of the Wisconsin ice sheet. That thaw left behind the huge basins of the Great Lakes and the rivers and channels that connected them and provided their outlet to the sea. As the water poured over the Niagara Escarpment near what is now the town of Lewiston, New York, it carved a pathway over the rock—the original Niagara Falls. Continuously eating away at the bedrock, the surging waters have gradually moved the escarpment back until the falls are some seven miles upriver from their original location.

Today the waters of the Niagara River descend a mere 22 feet as they drain from Lake Superior to Lakes Huron and Michigan. The flow from Lake Huron to Lake Erie steps down only eight feet. Between Erie and Lake Ontario, the waters roll across the Tonawanda plain and pour onto the Ontario plain, dropping from a height of 575 feet at Buffalo to 250 feet at Fort Niagara, 35 miles away. Most of that descent is over the twin cataracts.

SWIRLING WHIRLPOOL

But the falls are not Niagara's only watery wonder. About 12,000 years ago, as the forces of erosion inched the cascades upstream, the Niagara River made a curious dogleg turn. It etched out a deep shale bowl where the water, rushing down from the falls and the ensuing rapids, was thrown into a great spiral. The water wraps around and dives under itself and then breaks free for its journey to the lower gorge. Next to the falls, the Whirlpool is probably Niagara River's most spectacular feature. It can be viewed up close either from the jet boats that motor through the rapids or from the open Niagara Spanish Aero Car that dips as low as 150 feet directly above it on the Canadian side of the gorge, as well as from Whirlpool State Park in New York.

The entire sweep of the gorge can be taken in quickly by hired helicopter or, at a more leisurely pace, by automobile. The falls are lined with sites, some of which intrude on Niagara's majesty while

others preserve its rich history. At the IMAX Theatre and Daredevil Adventure in Niagara Falls, Ontario, the audience can view the insane stunts of thrill seekers who have walked tightropes across the gorge and tumbled in barrels over them. The 1725 French Castle of Old Fort Niagara in Youngstown, New York, was built to resemble a manor to deceive the Indians. The fort played a strategic role in the French and Indian War, the American Revolution, and the War of 1812.

There are many vantage points from which to take in the falling waters: the New York State Park, which includes Goat Island, the Cave of the Winds, Luna Island, and Prospect Point; the towers and high-rises of Ontario; the Queenston–Lewiston Bridge; and, of course, the *Maid of the Mist*, which was named after Niagara's most beloved myth.

As told by the people of the Six Nations, the maid referred to in the boat's name was said to be mourning the death of her husband when she decided to take her life by going over the falls in a canoe. But when she jumped, the thunder gods, who lived in a cave under the falls, intervened by lowering her gently to the basin below. The gods convinced the maid that all life is sacred and she eventually returned to her tribe to remarry and raise a large family. In another version of the story, the maid was the daughter of an Indian chief who was sent over the falls as a sacrifice to appease

the thunder gods. Some scholars now argue that this second version was made up by Europeans since cruel gods and human sacrifice are foreign ideas to the people of the Six Nations.

At dusk floodlights illuminate the watery temple, and the churning waters seem haunted by mysterious spirits. The thundering waterfalls are strangely peaceful, making travelers feel uplifted rather than diminished by a force that is so much greater than they are.

INTO THE MAW OF THE BEAST
Visitors to the Cave of the Winds, above, on the American side of the River, follow the sturdy boardwalk for a close-up view of Bridal Veil Falls.

NEARBY SITES & ATTRACTIONS

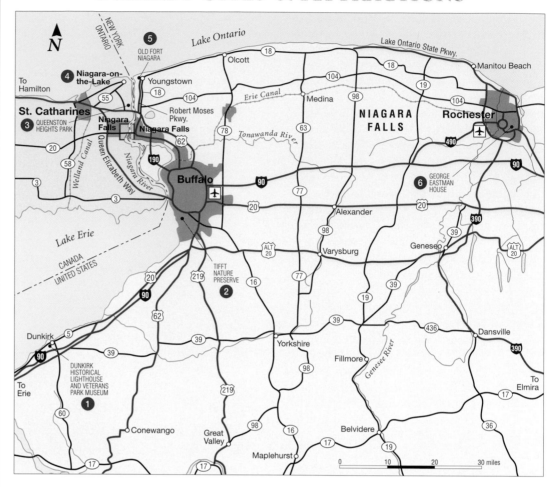

1 DUNKIRK HISTORICAL LIGHTHOUSE AND VETERANS PARK MUSEUM, NEW YORK

This 61-foot-tall lighthouse, equipped with a French-made Fresnel lens, was erected in 1876 to help guide ships into Dunkirk Harbor. A walk up the circular, cast-iron staircase offers a spectacular view of Lake Erie some 80 feet below. The Veterans Museum contains exhibits dedicated to the five branches of the armed forces: Navy, Army, Air Force, Coast Guard, and Marine Corps. Also on display are a lighthouse keeper's kitchen and bedroom, as well as exhibits on maritime history and the Vietnam War. On the grounds are a Civil War cannon, a 21-foot rescue boat, and several anchors. Located in Dunkirk off Hwy. 5.

2 TIFFT NATURE PRESERVE, NEW YORK

This 264-acre preserve of ponds, marshes, and woodlands, located just three miles from downtown Buffalo, is a refuge for a variety of plants and animals. The land was once owned by entrepreneur George Washington Tifft, who used it as a dairy farm. It became a transfer point for shipments of iron and ore at the turn of the century, a dump in the 1950's, and, in the 1970's, a landfill site. The preserve was opened in 1976, after an extensive cleanup and the replanting of vegetation. Several ponds and a 75-acre freshwater cattail marsh attract numerous migrating birds to the area. Visitors can follow five miles of hiking trails, walk along three boardwalks, picnic and fish in designated areas, and watch life in the marsh from the observation area. The preserve also offers numerous nature programs. Trails are open for snowshoeing and cross-country skiing in winter. Located on Fuhrmann Blvd. in Buffalo.

The flags of the three nations that have held Old Fort Niagara—France, Britain, and the United States—fly before the French Castle, below.

③ QUEENSTON HEIGHTS PARK, ONTARIO

On October 13, 1812, an American force crossed the Niagara River and landed near the village of Queenston intent on invading the British territory of Upper Canada. Some 60 American soldiers climbed the 360-foot-high Niagara Escarpment and gained control of the powerful cannon that was firing 18-pound cannonballs at the troops across the river. Nevertheless, a fierce counterattack by the British, under Maj. Gen. Isaac Brock, forced the Americans to surrender. Brock died on the battlefield that is commemorated in this park, and his statue, which stands atop a 64-foot column, looks out over the territory his men defended during that pivotal battle in the War of 1812. Plaques along a self-guided walking tour that leads past reconstructed fortifications describe critical events in the battle. Located at Queenston Heights.

Seen from Niagara-on-the-Lake, the Niagara River, left, cuts a blue swath through the lush vegetation of the surrounding countryside.

④ NIAGARA-ON-THE-LAKE, ONTARIO

More than 40 historic buildings, many of them from the early years of the 19th century can be seen in Niagara-on-the-Lake. The Masonic Hall—which is believed to have been built out of the rubble left after the devastation of the city in the War of 1812—housed the first Masonic lodge in Upper Canada. In 1792 the first session of the parliament of Upper Canada convened on the site. Just down the street, the Niagara Apothecary operated as a dispensary between 1866 and 1964. The Victorian structure now houses a pharmacy museum. The 1847 Court House became the town hall in 1862. Today its displays include the Lord Mayor's chambers and the town's original jail. At nearby Fort George, costumed interpreters stage mock battles and reenact the daily tasks of fort personnel prior to the War of 1812, when the fort was occupied by the British Army. All but abandoned after 1820, the fort fell into disrepair until preservation efforts began in 1937. Its reconstructed buildings include officers' quarters, barracks, a guard room, and a stone powder magazine. Located on the Niagara Pkwy.

⑤ OLD FORT NIAGARA, NEW YORK

Three flags have flown at this 300-year-old fort, which served as a military post until 1963. In 1679 the French established a trading post on the site, called Fort Conti, and erected a fortification 47 years later. During the French and Indian War, in 1759, the British gained control of the fort, and 37 years later, the British ceded the fort to an independent United States before recapturing it again, briefly, during the War of 1812. Tours of the fortification include the Powder Magazine, which was so well designed by the French that it continued to serve as an ammunition dump until 1929; the Provision Storehouse, which could store up to 7,000 barrels of food; and the French Castle, which has been restored to its original 1727 appearance. Also on display at the fort are two British redoubts, or guard towers, dating from 1770–71 that are unique to North America. Located 15 miles north of Niagara Falls off the Robert Moses Pkwy.

⑥ GEORGE EASTMAN HOUSE, NEW YORK

A wonderful mix of classical elegance and modern convenience, this 50-room mansion once belonged to George Eastman, founder of the Eastman Kodak Company. The house was built in 1905 and boasts a mahogany staircase, a built-in vacuum cleaning system, nine fireplaces, 13 baths, and an elevator. A building attached to the house holds 500,000 prints and negatives, 4,000 cameras, the first motion picture system, the first miniature camera, and numerous novelty cameras. Pictures by more than 8,000 photographers belong to its archives. The museum's changing exhibits have included the work of Ansel Adams, Margaret Bourke-White, and the inventor of the daguerreotype, Louis Jacques Mandé Daguerre. The motion picture display has highlighted silent films and international movie posters. Located in Rochester.

The terrace garden of the George Eastman House, above, has been restored to its former splendor, reminding visitors of the days when the founder of Eastman Kodak resided at the mansion.

El Yunque

*Puerto Rico's mountainous rain
forest protects a fascinating
diversity of flora and fauna.*

In this verdant refuge, 25 miles east of San Juan's
bustling city streets, the air is thick and moist
with the breath of a million leaves. It is the realm
of El Yunque—the anvil, named for the shape of
its blunt peak. Within the surrounding 28,000-
acre tropical woodland of the Caribbean National
Forest wind miles of shadowy trails. They begin
among the majestic tabonuco trees and climb
through forests of gnarled swamp cyrilla, or palo
colorado, draped with dangling liana and clus-
tered with bromeliads shot with bright red blossoms. The trails slip by the plumed fronds of
sierra palms as they ascend into the cool misty
cloud forest that crowns the steep Luquillo
Mountains, where the tallest trees grow no more
that 20 feet high. Along the way, hikers breathe
in the rich earthy smell of decomposing plant
life, their hearts pounding as they catch a rare
glimpse of an endangered green Puerto Rican
parrot, its blue-tipped wings visible in flight.
Pausing to rest by a moss-covered tree trunk, a
hiker may be captivated by the sight of a spider's
web, stretched across a hollow in the log and glistening in the dappled sunlight.

Rain falls almost daily in El Yunque, drenching the slopes that rise 1,000 to more than 3,500 feet above sea level. As much as 200 inches of rain falls on the forest's highest peaks each year, amounting to an astounding 100 billion gallons of water in some 1,600 showers. Mild temperatures combine with this abundant moisture to produce luxuriant tropical rain forest vegetation, including at least 225 species of native trees. This variety compares dramatically with the approximately 400 species of trees that grow in all of temperate North America. The forest also harbors about 50 species of native orchid and more than 150 of fern, including a giant tree fern that grows up to 40 feet tall and evokes the age of the dinosaur.

Unlike continental tropical rain forests, which contain a remarkable diversity of animal life, El Yunque's native mammals today are limited to 11 species of bat. Before human settlement, only animals that could reach Puerto Rico by air or by water populated the island, although bones found in the region suggest that the forest may once have been inhabited by a large ground sloth. In contrast, there are almost 80 bird species here, some of which are endemic, such as the Puerto Rican tody and screech owl; others, such as the American redstart and the Cape May warbler, pause here during their annual spring and fall migrations.

When Christopher Columbus first visited Puerto Rico in 1493, on his second voyage to the New

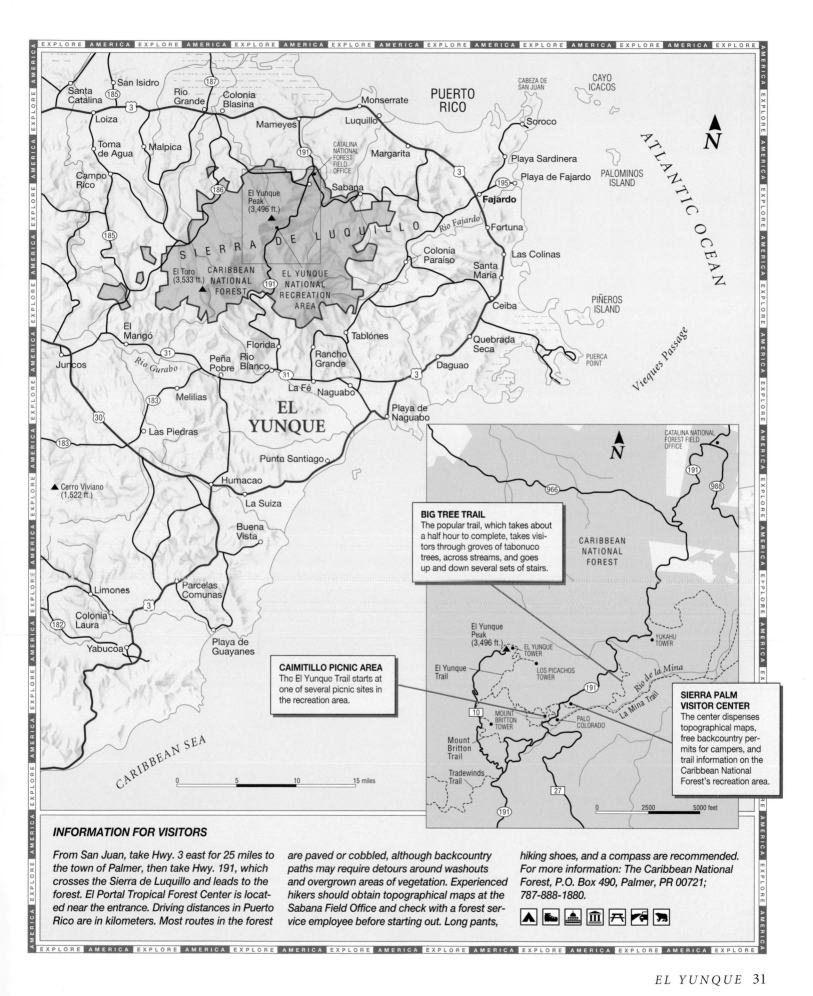

EXPLORE AMERICA *(decorative border repeated along top, sides, and bottom margins)*

PUERTO RICO

CABEZA DE SAN JUAN

CAYO ICACOS

ATLANTIC OCEAN

Santa Catalina
San Isidro
Rio Grande
Colonia Blasina
Monserrate
Soroco

Loiza
Mameyes
Luquillo
Playa Sardinera
PALOMINOS ISLAND

Toma de Agua
Malpica
Margarita
Playa de Fajardo

Campo Rico
CATALINA NATIONAL FOREST FIELD OFFICE
Sabana
Fajardo

El Yunque Peak (3,496 ft.)
Fortuna

SIERRA DE LUQUILLO
Rio Fajardo
Las Colinas

El Toro (3,533 ft.)
CARIBBEAN NATIONAL FOREST
EL YUNQUE NATIONAL RECREATION AREA
Colonia Paraíso
Santa Maria

PIÑEROS ISLAND

El Mangó
Tablónes
Ceiba
Quebrada Seca

Florida
Rancho Grande
Daguao
PUERCA POINT

Juncos
Rio Gurabo
Peña Pobre
Rio Blanco
La Fé
Naguabo

Vieques Passage

Melilias

Las Piedras
EL YUNQUE
Playa de Naguabo

Punta Santiago

Cerro Viviano (1,522 ft.)
Humacao
La Suiza

Buena Vista

CARIBBEAN NATIONAL FOREST

BIG TREE TRAIL
The popular trail, which takes about a half hour to complete, takes visitors through groves of tabonuco trees, across streams, and goes up and down several sets of stairs.

CATALINA NATIONAL FOREST FIELD OFFICE

Limones
Parcelas Comunas

Colonia Laura
Yabucoa
Playa de Guayanes

El Yunque Peak (3,496 ft.)
EL YUNQUE TOWER
YUKAHU TOWER

CAIMITILLO PICNIC AREA
The El Yunque Trail starts at one of several picnic sites in the recreation area.

El Yunque Trail
LOS PICACHOS TOWER

Rio de la Mina

MOUNT BRITTON TOWER
PALO COLORADO
La Mina Trail

SIERRA PALM VISITOR CENTER
The center dispenses topographical maps, free backcountry permits for campers, and trail information on the Caribbean National Forest's recreation area.

Mount Britton Trail

Tradewinds Trail

CARIBBEAN SEA

0   5   10   15 miles

0   2500   5000 feet

INFORMATION FOR VISITORS

From San Juan, take Hwy. 3 east for 25 miles to the town of Palmer, then take Hwy. 191, which crosses the Sierra de Luquillo and leads to the forest. El Portal Tropical Forest Center is located near the entrance. Driving distances in Puerto Rico are in kilometers. Most routes in the forest are paved or cobbled, although backcountry paths may require detours around washouts and overgrown areas of vegetation. Experienced hikers should obtain topographical maps at the Sabana Field Office and check with a forest service employee before starting out. Long pants, *hiking shoes, and a compass are recommended. For more information: The Caribbean National Forest, P.O. Box 490, Palmer, PR 00721; 787-888-1880.*

The roots of the sierra palm, right, which thrives on the slopes of the Sierra de Luquillo, emerge from its trunk six feet above the ground to batten down the plant against tropical winds.

Bromeliads, visible in the foreground below, bloom throughout the year. The plant is distinguished by its bright blossoms and the way its leaves grow in a rosette around a cup-shaped feeding tank. A rich population of rain forest wildlife—including beetles, frogs, spiders, and pseudoscorpions—is attracted to the rainwater, dew, and debris that collect in the plant's tank.

World, there were about 30,000 Taíno living on Borinquen, the island's Amerindian name. After about 300 years of colonization, only about 2,000 Taíno remained, their once vibrant culture reduced by disease and inbreeding.

The Taíno believed in a benign spirit named Yuquiyu who reigned from El Yunque Peak and the other mountains protruding above the rain forest. From his fog-enveloped summits Yuquiyu was said to protect the inhabitants of the island. When evil spirits sent violent storms from the east to ravage the island, Yuquiyo took the brunt of their rage, lessening the devastation of the settled land to the west.

The Sierra de Luquillo continue to suffer the worst effects of hurricanes. Hurricanes Hugo, Fran,

and Hortense all have wreaked havoc on El Yunque and, as a result, created tough challenges for the teams of managers and scientists from the Caribbean National Forest, as well as the International Institute of Tropical Forestry, whose job it is to protect this preserve for future generations.

Public concern about the area's survival has a long history. In 1876 the Spanish Crown set aside El Yunque as one of the first forest reserves in the Western Hemisphere. Several years after Puerto Rico's crown lands passed to the United States in 1898, the region was placed under the guardianship of the US Department of Agriculture, which, from 1931 to 1978, undertook the task of reforesting 10,000 acres, much of which had been cleared by settlers for subsistence farms

and coffee and tobacco plantations. In 1976 the Luquillo Experimental Forest Reserve section of the rain forest was made part of the Man and the Biosphere Reserve Program by the United Nations.

DIVERSE FOREST TYPES What makes El Yunque of special interest internationally is that it contains four general types of rain forest—tabonuco, palo colorado, sierra palm, and cloud. The tabonuco, which is found in the foothills and slopes of the Luquillo Mountains below 2,000 feet, extends for more than half of the reserve. It most closely resembles the rain forests of South America. The forest contains some 160 tree species but is dominated by the tabonuco, which exhibits dark green foliage, a smooth whitish bark, pungent resin, and enormous roots that often wrap around boulders on the slopes. Sometimes the roots graft to neighboring roots, making the stands of tabonucos strong enough to survive hurricanes.

Where the tabonuco forest was thinned for coffee plantations, clumps of pioneering species have taken root, such as the yagrumo, or hypocrite trees, so called because their large leaves show two faces: rich green above and silvery green beneath. Red-tailed hawks are often sighted circling above the treetops, scanning for a rat or one of several species of anole that reside in the preserve.

Amphibians are mostly represented by 12 species of small frogs, or coquís, that are without doubt the forest's noisiest denizens. An inch long, these nearly translucent tree frogs produce the signature sound of Puerto Rico: an incessant birdlike chanting that transforms Caribbean nights into raucous, two-note polyphonies: "co-KEE co-KEE." At night the coquís feed on insects high in the treetops, while tarantulas and other predators lurk on the tree trunks below. It has been estimated that as many as 10,000 coquís inhabit each acre of the forest.

The valleys and gentle slopes at elevations above 2,000 feet are named for the palo colorado, a huge, canopy-forming tree with a distinctive broom-shaped crown and a thick, twisted trunk up to 20 feet in diameter. Colorados can live for up to 1,000 years, although few trees that old survive today. Their cavities provide nesting sites for Puerto Rican parrots, the island's only native parrot. At one time nearly a million of these exquisite foot-long green birds filled the island skies. Much prized by the Spanish as pets, the bird was heavily hunted from the earliest days of colonization. But it was the century-long practice of cutting back the rain forest for agriculture that reduced the flock to just 13 birds by 1972. Three years later, a combined effort by the World Wildlife Fund and various government agencies set out to restore the nesting

habitat and to protect the parrot from the pearly-eyed thrasher, its primary predator. The thrasher preys on parrot eggs and chicks and competes with the parrot for nesting sites, often usurping its rival. The team designed nests for the parrots that were deep enough to protect their eggs and young birds. They also built nests for thrashers close by so that when the thrashers defend their turf against encroachment, they also defend parrot nests.

STAIRWAY TO HEAVEN
Rocky steps, below, many of which were built by the Civilian Conservation Corps in the 1930's, help travelers negotiate the slippery trails that crisscross the Caribbean National Forest.

By early 1989 biologists had tallied 99 parrots: 52 in an aviary in the Caribbean National Forest and 47 in the wild. Later that year Hurricane Hugo struck, defoliating the forest and wiping out 23 individuals from the wild population. Although the wild flock is now approaching its pre-Hugo numbers, the birds' survival remains precarious.

The palo colorado forest gradually shifts to a forest of sierra palm, named for the hardy trees that are

AFRICAN IMMIGRANT
*An African tulip tree, above, shows
off its scarlet flowers. The trees,
which were probably brought to
Puerto Rico by the ships that carried
slaves from Africa, now grow along
the roadsides and near abandoned
homesteads in the national forest.*

easily recognizable by their smooth trunks, plumed fronds, white flower spikes, and erect prop roots. The palm grows among all the forest types but it dominates the steep slopes and streambeds that are inhospitable to most other trees.

From the sierra palm forest to the cloud forest on the peaks and ridges above 2,790 feet, El Yunque looks much as it did when the Spanish arrived in Puerto Rico five centuries ago. Brief and intense rain showers occur 350 days a year at this eleva-tion. The average temperature is 65°F. Trade winds from the east carry moisture that produces myri-ad clouds and fog banks, which hang just above the ground. Beneath this cottony cover, the envi-ronment stays perpetually wet. Camasay, nemo-ca, limoncillo, and oak trees grow here, gnarled and dwarfed by exposure to winds, frequent cloud cover, an extremely low transpiration rate, and soils saturated with water.

A striking characteristic of the cloud forest is its profusion of epiphytes—plants that grow on oth-er plants. In some places every conceivable vege-tative surface is smothered by vines, mosses, liverworts, algae, and bromeliads. Epiphytes are benign tenants that do not harm their host. They make remarkable adaptations to survive, collect-ing rain along with air- and waterborne nutrients in modified leaves, roots, and bulbous stems.

The ground layer of the cloud forest is a tangled mass of roots, forbs, and grasses. Giant tree ferns resembling lacy parasols are found in protected areas. This is also the realm of the rare elfin woods warbler and the endemic burrow coquís, one of the 12 species of coquís in the region.

EXPLORING
EL YUNQUE

El Yunque is easy to reach and explore. Visitors can drive Highway 191 to the heart of the preserve in mere minutes, or they can take their time and stop along the way at the observation areas and parking lots that mark the starting points for hikes into the rain forest. Most travelers begin their explorations at El Portal Tropical Forest Center, located at the northern end of the rain forest preserve, which uses displays and interactive exhibits to give an introduction to both the human and natural history of El Yunque. Water circulates through the airy and light-filled center along a specially designed moat and waterfall, and an elevated walkway provides visitors with a sen-sational perspective on the wonders of the lush rain forest canopy.

South of El Portal, near the Catalina ranger sta-tion, kadam and mahogany plantations offer diverse habitats that attract black-cowled orioles, Puerto Rican bullfinches, red-legged thrushes, and pearly-eyed thrashers. On rare occasions visitors have caught sight of one of the preserve's several seven-foot Puerto Rican boas sunning itself a few hundred yards west of the parking lot.

Newlyweds pose for pictures in front of La Coca Falls, which spills 85 feet over mossy green cliffs near the road. Green mango hummingbirds hover nearby among the scarlet bromeliad blossoms, sipping the sweet nectar. Hikers can park their cars in the lot then follow La Coca Trail into the stream-webbed forest, a route popular with rock-hoppers. The forest shelters waterfalls and limpid pools cupped by mossy boulders and fringed by giant tree ferns, mountain palms, and bamboo.

Farther along Highway 191, Yokahu Tower provides views of Culebra, Vieques, and other islands off the eastern tip of Puerto Rico, as well as the extensive tabonuco and palo colorado forests of the remote Mameyes River valley. The Mameyes is the only sizable island waterway that has not been dammed.

A parking lot at the entrance to the El Yunque Recreation Area serves as a departure point for the one-hour round-trip Big Tree/La Mina Trail, which gently weaves south through elegant stands of tabonuco trees. The trail leads past La Mina Falls, which funnels through a narrow cleft and spills into a rock-walled basin. It then parallels the often thunderous La Mina River, named for a nearby colonial gold mine, to emerge at the Palo Colorado picnic area. The river's clear pools support fresh-water shrimp and the goby, a fish equipped with suction cups on modified pelvic fins that enable it to grip onto slippery rocks as it negotiates rapids and small waterfalls.

A hundred yards south of Sierra Palm, the steep El Yunque Trail includes three of the preserve's most spectacular lookouts as it zigzags up through palo colorado, sierra palm, and cloud forest. One branch of the trail ascends through the cloud forest to a tower atop 3,075-foot Mount Britton that provides expansive views to the north and east. Another branch goes north and climbs up the 3,496-foot El Yunque Peak. On clear days hikers are rewarded with spectacular views of San Juan, the island's Atlantic coast, and, about 75 miles to the southeast, the Virgin Islands.

Hikers can join the El Toro/Tradewinds Trail from Highways 186 or 191. It winds in an east–west direction through Puerto Rico's deepest wilderness, offering occasional glimpses of El Toro Peak, which at 3,533 feet is the highest point in the national forest.

The Caribbean National Forest, like all rain forests, plays a critical role in replenishing vital moisture to the earth's atmosphere. Its trees and wildlife must be protected. Fortunately, El Yunque is one of the best-managed tropical forests in the world. Here visitors can explore the wilderness, knowing that their presence will not disturb the delicate balance between humans and nature.

NEARBY SITES & ATTRACTIONS

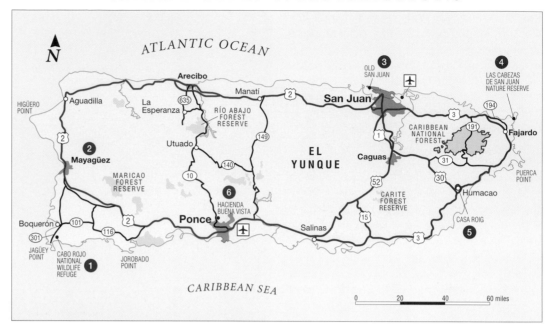

Ospreys, sea turtles, and an occasional manatee can be sighted from the rocky beaches and promontories at Las Cabezas de San Juan Nature Reserve, below.

① CABO ROJO NATIONAL WILDLIFE REFUGE

In the 1970's, when a government communication post became obsolete due to satellite technology, 587 acres of upland habitat were transferred to the Caribbean Islands National Wildlife Refuge complex, including seven wildlife refuges in Puerto Rico and the U.S. Virgin Islands. Now called the Cabo Rojo National Wildlife Refuge, the habitat encompasses some 320 acres of forest, 210 acres of grassland, and 50 acres of brush. A total of 245 plant species and 145 bird species have been identified in the refuge, including the snowy egret, great blue heron, common moor hen, and the endangered yellow-shouldered blackbird. Heavy cattle grazing damaged the habitat until cattle were excluded from the area in 1978. Now the refuge is being reforested with ucar, black cobana, and lignum vitae, native hardwood trees that once flourished here. Located about five miles south of Boquerón on Hwy. 301.

② MAYAGÜEZ

The third-largest city in Puerto Rico, the western port of Mayagüez takes its name from *majagua,* meaning "a town between two rivers" in the language of the Taíno Indians. Most of the city was destroyed by an earthquake in 1917. But one of the surviving buildings was the Yaguez Theater, which was declared a historic monument in 1977 and has been renovated and expanded. The town center is dominated by Plaza de Colón, with its statue of Christopher Columbus. The birds, mammals, and reptiles at the Mayagüez Zoo include Bengal tigers and the capybara, the world's largest rodent. The Tropical Agricultural Research Station, located on the site of a former plantation just outside of town, displays tropical vegetation such as pink torch ginger and the Sri Lankan cinnamon tree. Located on Hwy. 2.

36

③ OLD SAN JUAN

Spanish-built forts, gracious plazas, and 16th-century churches draw visitors to the seven-block neighborhood of Old San Juan. The elegant La Fortaleza, built in 1537, is the oldest of the forts and now serves as the home of the governor of Puerto Rico. Its successor, Fort San Felipe del Morro, was built in 1548 to defend San Juan Harbor against naval attack by English, French, and Dutch forces. To guard the land approaches to Old San Juan, construction of the nearby fort of San Cristobal was begun in 1634. Larger than El Morro, its imposing size and intricate design make it a strategic masterpiece. An 18th-century Spanish troop quarter has been restored inside one vault. Four historic plazas grace Old San Juan, including Plaza de Armas with its 1602 city hall, or Alcadia. Visitors can attend services at San José Church. Built in 1532, it is the second-oldest church in continuous use in the New World. The best way to see Old San Juan is by walking its narrow cobblestone streets, made of adoquine, a blue stone cast from furnace slag and used as ballast on Spanish ships. Located in San Juan.

④ LAS CABEZAS DE SAN JUAN NATURE RESERVE

Las Cabezas, which means heads, refers to this reserve's location on three windswept promontories off Puerto Rico's northeastern tip. The peninsula is managed by the island's Conservation Trust and protects seven different ecological systems, including dry forest, mangroves, and coral reefs. Trails and boardwalks wind through the areas, and guides explain the ecology. One promontory is capped by a restored 1882 lighthouse, El Faro, which houses exhibits. From its observation tower, visitors can see El Yunque and neighboring islands. Located 10 miles north of Fajardo off Hwy. 194.

⑤ CASA ROIG

When wealthy Humacao businessman Antonio Roig Torrellas asked his influential San Juan friends whom he should hire to design his home, their response was unanimous: Antonin Nechodoma. The work of this well-known Czech architect was strongly influenced by the prairie style of Frank Lloyd Wright. His clean, simple design for Casa Roig was in harmony with its tropical setting. Walls were made of thick concrete to keep the interior cool, and windows were set to make the most of island breezes. An overhanging roof protected the interior from rain and the sun's glare, and leaded stained glass muted what sun did shine through. The house was completed in 1920 and remained occupied until the death of Torrellas' wife, Doña Eulogia, in 1956. For almost 30 years, the house was left to deteriorate until experts began a painstaking restoration. In 1989 it opened to the public. The upstairs bedrooms have been returned to their former glory, as have the kitchen, servants' quarters, sewing room, and guest room on the ground floor. The house is now an art gallery and there is a permanent exhibit of Nechodoma's work in the former library. Located in Humacao.

⑥ HACIENDA BUENA VISTA

Hacienda Buena Vista is a restored 19th-century plantation set in a subtropical forest on the Canal River. Salvador de Vives established this mountain farm in 1833 to produce corn, coffee, flour, and citrus fruit. For the next 120-odd years, the plantation was operated by the Vives family. It is now an agricultural museum managed by the Conservation Trust of Puerto Rico. Many of the original farm buildings and machinery have been restored, as has the manor house with its 1850's furniture and pretty rose garden. Located in Ponce on Hwy. 10.

The walls of the six-level San Felipe del Morro Fortress, left, rise 140 feet above the ocean and are 18 feet thick. One of its large bombproof vaults has been converted into a museum of the fort's history.

Outdoor displays at Hacienda Buena Vista, below, include a 60-foot waterslide, a waterwheel, canal system, and a coffee and corn mill that was used by plantation farmers in the 19th century.

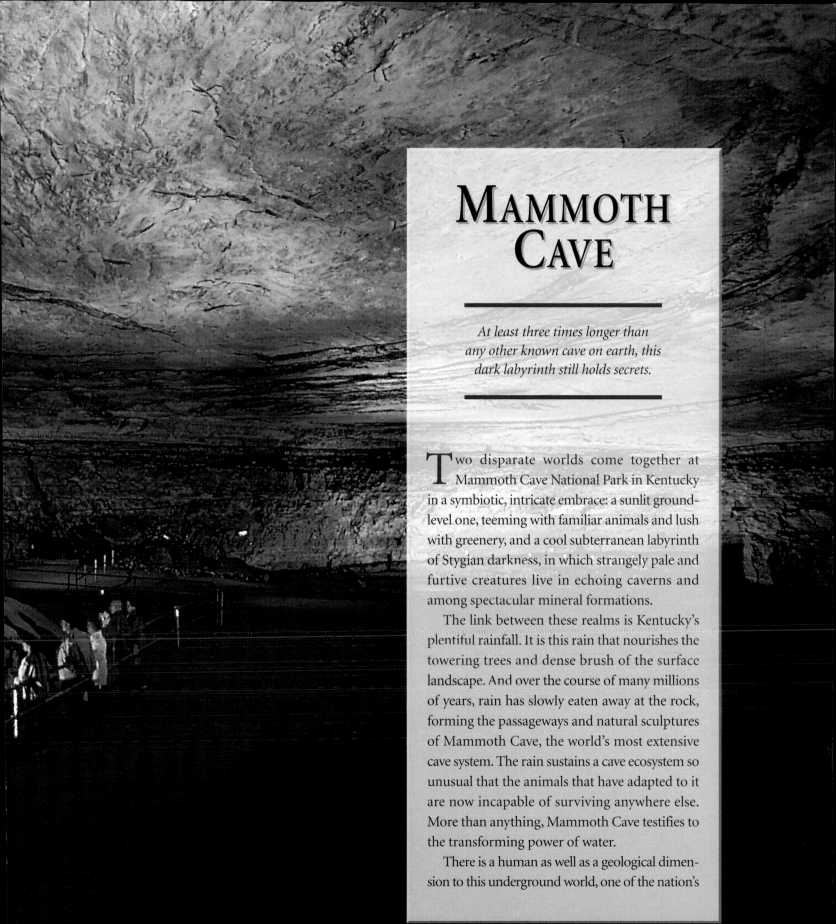

MAMMOTH CAVE

At least three times longer than any other known cave on earth, this dark labyrinth still holds secrets.

Two disparate worlds come together at Mammoth Cave National Park in Kentucky in a symbiotic, intricate embrace: a sunlit ground-level one, teeming with familiar animals and lush with greenery, and a cool subterranean labyrinth of Stygian darkness, in which strangely pale and furtive creatures live in echoing caverns and among spectacular mineral formations.

The link between these realms is Kentucky's plentiful rainfall. It is this rain that nourishes the towering trees and dense brush of the surface landscape. And over the course of many millions of years, rain has slowly eaten away at the rock, forming the passageways and natural sculptures of Mammoth Cave, the world's most extensive cave system. The rain sustains a cave ecosystem so unusual that the animals that have adapted to it are now incapable of surviving anywhere else. More than anything, Mammoth Cave testifies to the transforming power of water.

There is a human as well as a geological dimension to this underground world, one of the nation's

oldest tourist sites, popular since the days when the country was forging its identity. Mammoth Cave helped establish that this continent had natural attractions as magnificent as any cultural or artistic landmark in Europe. The cave offered grandeur, mystery, and danger. "The word goes forth in these colossal chambers like a bird," wrote naturalist John Burroughs in the mid-1800's. "When no word is spoken, the silence is of a kind never experienced on the surface of the earth, it is so profound and abysmal. This, and the absolute darkness, [makes one] feel as if he were face to face with primordial nothingness."

The story of Mammoth Cave begins more than 300 million years ago when a shallow tropical sea covered most of what is now the southeastern United States, including this part of south-central Kentucky. In these waters lived tiny organisms such as shellfish and coral. As the animals died, their shells, along with other sediments, accumulated on the seafloor and were compacted into layers of limestone. Millions of years later, a large river system to the north carried silt and sand to the region and deposited layers of sandstone and shale on top of the limestone. About 280 million years ago the earth underwent a period of global cooling. As

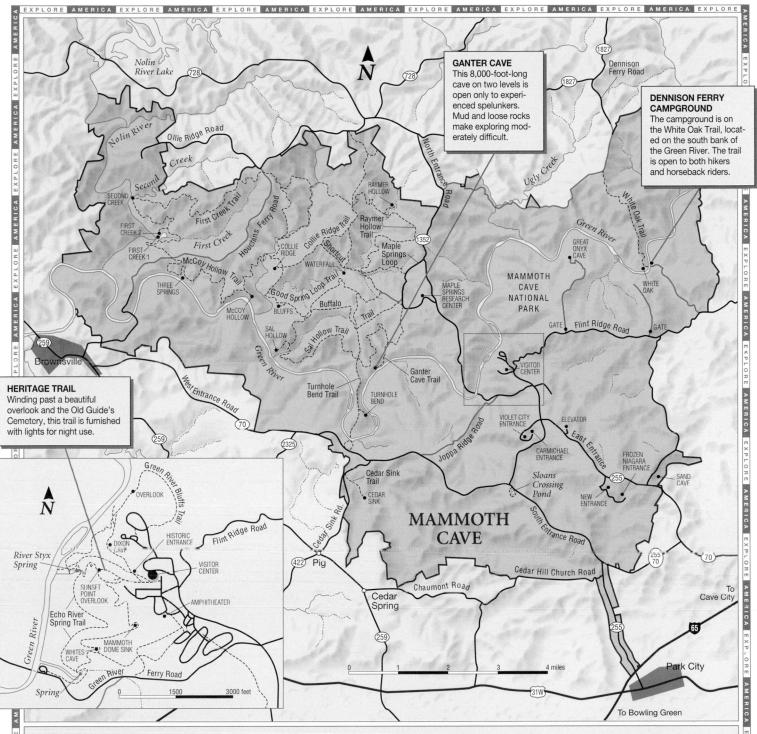

GANTER CAVE

This 8,000-foot-long cave on two levels is open only to experienced spelunkers. Mud and loose rocks make exploring moderately difficult.

DENNISON FERRY CAMPGROUND

The campground is on the White Oak Trail, located on the south bank of the Green River. The trail is open to both hikers and horseback riders.

HERITAGE TRAIL

Winding past a beautiful overlook and the Old Guide's Cemetery, this trail is furnished with lights for night use.

INFORMATION FOR VISITORS

To reach Mammoth Cave from Louisville, head south on Hwy. 65 to Exit 53 at Cave City. From Bowling Green, take Hwy. 65 north to Exit 48 at Cave City. The park is open year-round, except Christmas Day. Visitors must join a tour to view the caves, with the exception of the short, self-guided Discovery Tour. A variety of ranger-led tours are offered, ranging from 75 minutes to 6 hours in length. Tickets for all tours except the Wild Cave Tour can be purchased up to five months in advance at the visitor center or by calling 800-967-2283. Visitors under the age of 16 must be accompanied by an adult. In summer children ages 8 to 12 can go on a special guided tour of the surface and a small cave. Because cave tours can be strenuous, people with heart or lung problems should consult a ranger about less-taxing tours. Sturdy shoes and a light jacket are recommended. Three campgrounds are available above ground on a first-come, first-served basis for maximum stays of 14 days. The campgrounds may be closed December through February. Backcountry camping is available at 12 sites. Wear high boots and long pants to deter ticks. For more information: Superintendent, Mammoth Cave National Park, Mammoth Cave, KY 42259-0007; 502-758-2328.

KEY LINK IN THE FOOD CHAIN
A long-legged cricket, below, feels its
way in the dark with its antennae.
Leaving the cave at night to forage
for food, crickets are an important
source of sustenance for other ani-
mals in the cave.

water was drawn into growing ice caps, sea levels dropped to reveal large areas of land. In some places erosion dissolved the resistant sandstone and shale caprock, exposing the underlying limestone layers. Over the course of many millions of years, rainwater worked under the surface. The moisture collected carbon dioxide from the air and from decaying organic matter, forming a weak solution of carbonic acid—less potent than the fizz of soda pop—that seeped through cracks and fissures in the landscape. That slight acidity dissolved some of the limestone beneath the surface, resulting in a vast cave system protected by rain-resistant caprock. The region became dimpled with depressions and sinkholes and streaked with sinking streams that dive underground. As the water table gradually

dropped in elevation over the centuries, five levels of interconnected passageways were created in the ridges lining the Green River. Stalactites and stalagmites, constructions of mineral deposits left by dripping water, are relatively rare here, as is flowstone, which is formed from water seeping along cracks in the sloping ceilings. In places it has created thin draperies of rock. Delicate gypsum "flowers" curl from many of the cave walls and ceilings like decorations on a cake.

Today water continues to course through the lowest reaches of Mammoth Cave—some 400 feet below ground—collecting in underground streams and rivers that eventually wind their way to the Green River. The water levels inside the cave vary considerably. During periods of heavy rain, the

SUNSET SPLENDOR
Above the surface of the cave,
Sloans Crossing Pond, right, is
awash in delicate evening colors.
Mammoth Cave National Park
offers everything from horseback
trails and camping to first-rate
fishing and backcountry hiking.

Green River floods and sometimes reverses the flow of the cave's streams so that they pour into rather than out of the passageways.

In-flowing surface water can be a hazard as well as a boon to the cave's delicate wildlife. The water—some of it originating from as many as 15 miles away—accumulates farm runoff, human waste, hazardous spills along roadways, and other pollutants, which all are washed into the cave's drainage system. Within the last few years steps have been taken to preserve the cave's ecosystem. New sewage treatment facilities have been built in the park and surrounding towns, and both farmers and industries have coordinated an effort to reduce groundwater contamination. In 1990 the United Nations Educational, Scientific and Cultural Organization (UNESCO) named the entire area a unit of the International Network of Biosphere Reserves, recognizing it as a fragile environment and targeting it as an area for further research, monitoring, and educational initiatives.

LIFE IN THE DEPTHS Winding their way through the dark, silent passageways of Mammoth Cave, it is easy for visitors to imagine that the cave is devoid of living creatures. In fact, almost 130 animal species can be found inside. Some, like frogs and raccoons, do not live in the cave but wander into and out of it. Others, such as crickets and bats, inhabit the cave but frequently feed outside its confines. Perhaps the most fascinating of the cave creatures are the 25 species of troglodytes—animals that have adapted exclusively to life in the darkness. Biologists from around the world come to Mammoth Cave to study the world's most biologically diverse cave habitat.

With no sunlight and little food, animals such as fish, millipedes, crayfish, and shrimp make ingenious adaptations to ensure their survival. Because they require neither camouflage nor protection from the sun, many of them have lost their pigmentation and are pale white. Some, such as the cave fish (*Amblyopsis spelaea*), are eyeless. Others have evolved highly developed sensory organs to detect prey and predators in the dark. Because their food sources are scarce, the cave dwellers have slow metabolisms and require less food to survive. They also tend to live longer than their surface relatives. Rarely seen by either cave visitors or rangers, the creatures deep in the cave's belly live out a life dictated by the rainwater that will bring them essential nutrients from the upper world.

The profusion of life above ground contrasts starkly with the spareness of life below. The 52,830 acres of eastern hardwood forest that lie within the park's boundaries are home to a wide variety of plant and animal species. A thick undergrowth and immense trees—including 300 acres of old-growth forest—shelter white-tailed deer, coyotes, wild turkeys, raccoons, beavers, and more than 200 species of birds. Green River, which cuts through the center of the park, supports 82 fish species and more than 50 species of freshwater mussels—7 of them on the endangered list.

No one knows precisely when the first humans encountered Mammoth Cave, but archeological evidence indicates that at least 4,000 years ago, Native peoples collected crystals and other minerals from its twisting passageways. These early spelunkers left behind the remnants of the cane reed torches they used to light their way. About 2,000 years ago those explorations stopped, and the cave lay undisturbed until its rediscovery in

RELICS OF HUMAN ENDEAVOR
The tuberculosis huts, above, built in the 1840's, are the remains of one doctor's experimental treatment for people inflicted with the disease. The processing vat, below, was used during the War of 1812 to glean saltpeter from cave sediments for gunpowder.

traveled to see the cave's wonders. The actor Edwin Booth recited the soliloquy from William Shakespeare's *Hamlet* inside the cavern so he could hear the words resonate to their fullest effect.

The first person to map extensive parts of the cave was a self-educated slave named Stephen Bishop, who in 1838, at the age of 17, began guiding visitors through its passageways. An enthusiastic explorer who reveled in uncovering the cave's subterranean mysteries, Bishop was the first person to cross such underground landmarks as the Bottomless Pit. Two other slaves, the brothers Mat and Nick Bransford, also explored the cave and acted as guides. Descendants of the Bransfords carried on the family tradition at Mammoth Cave for more than 100 years.

One of the oddest chapters in the cave's history began in 1839, when prominent Louisville physician John Croghan purchased it from Franklin Gorin, a well-known lawyer who hailed from Glasgow, Kentucky. In addition to running tours, Croghan investigated medicinal uses for the cave. After reading of Europe's underground tuberculosis hospitals, he erected two wood and two stone huts in the cave for 15 people suffering from the disease. After several months of "treatment," two patients died, and within a year Croghan abandoned the experiment. Although the wooden huts have been dismantled and removed, the stone huts stand as a grim reminder of the lengths to which sufferers went in seeking a cure.

SUBTERRANEAN LAKE
Lights, positioned beneath the clear water, set Crystal Lake aglow at the bottom of the Moonlight Dome, above. The lake lies some 150 feet underground.

1798 by European-American settlers. Legend has it that a hunter happened upon the cave when he tracked a wounded bear to its entrance.

Soon thereafter, the cave was mined for saltpeter, a key ingredient in the production of gunpowder. The War of 1812 caused a greatly increased demand for the mineral, and as many as 70 slaves were brought in to mine the valuable material in large quantities. The remains of the leaching vats and wooden waterlines used in these mining operations can still be seen today.

EARLY TOURISM

In the 19th century Mammoth Cave, along with Niagara Falls, became one of the nation's first major tourist attractions. The cave's natural entryway, a massive arch with a delicate waterfall, opens up to a gaping passageway with vaulted ceilings, an underground avenue that elicits gasps. Famous figures of the era, from Ralph Waldo Emerson to visiting European royalty,

Miles of the cave continued to be probed by intrepid explorers, often under extremely difficult circumstances. These early investigators used open-flame lanterns to light their way; to illuminate large spaces they took oil-soaked twisted rags, set them afire, and threw them up into the air. It was the death of Floyd Collins, an avid spelunker and part-owner of nearby Crystal Cave, that led to the establishment of Mammoth Cave as a national park. In 1915 Collins became trapped in a narrow passage when a huge rock fell on his ankle. For 15 long days, he was the subject of an exhaustive search-and-rescue attempt that was reported in great detail by the new medium of radio. After drilling a shaft, rescuers finally reached Collins—but it was too late to save the unfortunate adventurer. However, the resulting publicity sparked nationwide interest in the cave, and in 1926 Congress designated it the nation's 26th national park, with formal establishment coming in 1941. Another honor was accorded in 1981, when UNESCO designated Mammoth Cave as a World Heritage Site.

MODERN EXPLORATION

Exploration continues today, as spelunkers wearing lighted helmets inch their way through the underground wilderness. Though more than 350 miles have been explored to date, scientists speculate that hundreds more miles of passageways are yet to be found.

The 2 million visitors who come here each year follow some 10 miles of passages that take them past an astonishing range of formations and caverns. Tours highlight the distinct facets of this underground wilderness, from the Frozen Niagara Tour, with its stalactites, stalagmites, and dripstone formations, to the Historic Tour, which winds past the remains of mining operations and describes Native American activities in the cave. Visitors who enjoy adventure and don't mind narrow, enclosed spaces can experience caving firsthand on the Wild Cave Tour, crawling through passageways off the usual routes.

Though the cave has been explored time and again by countless visitors, explorers, and scientists, its mysteries continue to be uncovered. How many more miles of passageways lie under the Kentucky woodlands? What strange forms of life occupy its darkest reaches? The answers are as surprising today as they were more than 200 years ago.

CAVE ODDITIES
A sightless Mammoth Cave crayfish, left, rests in the dark waters. The crayfish has only a vestigial eye structure and locates food with its highly sensitive antennae. Delicate gypsum flowers like the one below are created when gypsum is extruded through fissures and pores in the bedrock in a process that is still poorly understood.

TRAILBLAZERS
The Gothic Avenue section of Mammoth Cave, left, displays pyramid-shaped piles of stones, erected by workers, explorers, and tourists as they cleared trails in the early 1800's.

NEARBY SITES & ATTRACTIONS

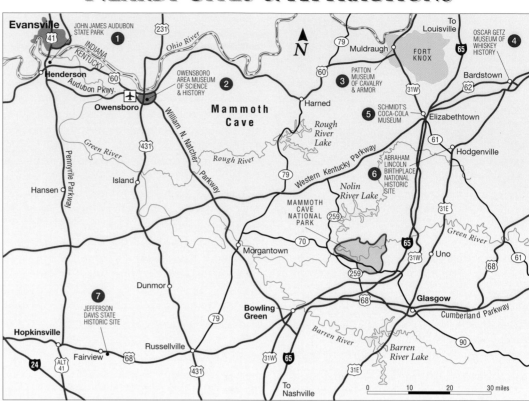

The construction of the Jefferson Davis monument, above, was begun in 1917 using crushed stone from a nearby quarry. Work on the monument continued until September 1918 when it was halted due to war-related shortages of building materials. It was eventually completed in 1924 and dedicated by the United Daughters of the Confederacy.

① JOHN JAMES AUDUBON STATE PARK

The park bearing the name of one of the nation's preeminent ornithologists preserves the quiet woods where he observed many of the birds that he rendered in paint. John James Audubon was born Jean-Jacques Fougère Audubon in Haiti. During his boyhood in France he developed an interest in drawing birds, which he kept up when he came to the United States in his late teens to avoid conscription into the French army. He lived in Henderson from 1809 to 1819, and it was here that his goal to catalog every species of American bird really began. Audubon's famous four-volume work *The Birds of America* contains 435 hand-colored plates. He was one of the first artists to depict life-size birds and animals set in their natural surroundings. A highlight of the park is the newly renovated John James Audubon Museum, whose four galleries feature a collection of the artist's watercolors, oils, engravings, and personal memorabilia. The adjacent Nature Center comprises three areas: a Learning Center, where a park naturalist and an art educator conduct environmental and art programs, a Discovery Center with hands-on exhibits, and a wildlife Observation Room. Located on Hwy. 41 at the northern boundary of Henderson.

② OWENSBORO AREA MUSEUM OF SCIENCE & HISTORY

This museum, which focuses on the region's natural and human history, is contained within a complex of three separate structures, one of which was a theater in the 19th century. The buildings house a hands-on science center, called Encounter, and a natural-history hall, which includes fossil displays and a life-size painting of a woolly mammoth. The picture serves as a reminder that this largest land mammal roamed the area from 1.7 million years ago until about 10,000 years ago. Temporary exhibits focus on local and regional history and have included such displays as "Women at Work—Tools of the Trade," "Yellowbanks Goes to War, 1941–1945," and "Wield the Power—Election Politics." The museum also serves as the host site for many community events and sponsors an annual family event in June entitled "Day of the Dinosaur." Located in Owensboro.

③ PATTON MUSEUM OF CAVALRY & ARMOR

One of the centerpieces of this military museum is a 14-foot section of the Berlin Wall that the United States acquired in 1989, when Berliners tore down the barrier and East and West Germany were unified. The museum, which is administered by the US Army Armor Center in Fort Knox, was established in 1949 for the preservation, study, and exhibition of historical material relating to cavalry and armor. The galleries feature displays of armored equipment and vehicles, weapons, and art that give a picture of the evolution of the US Armor branch of the military from World War I through its involvement in the Persian Gulf conflict. Represented in the museum are a British Mark V, the first combined infantry and tank vehicle dating from World War I; an M4 Sherman tank and a Panzer-kampfwagen from World War II; a cutaway model of the US M47 "Patton" tank from the Korean War; a prototype of the Cobra Attack helicopter from the Vietnam War; and a Soviet-built T72 tank configured for use in Kuwait in Operation Desert Storm. In the museum's Patton Gallery many of Gen. George S. Patton's personal effects are on display, including an impressive array of his medals. Patton was a dedicated soldier whose brilliant military career spanned 36 years. He served as a member of Gen. John J. Pershing's staff during both the Punitive Expedition to Mexico and World War I. When he died in 1945, as a result of a car crash, he was commander of the 15th Army in American-occupied Germany. Adjacent to the museum is the Armor Memorial Park, which is dedicated to the soldiers who fought with the Armor branch of the army in the two world wars. Located on Fayette Ave. near the Chaffee Ave. entrance to Fort Knox.

4 OSCAR GETZ MUSEUM OF WHISKEY HISTORY

This collection presents the history of the American whiskey industry from pre-Colonial days through Prohibition to the present day. The museum was made possible by a gift to the people of Bardstown from Emma Getz, wife of the philanthropist and collector Oscar Getz, who owned the Barton Brands Ltd. distillery. Visitors can see a copy of the 1833 liquor license that was obtained by Abraham Lincoln when he owned a tavern in New Salem, Illinois. A moonshine still, confiscated in the Kentucky hills, is also on display along with a handsome collection of copper distilling vessels. Another exhibit focuses on Carrie Nation, the infamous ax-wielding Kentuckian who destroyed taverns during the Temperance Movement in the early 1900's. Located in Spalding Hall in Bardstown.

5 SCHMIDT'S COCA-COLA MUSEUM

Spurred by their interest in the history of Coca-Cola, the Schmidt family, which has been producing the soft drink in Kentucky since 1901, has built up a collection of Coca-Cola products and memorabilia that is considered to be the largest privately owned collection of its kind in the world. Their museum displays thousands of items bearing the familiar Coca-Cola trademark, including everyday objects such as calendars, jewelry, serving trays, beverage glasses, toys, playing cards, and sheet music, and ephemera such as cigar bands, candy boxes, and chewing gum wrappers. Coca-Cola magazine ads and posters will remind visitors of styles and fashions that go back nearly 100 years. Of particular interest is an authentic 1890's soda fountain. While at the museum, visitors can also view the family-owned Coca-Cola production facility and learn about modern bottling and canning procedures. Located at the Coca-Cola Bottling Co. on Hwy. 31W in Elizabethtown.

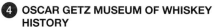

6 ABRAHAM LINCOLN BIRTHPLACE NATIONAL HISTORIC SITE

Abraham Lincoln was born here on February 12, 1809, in a log cabin on Sinking Spring Farm. The family lived on the 348-acre homestead until Lincoln was two and then moved to another farm at Knob

Creek a few miles away. In 1916 a 116-acre park on the site of Sinking Spring Farm was established as a historic site by Congress. Its heart is an early 19th-century Kentucky cabin, enshrined in a large granite memorial building near the spring that gave the farm its name. Although the cabin is not the one the nation's 16th president was born in, it is a vivid reminder of his humble roots—the cabin has an earthen floor and measures only 12 by 17 feet. The park museum features Lincolnalia and exhibits, including the family Bible, a diorama of the farm, and an 18-minute film, "Lincoln: The Kentucky Years." Within the park there are picnic facilities, meadows, and hiking trails through a small forest where young Abraham might well have played. Demonstrations of quilting, basket making, and rail splitting are given in July. Located in Hodgenville.

7 JEFFERSON DAVIS STATE HISTORIC SITE

Jefferson Davis, the president of the Confederate States during the Civil War, was born in 1808 on the site now dedicated to his memory. At the center of the 19-acre park stands one of the nation's tallest monuments, the idea for which was proposed by Gen. Simon Bolivar Buckner, a famous Confederate soldier from Kentucky. The 351-foot obelisk has walls seven feet thick at the base that taper to two feet thick at the apex. The historical marker at the base of the monument bears the address presented by Jefferson Davis on his last visit to his Kentucky birthplace in November 1886. Three years later, Davis died, never having regained his American citizenship; it was restored posthumously in 1978. A room inside the monument contains a life-size sculpture of Jefferson Davis. Visitors can ride the elevator to an observation room at the top for a breathtaking view of the surrounding countryside. The monument site offers covered picnic shelters and a playground. Located east of Hopkinsville on Hwy. 68.

The neoclassical structure, located at the birth site of Abraham Lincoln, above, was erected by the Lincoln Farm Association in 1911 as a memorial and shrine.

A selection of medicinal whiskey bottles dating from 1914–33 is on display in the Oscar Getz Museum of Whiskey History, below. One item in the museum's collection, an 1854 E. G. Booze bottle, is the origin of the word "booze" for liquor.

BIG THICKET NATIONAL PRESERVE

The 12 ecosystems in this ancient land support the greatest diversity of flora and fauna in the nation.

By itself, the Neches River is a waterway of no particular distinction. It carries no shipping traffic, powers no hydroelectric generators, and passes through no great metropolis. Its single distinction is that, in the last 50 miles before it reaches the Gulf of Mexico, it cuts through the heart of one of the most extraordinary pieces of property in North America—a primitive, hauntingly beautiful land known as the Big Thicket. On its relatively short, due-south course from a man-made lake in the Piney Woods of East Texas to Sabine Pass on the coast, the Neches flows through landscapes of vivid incongruity. These are timeless hills of fragrant magnolia and loblolly pine, savannas sprinkled with insect-eating flowers, murky bogs abloom with orchids, floodplain forests of thick palmetto, and dunes spiked with cacti and yucca. Along the riverbanks tower 100-year-old bald cypress trees, and close by wild azaleas flower in shallow canyons.

WADING GIANTS
Stately bald cypress trees, above, stand ankle-deep in a slough. Damming of the Neches River has altered the traditional seasonal fluctuations of water, so that the area stays wetter throughout the year.

WATERY REALM
Overleaf: An early morning fog settles over Village Creek in a heavy mantle. The wet climate nourishes the diverse plant life that thrives in the preserve.

AMERICAN ARK

Four of North America's natural environments converge, overlap, and coexist in the thicket, making it one of the most important biological crossroads on the continent. Eastern forests, Southeastern swamps, Southwestern desert, and Midwestern prairie exist here, and the thicket's diversity has led to it being called an American ark. A canoe trip down the tenebrous waters of the Neches River is a journey through the quirky artistry of the ice ages, when the rise and fall of sea waters during four glacial periods 2 million years ago pushed terraces of sediment bearing nearly 100 different soil types and diverse plant species southward into Texas.

The region's current average rainfall of 55 to 60 inches per year provides a moist environment for the nourishment of a wide array of flora and fauna. A change in elevation of just a few feet alters the moisture level, creating different habitats that support their own types of vegetation. Where two or more of the habitats overlap, life forms are the most varied—a natural phenomenon known as an ecotone. Big Thicket encompasses one of the most diverse collections of ecotones for an area of its size anywhere on earth.

Southwestern deserts bump into palmetto and tupelo swamps that are usually found in the Southeast, and dense hardwood forests typical of the Northeast rise above areas that are characteristic of the Central Plains. Roadrunners and eastern bluebirds share a common habitat, alligators and coyotes dwell in the same backyard, and armadillos and coral snakes forage for food side by side.

The precise boundaries of the thicket were never universally agreed upon by either scientists or surveyors. It has been said that the thicket represents an idea more than a reality and therefore its true locale and dimensions are irrelevant. The thicket is usually defined as a 3.5-million-acre subtropical tract that stretches west from the Sabine River on the Louisiana border toward the Texas Hill Country. This teeming biological community is home to nearly 200 species of trees and shrubs, some 550 varieties of flowering plants, 175 species

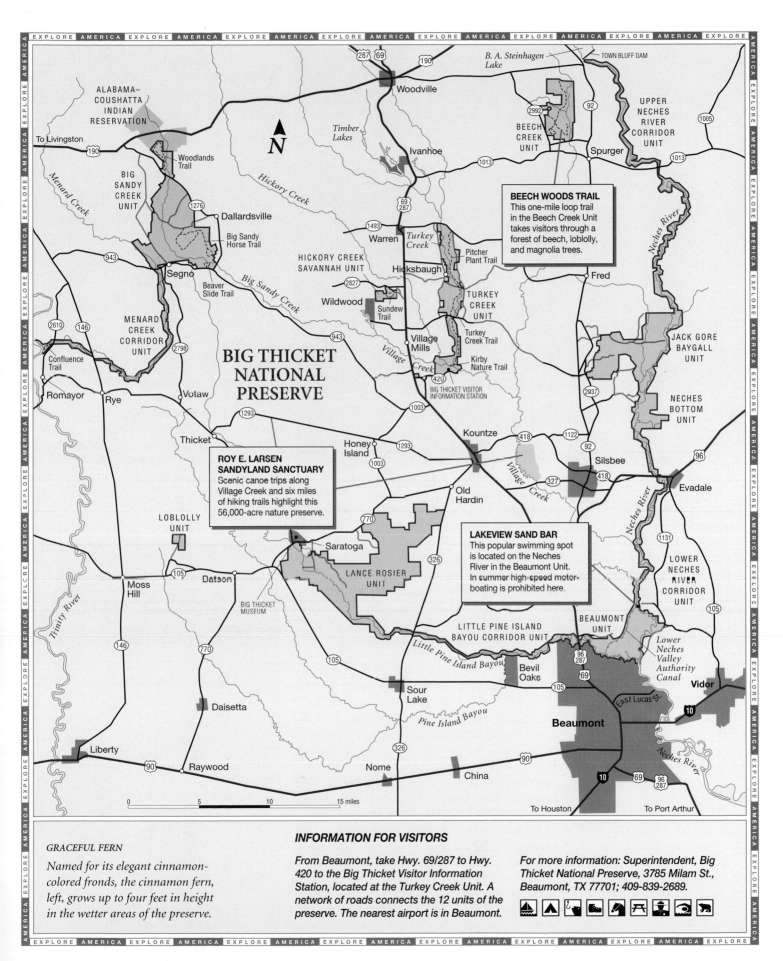

BIG THICKET NATIONAL PRESERVE

BEECH WOODS TRAIL
This one-mile loop trail in the Beech Creek Unit takes visitors through a forest of beech, loblolly, and magnolia trees.

ROY E. LARSEN SANDYLAND SANCTUARY
Scenic canoe trips along Village Creek and six miles of hiking trails highlight this 56,000-acre nature preserve.

LAKEVIEW SAND BAR
This popular swimming spot is located on the Neches River in the Beaumont Unit. In summer high-speed motorboating is prohibited here.

GRACEFUL FERN

Named for its elegant cinnamon-colored fronds, the cinnamon fern, left, grows up to four feet in height in the wetter areas of the preserve.

INFORMATION FOR VISITORS

From Beaumont, take Hwy. 69/287 to Hwy. 420 to the Big Thicket Visitor Information Station, located at the Turkey Creek Unit. A network of roads connects the 12 units of the preserve. The nearest airport is in Beaumont.

For more information: Superintendent, Big Thicket National Preserve, 3785 Milam St., Beaumont, TX 77701; 409-839-2689.

INSECT EATER
The funnel-shaped leaves of the pitcher plant, above, are lined with fine hairs that prevent insects from escaping once they land on the plant. As the trapped insects decompose, they are absorbed by the plant's cells.

ALONG THE NECHES RIVER
A solitary motorboat cruises along the Lower Neches River, right. A sandy beach on the left bank is a popular spot for swimming and fishing for bass, catfish, and white perch.

of birds, 50 species of reptiles, including 4 types of poisonous snakes, and a wide array of mammals—all living within an area a little larger than the state of Connecticut.

"The whole heterogeneity of the earth compressed in a small space" is how Dr. Pete Gunter, a professor at the University of North Texas, once described the area. "An incredible storehouse of genetic information. Someday, a cure for a major disease will be found in the Thicket."

THREATENED LAND

In 1974, 86,000 acres of the thicket were placed under the protection of Big Thicket National Preserve. Its establishment was essential if the unique character of the region was to be saved. Many of the region's species had vanished and others were slowly becoming extinct. Second-growth forests have largely replaced virgin timberlands, and hardwoods have almost all disappeared outside the preserve, as have some species of wildflowers. Panthers, red wolves, and black bears are long gone, lost to hunting and diminished habitats. As recently as the 1980's there were occasions when visitors emerged from the depths of the thicket with news of having spotted the rare ivory-billed woodpecker, once the largest woodpecker on the continent. These claims have been greeted with skepticism by

ornithologists; since the early 1970's, there has not been a confirmed sighting of the ivory-billed in the United States.

Nature produced this ecological phenomenon over the course of 2.5 million years; but after a mere 150 years of human contact the marvel of the Big Thicket's creation may well be eclipsed by the fact of its survival. A trickle of settlers in the mid-19th century became, by the 20th century, waves of lumbermen and sawmill workers, oil drillers, soldiers, outlaws, and trophy hunters. Big Thicket has been scarred by the building of dams and highways and subjected to the natural force of fires and hurricanes. In short, it has been ravaged as thoroughly as any area in the nation.

Yet, parts of the thicket have survived intact. Perhaps 300,000 acres, probably fewer, bear some resemblance to the spectacular wilderness that nature created. A much smaller allotment—the 86,000 acres in 12 units of the Big Thicket National Preserve scattered between the Neches and Trinity rivers—appears in places untouched by time and human hands.

As a national preserve, as opposed to a national park, Big Thicket performs a delicate balancing act: to keep the wilderness wild and the habitats from being spoiled, while allowing limited commercial exploitation. Logging is prohibited but oil and gas exploration are allowed and hunting is permitted within some of the units.

One of the most striking and pristine of the habitats is the Jack Gore Baygall Unit, a 12-square-mile bog stretching west from the Neches River halfway between B. A. Steinhagen Lake in the north and the Beaumont Unit in the south. The floodplain of this unit with its low, watery lands, towering trees, and dense underbrush deters human trespass, let alone habitation. It remains a noble wilderness where beavers, otters, and the occasional alligator share creeks, sloughs, and oxbow ponds. Where deer deftly pick their way across a surface of mattress-soft seeps and decaying vegetation, squirrels, hawks, and owls nest among the moss that hangs from 100-foot tupelos, bald cypresses, black gums, and water oaks. Magnolia, loblolly pine, and beech trees grow on the slopes and ridges of the upper floodplain.

An unofficial unit of the preserve, Bear Hunter's Thicket is a triangular section of land anchored by the towns of Kountze, Saratoga, and Sour Lake. Famed for its big bear hunts of a century ago, this habitat takes in the 25,025-acre Lance Rosier Unit, named after renowned conservationist and self-taught botanist Lance Rosier, who guided scientists on field trips to catalog species in the thicket from the 1930's to the 1950's. The forests here are so impenetrable that local mythology has it that even snakes traverse it with difficulty.

NATURE TRAILS

While wildlife still abounds in the Big Thicket preserve, the region's primary attraction is its multiple ecosystems. The two-and-a-half-mile Kirby Nature Trail, which begins at the Big Thicket Visitor Information Center at the south end of the Turkey Creek Unit, provides travelers with an overview of this naturally diverse area. Descending into the Village Creek floodplain under an umbrella of beeches and pines, the trail passes through an acidic swamp called a baygall—because of the gallberry holly, red bay, and sweet bay trees that grow there—then through a forest of oaks and sweet gums that overhang the approach to several sloughs.

The longer Turkey Creek Trail goes for 17 miles all the way to the northern end of the Turkey Creek Unit. The winding hike takes in the most diverse vegetation in the preserve. It traverses a mixed pine-hardwood forest, passes through a forest of loblolly pines, white and red oaks, beeches, and magnolia trees, and then through a floodplain forest of sweet gum and water and basket oaks.

RIVER INHABITANT
A water snake, left, glides silently through the Neches River. Boaters are advised to be on the alert for snakes, which sometimes fall out of the trees along the waterway and into boats. Most of the water snakes are not poisonous.

GROUND COVER
Magnolia, sassafras, and oak leaves mixed with pine cones, above, make a decorative carpet for the floor of the Turkey Creek Unit.

Boardwalks cross baygalls where the usual plant life is enhanced by black titis, black gums, and azaleas. The Sundew Trail in the Hickory Creek Savannah Unit is named for the sundew plant that, along with the pitcher plant, bladderwort, and butterwort, has adapted to the acidic nutrient-poor soils of the savanna wetland by developing the ability to digest insects. In this unit and elsewhere in the preserve, lilies, flowering dogwoods, bluebonnets, and 17 varieties of orchids flourish in a tapestry of sunlight that filters through the tall trees.

EARLY SETTLERS

The legends and lore of the thicket are nearly as colorful as its habitats. Long before any Europeans arrived, four Indian tribes claimed domain over various parts of the thicket. Befitting a land of striking diversity, the Indian tribes adhered to different traditions and beliefs. Living along the Gulf were the Atakapa people, who were said to eat the flesh of those they killed in combat. The northern regions were occupied by the Caddos, who were proficient farm-

ENTICING CARNIVORE
The spoonbowl sundew plant, above, grows in the wetlands of the Hickory Creek Savannah Unit. The leaves of the plant are covered with fine hairs that exude a sticky substance. Insects that become stuck on the leaves are slowly digested by the plant.

SYLVAN TRAIL
Thick foliage shades a back road in the Lance Rosier Unit, right, named for the man who played such a prominent role in the fight to protect Big Thicket. It has been said that Rosier, who often walked the area with his talking crow, could charm a copperhead snake so that visitors could take a close look at it.

ers, fishermen, and craftsmen. Much later, in the early 1800's, the Coushatta and Alabama tribes arrived from the Southeast and established villages on the Neches and Trinity rivers. They exhibited a gentler nature than the other two tribes and were more inclined to associate and cooperate with the colonists who began to stream into Texas. While the tribes remained neutral during the Texas Revolution, they gave sanctuary to Texans fleeing from Mexican forces. Today the Alabamas and Coushattas live on a reservation that adjoins the Big Sandy Creek Unit of the preserve.

The first white settlers were mostly Anglo-Americans from the East who arrived about 1820. Because of the density of the thicket, they claimed land outside the forest, ceding the interior to outlaws, outcasts, and loners looking for a place to hide or to escape the society of other Americans migrating westward through the area. Within a decade, however, settlers began to move into the thicket, clearing plots for cabins and gardens. It wasn't until almost 1850 when loggers, having depleted vast areas of the forests to the north, descended on the thicket, cutting down several million acres in a brief 60 years.

DISCOVERY OF OIL

On January 10, 1901, with the thicket already under siege, oil was discovered near the town of Beaumont, under a dome of land called Spindletop along the southeastern fringe of the region. Spindletop was a colossal find, the first major oil discovery in Texas. By 1902, 285 active wells were pumping oil from the Spindletop field. Unfortunately, lack of experience in dealing with such a massive well led to more environmental damage. The Lucas Gusher, as the first well was called, spewed nearly 100,000 barrels a day for nine days before the drillers were finally able to cap it.

Within weeks of the discovery, chaos overtook the thicket as drillers arrived in droves and fanned out across the land in search of new wells. It was the beginning of a destructive era that would further scar the land. Wide tracts were cleared for pipelines, and the natural gas from the wells killed birds and plants. The saltwater used for drilling destroyed the vegetation and contaminated streams.

Preservationist passions were inflamed by the 1938 publication of the *Biological Survey of the East Texas Big Thicket Area*. Scientists, academics, students, and nature lovers streamed into the area, many of them under the direction of Lance Rosier, who had assisted the authors of the survey. In 1964 the Big Thicket Association of Texas was formed to save what remained of the wilderness. It met the inevitable opposition of those bent on exploiting the thicket's valuable resources.

Ironically, the opposition gave the preservationists what was perhaps their strongest case for federal intervention by destroying the Witness Tree, a stately, 1,000-year-old Southern magnolia that had acted as a landmark and meeting place for generations of Native Americans, explorers, settlers, and soldiers. The tree had acquired its name because of the centuries of history that had taken place beneath its outstretched branches.

In 1966 US Supreme Court Justice William O. Douglas went to see the famous tree with Lance Rosier. By then it was an ashen corpse standing 50 feet above the forest floor. Rosier explained that someone who had wanted to scare people into giving up the idea of a national park for the Big Thicket had killed the tree by drilling five holes into it and filling them with arsenate of lead.

The preservation campaign gathered momentum, and in 1974 Congress passed legislation to create the first national preserves in U.S. history: Big Cypress, Florida, and the Big Thicket. Eight years later the United Nations added Big Thicket to its list of International Biosphere Reserves, deeming it worthy of protection worldwide. Francis Edward Abernathy, author of *Tales from the Big Thicket*, wrote in 1966, "There are times when this clear flowing part of the Big Thicket affords a sense of peaceful and primitive immediacy. One feels separated . . . from the steel and plastic of modern cities, from the sharp corners and raw edges of modern living." Visitors to this unique wilderness area will be rewarded with a similar experience. For here the trappings of civilization fall away, and nature in all its glory takes over.

CACTUS BLOOM
Flowering prickly pear cacti and pine cones, above, nestle at the base of a tree trunk in the Larsen Sandyland Sanctuary.

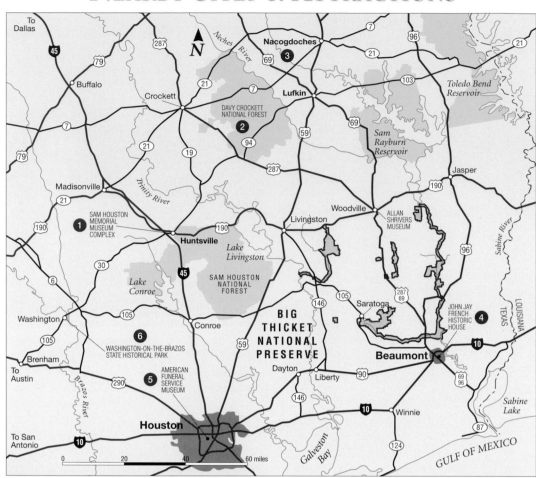

Established in Nacogdoches in 1838, the cemetery of the Old North Church, below, contains the graves of many of the area's early settlers.

1 SAM HOUSTON MEMORIAL MUSEUM COMPLEX

This museum is dedicated to the memory of Sam Houston (1793–1863), who led the fight for Texas independence and then served as president of the Republic of Texas, United States senator, and governor. The complex includes Houston's 1848 Woodland Home, where four of his eight children were born; his Law Office, which also served as a Masonic lodge; and the Exhibit Hall, which displays 19th-century artifacts from the early days of the Texas frontier. The Texas Memorial Museum building houses memorabilia from Houston's life. Of particular note are Houston's leopard skin vest and the horse saddle of Mexican general Antonio López de Santa Anna, who was captured in 1836 when the Texans, led by Houston, defeated the Mexicans at the Battle of San Jacinto. Located in Huntsville.

2 DAVY CROCKETT NATIONAL FOREST

The centerpiece of the national forest is a 45-acre lake that served as a log pond and a water source for a local sawmill in the early years of the century. The lake's clear waters are open for boating, fishing, and swimming. Piney Creek Horse Trail offers more than 50 miles of picturesque paths that wind through the 160,567-acre forest. The forest is dominated by pine and bottomland hardwoods and visitors may glimpse white-tailed deer, doves, quails, and endangered red-cockaded woodpeckers. The Big Slough Canoe Trail takes visitors on an exhilarating trip along the Neches River. For a panoramic view of the river, hikers should climb to the Neches Bluff Overlook. Located eight miles east of Crockett on Hwy. 7.

John F. Kennedy and Rev. Martin Luther King Jr., and the entertainers Judy Garland and Elvis Presley. The museum's collection of hearses includes an 1860 gold-trimmed German hearse and a funeral sleigh. A coffin built for three people, as well as a 1916 funeral bus—designed to carry the deceased, flower displays, pallbearers, and up to 20 mourners—are among the most unusual items on display. Located in Houston.

6 WASHINGTON-ON-THE-BRAZOS STATE HISTORICAL PARK

This park includes the site where the Texas Declaration of Independence was signed in 1836. The town of Washington also served as the capital of the republic between 1842 and 1845 when Mexican troops threatened the established capital of Austin. Today this 229-acre park contains a reconstruction of the original Independence Hall where Texas delegates met to sign the republic's declaration of independence, drafted a constitution, and formed an interim government. Also on the grounds is the home of Anson Jones, the last president of the Texas republic. The 1844 homestead was moved to the site for the 1936 centennial of Texas independence. The Star of the Republic Museum, which is designed in the shape of a five-pointed star, houses artifacts, exhibits, and an extensive research library relating to the history of Washington and the Republic of Texas. Located in Washington.

The Steamboat House, left, built in 1858, was the home of Sam Houston in the years after he was deposed as governor of Texas for refusing to swear allegiance to the Confederacy. Houston died in a downstairs bedroom in 1863.

Sunlight filters through stands of loblolly pine and sweetgum on the shores of Ratcliff Lake in Davy Crockett National Forest, below.

3 NACOGDOCHES

Nacogdoches is one of the oldest towns in Texas. It was a thriving Native American settlement long before Spanish explorers arrived in the 1540's. Its Native American past can be seen in the burial mound built by the Nacogdoches Caddo Indians approximately 700 years ago. The first permanent European settlement was established by the Spanish in 1716, but the oldest surviving building in town is the Adolphus Sterne House, erected in 1828, prior to the Texas Revolution. The Old University Building was used as a hospital by Confederate troops during the Civil War and by Union army veterans afterward. Today it is a furniture and silver museum. Many notable figures from Nacogdoches history are buried in the Oak Grove Cemetery, including four men who signed the Texas Declaration of Independence. Located on Hwy. 59.

4 JOHN JAY FRENCH HISTORIC HOUSE

At the beginning of the 19th century, when the Mexican government offered free land to anyone settling in Texas, John Jay French and his wife, Sally Munson, claimed 300 acres of prime farmland on the northern outskirts of Beaumont. French was a successful mercantile trader who saw the potential for economic profit on the frontier. In 1845 he built a grand home that was the town's first wooden house, and the first to have two floors. The building, Beaumont's oldest surviving structure, was restored in 1968. Original family furnishings and regional frontier artifacts such as a maple rocker, cherry bed and cradle, and mahogany sleigh are on display inside. Other household items include a rosewood piano, a mahogany Seth Thomas clock, and the family Bible. Located on Delaware St. off Hwy. 69.

5 AMERICAN FUNERAL SERVICE MUSEUM

This museum offers a unique display on the history of funeral rites and services. Included among the notable collection of coffins, hearses, and funeral attire are replicas of King Tut's sarcophagus and Pres. Abraham Lincoln's coffin. The "Funeral Directors" exhibit describes ancient Egyptian embalming techniques, and the "Funeral of the Famous Gallery" displays newspaper articles on the funerals of noted figures such as Pres.

DEATH VALLEY

---

*In this land of extremes,
snowcapped peaks rise above one
of the hottest deserts on earth.*

In 1849 a group of prospectors making their
way west to the Sierra Nevada goldfields in
California, decided to take a shortcut across a
parched and unnamed stretch of the southern
Nevada and California desert. Within a month
the wagon train was destroyed. Unable to find
sustenance, the emigrants were forced to slaugh-
ter their oxen, abandon all but one of their 29
wagons, and bury a member of their party in the
arid earth. When they finally escaped into the relative cool of the Panamint Mountains, one of the
miners looked back and spat out, "Good-bye,
Death Valley." The name stuck, and today it con-
jures up images of an expanse of salt-encrusted
desert where nothing lives or grows.

Although Death Valley's fearsome reputation
is well deserved—during the summer months,
temperatures on the valley floor regularly hit
120°F—it is also somewhat misleading. All kinds
of living things have scratched out niches for
themselves in this harsh land, from the tiny snail
species that has survived for over 10,000 years in

MIRROR IMAGE
Overleaf: A purple sky and the snowcapped heights of Telescope Peak cast their reflections on the still surface of Badwater Basin.

BEEHIVES OF ACTIVITY
With the discovery of silver in Death Valley in 1875, a series of kilns was constructed to make piñon pine and juniper charcoal for smelting. The insides of the kilns in Wildrose Canyon, below, are still redolent with resin and creosote, by-products of the burning process.

the brackish brine of Badwater, to the tenacious salt grass that sprouts along the edges of the glimmering desert salt pan.

<table>
<tr><td>BIRTH OF
THE VALLEY</td><td>These days Death Valley is a hauntingly quiet place. But it was born in a titanic geological tug-of-war. For millions of</td></tr>
</table>

BIRTH OF THE VALLEY

These days Death Valley is a hauntingly quiet place. But it was born in a titanic geological tug-of-war. For millions of years the basin and range region that encompasses portions of the states of Nevada, Utah, Oregon, and California has been pulling apart due to the shifting of the earth's crust. About 15 million years ago the Sierra Nevada began to drift to the west. So far, the range has moved 150 miles from its original location. This shift has taken place across many different breaks, or faults, in the region.

At the northern and southern ends of Death Valley lie strike slip faults, in which sections of bedrock slide past each other, mimicking the horizontal shift along the more famous San Andreas Fault to the west. A cinder hill near Shoreline Butte offers dramatic visual evidence of this tectonic movement. A volcano erupted here some 690,000 years ago, astride a fault; the cinder cone has since been pulled apart, its eastern side grinding a few hundred yards to the north.

Death Valley is flanked on the west and east by the Panamint and Black mountains. Most geologists concur that the two ranges were once docked alongside each other, with some experts claiming that the Panamint Mountains had been piled squarely on top of the Black Mountains. Over the past 10

DELICATE FLOWERINGS
The tiny yellow blossoms of desert velvet, above, contrast with the silvery green tinge of its leaves.

INFORMATION FOR VISITORS

From Las Vegas, take Hwy. 95 to Hwy. 373. Travel south to Death Valley Junction, then west along Hwy. 190. From Los Angeles, take Hwy. 395 to Hwy. 190 east. The Furnace Creek Visitor Center is located on Hwy. 190. The best time to visit is from October through May when the intense summer temperatures can be avoided. Even during cooler months, however, the area can be extremely hot. Before venturing into the park, visitors are advised to make sure that their cars are in good working condition and that their gas tanks are full. Water for radiators is available from water tanks situated at intervals along the park roads. In the event of a breakdown, visitors should stay with their car. Nine campgrounds are open year-round. Fuel for fires must be brought in. Visitors to the park should avoid travel in the low country during stormy weather as flash floods can wash out roads.
For more information: Superintendent, Death Valley National Park, Death Valley, CA 92328; 619-786-2331.

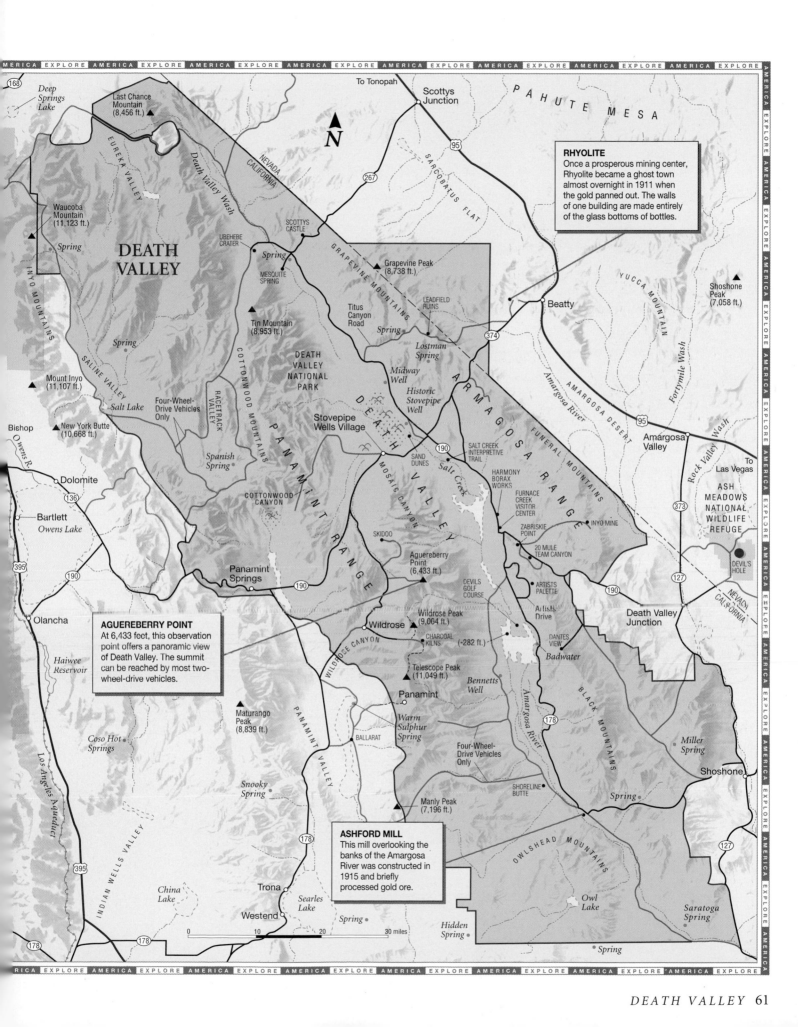

million years shifting plates have pulled the Panamints 30 miles away from the Blacks, creating Death Valley in the rift.

As these massive ranges separated, the intervening basins collapsed. Over time, rainfall and streams wore away the steep mountainsides, scooping steep canyons into the valley floor. A walk up Mosaic Canyon near Stovepipe Wells Village offers dramatic proof of the irresistible force of moving water. Flash floods have gouged out loose rock and soil and hurled the debris into the valley below. At the western foot of the Black Mountains, this alluvium has piled up in symmetrical fans that spread out for miles. On the other side of the valley, alluvial fans from adjacent canyons have converged to form bajadas that cover the valley floor along the entire eastern front of the Panamint Mountains.

The floor of Death Valley has dropped so low that water no longer flows out of it. One spot near Badwater is 282 feet below sea level, the lowest elevation in the Western Hemisphere. Water can leave the valley only by evaporation, and all sediment and minerals carried into the valley by rain runoff are trapped here forever. The floor of Death Valley gleams with sodium deposits that have collected here over the eons. Seismic tests reveal that the actual floor of the valley lies beneath some 8,000 feet of salt, calcite, and gypsum.

Visitors can get a spectacular view of this chemical desert by taking the 25-mile drive from the Furnace Creek Visitor Center to Dantes View, an overlook perched high up on the Blackwater Mountains. From the top, a coyote might be seen trotting by at a respectful distance, while a black raven wheels overhead and violet-green swallows slash through the air just beyond the cliffs. More than 5,000 feet below, Badwater Basin is merely a smudge of green. The valley floor, so harsh and unforgiving, is transformed at this height into a delicate tapestry of white salt and brown silt.

BITTER WATER

Death Valley is the driest place in the United States, averaging just over one and a half inches of rain a year. Much of the water in the valley is undrinkable due to its high salt content. The spring at Badwater, for example, is said to have gotten its name when a surveyor's thirsty mule refused to drink from the salty pool. It should come as no surprise that Death Valley's most significant watercourse, the Amargosa River, means "bitter" in Spanish.

But the valley wasn't always so parched. During the Pleistocene epoch, dating from about 2 million until 10,000 years ago, water from melting glaciers flowed into the basin faster than it evaporated, helping to form a massive lake that reached depths of 600 feet. Visitors can see the demarcation of the ancient lake's shoreline hundreds of feet up the mountain slopes above Badwater.

The force of wind erosion also gave shape and form to Death Valley. High winds howl down the mountainsides and across the floor, carrying with them great clouds of dust and sand. The dune fields

at Stovepipe Wells Village form where the wind eddies out behind Tucki Mountain, slowing down long enough to deposit more sand. The dunes, some of which are as high as 700 feet, are under constant construction, as, in storm after storm, the wind and rain dramatically reshape them. Other dune fields are found in similar pockets in the nearby mountains. The sand of the Eureka Dunes, at the extreme northern end of the park, sing. The singing is a deep, vibrating boom caused by grains of sand rubbing against each other in an avalanche. Oddly enough, avalanches are not usually initiated by the wind. Instead they are generally produced when a dune's angle of repose is too steep or when a dune is disturbed by people walking on it.

Some geographical changes are lightning-quick and violent. Three thousand years ago or so, molten magma rose to within a few hundred feet of the valley's surface north of Mesquite Spring. Then the magma hit a body of underground water, which instantly flashed to steam. The resulting explosion blew out Ubehebe Crater, half a mile in diameter and 750 feet deep. Volcanic ash was hurled into the sky, blanketing the landscape for miles. Today visitors can walk among the coffee-colored cinders left by the upheaval.

NATURAL MYSTERY

Racetrack Valley, located about 27 miles beyond the Ubehebe Crater, is home to one of the area's most enduring natural mysteries. Here, dozens of rocks lie scattered across the dry flat lake bed. Upon closer inspection, visitors notice that the rocks have gouged trails in the dry mud as if they had crawled across the surface. No one has ever seen the rocks move across the playa, but it is clear they do. Scientists speculate that the rocks are blown across the frozen mud during the winter by gusts of wind.

Death Valley is chameleonlike. At midday it can be one of the bleakest landscapes on earth: gray, austere, forbidding. But at sunrise and toward sun-

called the desert sunflower, brighten the sandy, rock-strewn areas above the valley floor. Sweet-smelling sand verbena and phacelias add splashes of pink and purple, interspersed with sprawling gold carpet, or Death Valley gilmania.

The vegetation has adapted in a variety of ways to its scorched environment. The leaves of many plants are sticky, coated, or hairy as protection from the relentless sun and to lessen evaporation. Cacti have done away with leaves entirely; instead they store most of their moisture in their thick, porous bodies. The mesquite tree sends its roots as far as 70 feet below the surface in the endless search for a water source.

The yellow flower of the Death Valley mohavea, which resembles a snapdragon, blooms in early spring, but its fragile beauty is short-lived. The plant germinates, flowers, and seeds in only three weeks, a pace that is kept up by many of the local annuals to take advantage of the rare wet periods. Seeds of annuals can remain dormant in the soil for years until, when the right combination of moisture and warmth occurs, the plants bloom and complete their life cycles.

Only plants that can tolerate the extremely high salinity of the soil in Death Valley survive. The

LIFE-BEARING WATER
The crystal-clear waters of Saratoga Spring, beside the Ibex Hills, above, support schools of tiny pupfish, a species that is found only in Death Valley.

set the valley comes alive with color. Artist's Drive leads to the Artists Palette where an explosion of volcanic rock in white, black, red, brown, turquoise, and yellow greets the eye. The one-way road passes through a jumble of rock formations, tilted every which way and highlighted by brilliant pastels.

	SPRINGTIME FLOWERING

Natural wonders abound in this unique valley. Despite the wilting heat—on July 10, 1913, the mercury hit 134°F—there are signs of life in every shaded nook and cranny. A startling number of plant species, nearly 1,000, can be found within the park's boundaries.

Heavy winter rainfalls set the scene for the normally austere canyons, mountains, and desert to blossom in spring with the vibrant colors of wildflowers. Among the showiest are the breathtaking desert mariposas, wild lilies with delicate satin petals of yellow and deep orange; the saucer-sized yellow flowers of Panamint daisies; and bear poppies so tender a mere touch sends the fragile white petals tumbling to the ground. Swaths of desertgold, also

small pickleweed shrub, with fleshy green stems that are bubbled like beads on a necklace, grows on the rim of the glaring white salt pan. But in spite of its hardy nature, even pickleweed is unable to live on the salt deposits of Devils Golf Course.

Bands of arrowweeds, alkali sacaton grasses, rushes, and desert holly grow here. During the hottest times of the year, the desert holly's toothed leaves thicken and take on the white or rose color of the crystallized salts that collect on their surfaces and reflect the sun's rays. The desert holly can survive two or three years with low rainfall, making it the most drought-tolerant plant in Death Valley. Mesquite, like pickleweed, must live where the water table is close to the surface so its roots can obtain water year-round. It occupies the outer edges of the salt flats and is also found on the alluvial fans around the springs.

A surprising number of plants burst forth wherever water can be found in Death Valley: stream orchids and maidenhair ferns thrive in wet places in the canyons, and maple trees are found in the Panamint Mountains. The pools of the salt flats attract tiny water snails. In particularly moist years, painted lady butterflies flutter through the valley in early spring on their northward migration. A forest of limber pines and ancient bristlecones grows in the highest reaches of the mountains.

LIVELY FISH Visitors can spot desert pupfish darting about in ponds in Death Valley. The name of these tiny fish comes from their puppylike activity, which is especially frenetic during spring spawning. At the end of the Pleistocene epoch massive Lake Manly dried up, leaving warm spring-fed pools, many of which are populated today by pupfish. Each pool claims a species or subspecies of pupfish with its own distinct shape and markings: four species and three subspecies of

SUN-BAKED MUD
The cracked playas of Death Valley, left, attest to the region's extreme dryness. Some 10,000 years ago, a 600-foot-deep body of water covered the valley.

DAINTY BUTTERFLY
A painted lady, above, helps pollinate the flowers during its annual migration to Death Valley.

PAINTED BY NATURE'S BRUSH
The misconception that deserts are colorless places is put to rest when visitors cast their eyes on the spectacular pink and turquoise shades of Artist's Palette, left.

ing in areas where there are a lot of kangaroo rats, especially around the growths of mesquite and saltbush on the sand flats and dunes.

Snakes are commonly sighted at higher elevations where temperatures are cooler and where rodents are more plentiful. In the lower reaches of the valley, sidewinders, or horned rattlesnakes, coil up under bushes during the day and venture out at night to hunt for food. Among the resident lizards are chuckwallas, banded geckos, whiptails, and collared lizards, which can be seen darting from shrub to shrub in search of shade.

HUMAN HABITATION

People have been forging lives in Death Valley for at least the last 8,000 to 10,000 years. Prehistoric petroglyphs etched into the rock at Titus Canyon attest to the presence of the earliest residents, the ancestors of the Shoshone Indians. They entered the valley in about A.D. 1000 and survived off the land, eating chuckwallas, mesquite beans, wild mustard greens, piñon nuts, Indian ricegrass seeds, cactus fruits, rabbits, deer, and bighorn sheep.

Soon after the first wagon trainers stumbled out of Death Valley in 1849, prospectors went to the region in search of gold, silver, copper, lead, talc, and borax. Evidence of their work is found everywhere. A mining strike of silver chloride was made in 1873 and gave birth to Panamint City, Death Valley's first boomtown. Two years later, a silver strike in the Argus Range led to the construction of some charcoal kilns in Wildrose Canyon, located within the Panamint Range, where piñon trees were burned for charcoal to fuel the smelters. Ten stone kilns still stand today.

Borax, a boron salt now used primarily in making soap, was discovered in the valley in 1873. William T. Coleman of San Francisco, recognizing a promising venture, bought a borax claim for $20,000 and proceeded to make a fortune. In order to haul the valuable borax 165 miles to the railhead, Coleman hitched 18 mules and 2 horses to a wagon, inventing the famous Twenty Mule Teams of Death Valley. These teams stretched 100 feet in front of the wagons and could pull two 16-foot loaded wagons—as well as

NATURAL AND MAN-MADE BEAUTY Scotty's Castle, above, displays the red-tiled roofs and stucco exterior typical of provincial Spanish architecture. The striking rock patterns of Cottonwood Canyon, right, are called breccia *in Spanish, which means "sharp rocks embedded in sandstone."*

pupfish have been identified in and around Death Valley, including Saratoga Spring and Cottonball Marsh, where visitors can view the lively fish from a boardwalk.

One of the most popular and populous denizens of Death Valley is the desert bighorn sheep. Visitors are afforded many opportunities to observe the rams with their great curling horns and the ewes protecting their lambs from potential predators. Bighorns browse among the stems of honey sweet. The best place to spot these magnificent animals is on the sides of cliffs, where they feel safe. The sheep are sometimes seen on Titus Canyon Road and at watering holes such as Willow Spring.

Visitors are even more likely to come across a member of Death Valley's large rodent population of squirrels, mice, pack rats, and rabbits. The rodents are preyed upon by hawks, snakes, and larger mammals. Tiny kit foxes, distinguished by their oversized ears, are often found prowl-

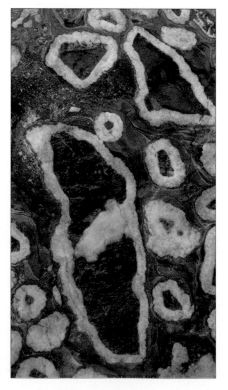

the essential 1,200-gallon water tank. From 1883 to 1889, some 10,000 tons of borax were transported by this method. Visitors can still inspect Harmony Borax Works, situated just north of Furnace Creek.

No story of Death Valley is complete without mention of Walter Scott. Scotty was a flimflam artist of the first water, who, for a surprising number of years, enticed gullible investors with tales of the untold riches in Death Valley. His publicity-grabbing stunts, such as cross-country train rides at record speeds, somehow convinced people of his credibility. One investor, Chicago insurance executive Albert Johnson, continued to support Scotty even after learning there was no gold mine. Johnson and his wife, Bessie, developed a passion for Death Valley and between 1915 and 1927 bought more than 1,500 acres in Grapevine Canyon as a vacation retreat. They built a sprawling Spanish-style castle complete with a chimes tower, guest house, and assorted outbuildings, including a powerhouse and solar water heater. Death Valley Scotty became a fixture at the ranch, holding court from his wicker rocking chair; he was such a frequent guest that Johnson's home in the desert soon became known simply as Scottys Castle. After Johnson's and then Scotty's death, the mansion and lands were bought by the National Park Service.

Visitors to Death Valley are astounded both by the severity of this land and the remarkable abundance of life it nourishes. Perhaps William Lewis Manly, one of the leaders of that ill-fated group of forty-niners, expressed it best when he said this is a place where "pretty near all creation was in sight."

SCAVENGER'S CALL
One of the most resourceful residents of Death Valley is the raven, below, which can be seen scavenging for food wherever people are found.

DEATH VALLEY OVERLOOK
Jutting above the Badlands, Manly Peak, left, was named after William Lewis Manly, a miner who walked all the way to Los Angeles to get help for a group of forty-niners stranded in Death Valley.

NEARBY SITES & ATTRACTIONS

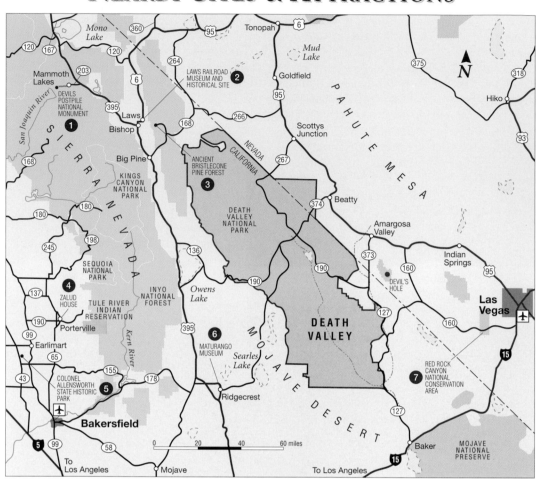

Battered by the elements, a bristlecone pine, below, clings tenaciously to life on California's White Mountains. Some of these trees were growing here at the same time that the Egyptians were completing the pyramids.

① DEVILS POSTPILE NATIONAL MONUMENT, CALIFORNIA

Encompassing 800 acres of the Inyo National Forest, the monument was established in 1911 to preserve two natural features: Devils Postpile and Rainbow Falls. Sixty-foot-tall Devils Postpile was created about 100,000 years ago when a cooling basalt lava flow cracked into six-sided columns that resemble the pipes of a massive church organ. Visitors who hike to the summit can see how perfectly these columns fit together. Some 10,000 years ago the top of Devils Postpile was scraped flat by a glacier, giving it the appearance of a meticulously laid tile floor. Other attractions at the monument include Rainbow Falls, which drops 101 feet over a cliff, and the mineral waters of Soda Springs. Visitors can fish for trout in the San Joaquin River and hike a section of the John Muir Trail. Located eight miles west of Mammoth Lakes off Hwy. 203.

② LAWS RAILROAD MUSEUM AND HISTORICAL SITE, CALIFORNIA

In 1880 the Carson and Colorado Railroad Company began building a narrow-gauge railway between Mound House and Carson River. The railroad never reached Carson River but instead made its terminus at Keeler. Knowing that the railway would pass

through the area, people established homesteads in what became the town of Laws. Laws declined with the shutting down of local mines, the increased use of trucks for transport, and the closing of the railroad in 1959. Many of the town's buildings were subsequently restored and are excellent examples of turn-of-the-century structures in a railroad town. Also on display are engines, cars, and cabooses from the early 20th century. Antique fire-fighting equipment is exhibited in the Fire Station, and Native American artifacts are on view in the Wells Fargo Building. Other exhibits include the Post Office and a restored 1900 ranch. Located on Silver Canyon Rd. in Laws.

③ ANCIENT BRISTLECONE PINE FOREST, CALIFORNIA

A grove of bristlecone pines has been growing for at least 4,000 years on the slopes of the White Mountains in the Inyo National Forest at an elevation of 10,000 feet. One bristlecone pine, known as Methuselah, is estimated to be 4,700 years old and is the oldest living tree on earth. Old Patriarch, with a trunk circumference of 36 feet, is the world's largest bristlecone pine. Blanched by the sun and scoured by the high mountain winds, these ancient trees resemble huge pieces of living driftwood. The trees secrete sap that fills the air with fragrance. During the summer, wildflowers carpet Patriarch

Grove. Hiking trails wind through the forest, and numerous picnic sites make perfect spots to rest and enjoy the scenery. Visitors can also take a forest road that affords spectacular views of the Sierra Nevada and Owens Valley. Located 22 miles northeast of Big Pine off Hwy. 168.

4 ZALUD HOUSE, CALIFORNIA

Listed on the National Register of Historic Places and the National Historical Registry of Old Houses, the Zalud House has not been altered in any way since it was built in 1891. The Zaluds, who were of Bohemian origin, are the only family to have lived in it. John Zalud was a shrewd businessman who made a small fortune in land investments. Complete with a spectacular garden planted according to its original design, this is one of the few museums in the nation to be furnished entirely with the possessions of its original owners. Located in Porterville.

5 COLONEL ALLENSWORTH STATE HISTORIC PARK, CALIFORNIA

In 1908 Allensworth became the only town in California founded, financed, and governed by African-Americans. Its founder, Allen Allensworth, was a former Kentucky slave, who escaped to the North and rose to the rank of lieutenant colonel in the army before moving here. He wanted to found a community where African-Americans could be self-sufficient and live free from prejudice. The town became a haven for black businessmen, artisans, ranchers, and farmers, and it thrived as an agricultural center until 1966. That year high levels of naturally occurring arsenic were found in the drinking water and the town rapidly declined. Eight buildings have been restored to their early 20th-century appearance and furnished in that style, including the town's school and Colonel Allensworth's home. Located eight miles west of Earlimart on Hwy. 43.

6 MATURANGO MUSEUM, CALIFORNIA

Established in 1962, this museum's cultural and natural history exhibits are complemented by its art collections and informative lectures. The natural history section focuses on desert flora, fauna, and geology. There are also displays of Native American artifacts, and paleontological specimens. Children especially enjoy the Discovery Area, which offers a variety of hands-on exhibits. The work of local artists is showcased in the museum's art gallery. The museum staff leads field trips to some of the most extensive Native American petroglyph sites on the continent. Located on East Las Flores Ave. in Ridgecrest.

7 RED ROCK CANYON NATIONAL CONSERVATION AREA, NEVADA

The centerpiece of this 196,000-acre conservation area is a steep-walled canyon composed of multicolored layers of sandstone and limestone that once was an ancient seabed. Millions of years ago the sea

Sixty-foot-tall basalt columns, left, sweep gracefully to the summit of Devils Postpile. The formations, found in only a handful of places worldwide, are remarkable for their geometric precision.

dried up, and subsequent geological upheaval covered the soft seabed with a protective cap of older limestone. The elements eventually wore away the formation's hard shell to expose the colorful layers of rock underneath. A 13-mile paved drive climbs along the lower rim of 7,000-foot Red Rock Escarpment, where bighorn sheep can be spotted climbing the cliffs. Trails lead to picnic sites and campgrounds. A visitor center provides an overview of the region's natural history, geology, and its flora and fauna. Located 20 miles west of Las Vegas off Hwy. 159.

The layers of rock in Red Rock Canyon National Conservation Area, below, testify to geological events in the region. The rust color was created by iron oxide staining.

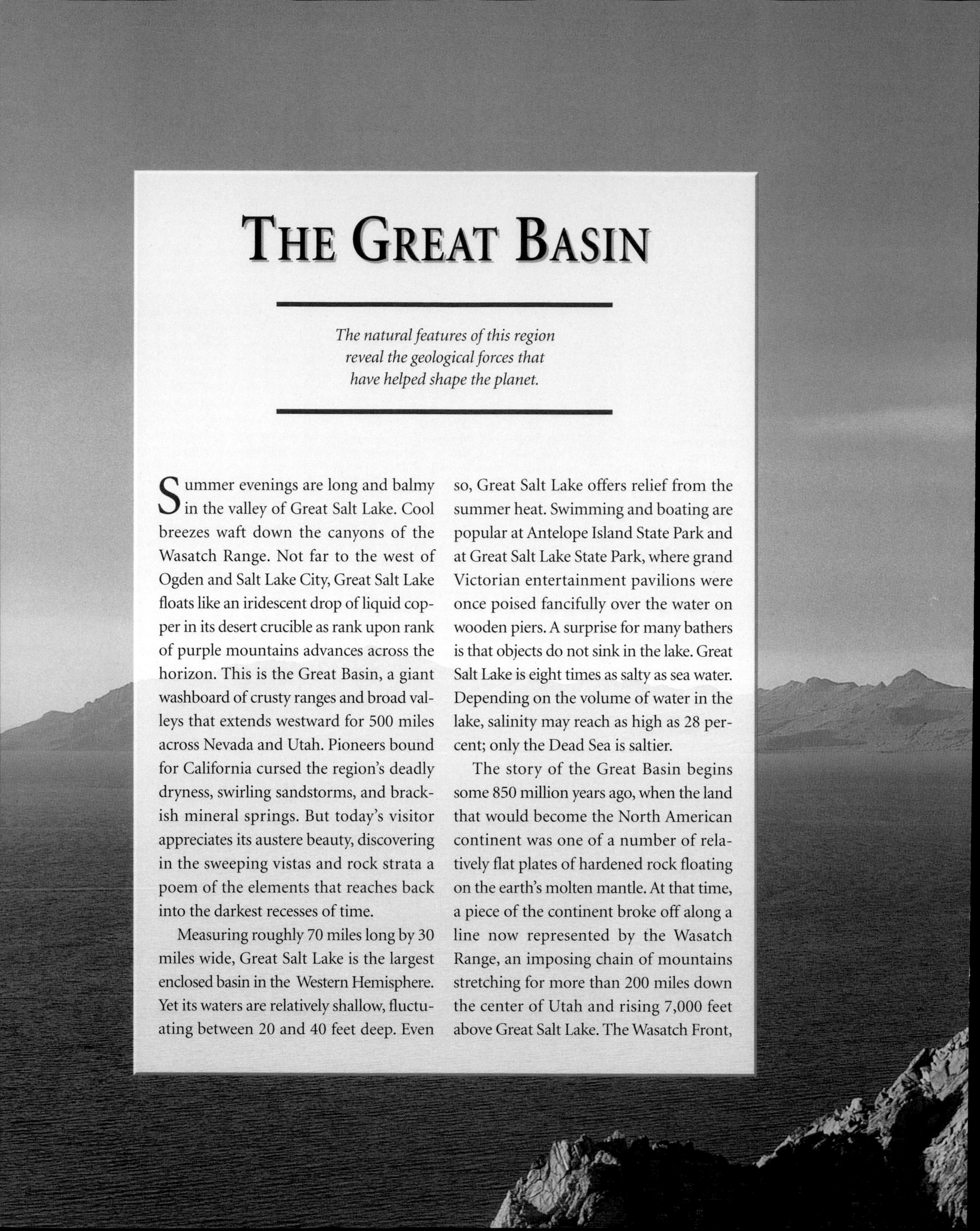

THE GREAT BASIN

---

*The natural features of this region
reveal the geological forces that
have helped shape the planet.*

Summer evenings are long and balmy in the valley of Great Salt Lake. Cool breezes waft down the canyons of the Wasatch Range. Not far to the west of Ogden and Salt Lake City, Great Salt Lake floats like an iridescent drop of liquid copper in its desert crucible as rank upon rank of purple mountains advances across the horizon. This is the Great Basin, a giant washboard of crusty ranges and broad valleys that extends westward for 500 miles across Nevada and Utah. Pioneers bound for California cursed the region's deadly dryness, swirling sandstorms, and brackish mineral springs. But today's visitor appreciates its austere beauty, discovering in the sweeping vistas and rock strata a poem of the elements that reaches back into the darkest recesses of time.

Measuring roughly 70 miles long by 30 miles wide, Great Salt Lake is the largest enclosed basin in the Western Hemisphere. Yet its waters are relatively shallow, fluctuating between 20 and 40 feet deep. Even

so, Great Salt Lake offers relief from the summer heat. Swimming and boating are popular at Antelope Island State Park and at Great Salt Lake State Park, where grand Victorian entertainment pavilions were once poised fancifully over the water on wooden piers. A surprise for many bathers is that objects do not sink in the lake. Great Salt Lake is eight times as salty as sea water. Depending on the volume of water in the lake, salinity may reach as high as 28 percent; only the Dead Sea is saltier.

The story of the Great Basin begins some 850 million years ago, when the land that would become the North American continent was one of a number of relatively flat plates of hardened rock floating on the earth's molten mantle. At that time, a piece of the continent broke off along a line now represented by the Wasatch Range, an imposing chain of mountains stretching for more than 200 miles down the center of Utah and rising 7,000 feet above Great Salt Lake. The Wasatch Front,

UTAH SAHARA

Little Sahara Recreation Area, right, contains 60,000 acres of dunes, trails, and sagebrush flats. The area's fragile dune fields were created from deposits left by the Sevier River, which 15,000 years ago flowed into ancient Lake Bonneville. The dunes are constantly on the move, shifting to the north and east between five and nine feet a year.

ISLAND TREASURES

Clumps of pink Indian paintbrush bloom in the rocky crevices of Stansbury Island, below, 1 of 10 islands in Great Salt Lake.

vaulted the mountain ranges of the region more than a mile into the sky, creating the Great Basin—a vast area of horsts and grabens.

ORIGIN OF GREAT SALT LAKE

The terraced hills of Antelope Island, the largest of Great Salt Lake's islands, offer important evidence as to the origin of Great Salt Lake. The terraces ring the Wasatch and other mountains like broad porch steps. Here and there, the rocks are coated with a chalky white substance known as tufa, which was deposited by wave action. The terraces and the tufa are visible reminders of Lake Bonneville, the prehistoric ancestor of Great Salt Lake. For centuries the island was a popular hunting ground for Native Americans. In 1845 Antelope Island attracted the attention of explorer Captain John C. Frémont, who, with his guide, Kit Carson, was mapping the American West. When the explorers came upon the island, they named it after the pronghorn antelopes that grazed on its lush grasslands. Today the antelopes are joined by a large herd of bison, as well as mule deer, bobcats, and a great variety of waterfowl.

Great blue herons perch in their nests, above, in the Fish Springs National Wildlife Refuge. The refuge, which is located along the Pacific Flyway, was established in 1959 for migratory birds.

VAST INLAND SEAS

Sediment cores taken by geologists reveal that bodies of water have occupied Salt Lake Valley many times over the past million years, but none was as extensive as Lake Bonneville. During the Pleistocene epoch, an ice age that lasted from roughly 2 million to 11,000 years ago, the earth's climate was much cooler and wetter than it is today. High rainfall turned Great Basin's grabens into lakes, and snows built glaciers in the mountain valleys. About 25,000 years ago, the lakes linked up to form two enormous inland seas: Lake Lahontan, a remnant of which still exists in the west, and Lake Bonneville in the east.

Lake Bonneville covered more than 20,000 square miles, extending from southern Idaho to southern Utah and from the Wasatch Front into eastern Nevada. The lake was more than 1,100 feet deep, and contained so much water that the earth's crust sagged nearly 200 feet under its weight. The strong rains of the Pleistocene epoch tore into the soft sedimentary blocks, depositing silt and gravel on the alluvial fans and deltas that today rise hundreds of feet above the water line.

Lake Bonneville held its peak water level for several thousand years before disaster struck. For some time, a small gap in the soft strata at Red Rock Pass in southeastern Idaho had served as a natural valve through which excess water from Lake Bonneville found its way to the Snake River and eventually to the sea. About 14,500 years ago, the opening gave way, disgorging an immense torrent of water onto the Snake River Plateau. The water scoured a deep gorge into the volcanic rock of the plain. At Massacre Rocks State Park in southeastern Idaho, trailer-sized boulders strewn across the grasslands recall the immense force of the raging waters. In the Great Basin the draining of Lake Bonneville lowered it by nearly 350 feet in a very short period of time. The waters rushing through the gap at Red Rock Pass hit resistant bedrock, and the lake level stabilized for the next 1,500 years, creating the prominent benchland that is now occupied by many of the cities of northern Utah, including Ogden, Salt Lake City, and Provo.

Climatic changes and renewed breakouts at Red Rock Pass caused lake levels to fluctuate. Geologists have discovered that the lake twice dried up completely before attaining its present level. Could it happen again? Probably not for some time. The lake reached low levels as recently as the early 1960's, when Antelope Island was connected to the shore by a sandbar that supported car traffic. Then, in 1987, the waters rose to a historic high. The high

TAKING ROOT
Great Salt Lake Desert, right, was once the floor of Lake Bonneville. The desert is aptly named: its salty crust ranges in depth from a fraction of an inch to four feet. The only vegetation here is found in extremely rare depressions where some soil has accumulated.

water swamped the causeway and forced the park to close. A new causeway to the park has been built, providing access once again, and a new man-made overflow valve has been installed that pumps excess water into the Salt Lake Desert. However, more recent climatic conditions have caused the lake level to fall once more.

As Interstate 80 rolls west from Salt Lake City, it skirts the southern shore of Great Salt Lake. Islands rise above the shimmering waters whose reflections mingle with those of clouds and distant ranges. The road leaves the shoreline, snakes through the Cedar and Lakeside mountains, and enters a dune field unrelieved by even a hint of plant life. It seems inconceivable that any human being could live out here, but the desert has been occupied on and off for more than 11,000 years.

On the western side of the Bonneville Salt Flats, a small road leads north to Danger Cave, a major archeological site now under development as a state park. The remains of tools and scraps of leather found at Danger Cave indicate that peoples of the Desert Archaic Culture, western Utah's earliest

people from the south who roamed the region, hunting game and gathering the piñon nuts of the wooded uplands.

WILDLIFE OASIS
The white-faced ibis, above, is one of the species of shore- and wading birds that visit the Fish Springs National Wildlife Refuge in spring and summer. The refuge provides an important stopover for migrating birds, some of which nest and rear their young here.

inhabitants, lived here when the cave was surrounded by marshland. They lived an itinerant life, moving between the wetlands, where they had a nutritious diet of cattails, pickleweed seeds, sedge, marsh birds, and deer, to the hills, where they hunted mountain sheep, deer, and bison. Centuries later tribes of the Fremont Culture built more permanent settlements on the alluvial fans of the Wasatch. They supplemented bison hunting and marsh gathering with the cultivation of corn, squash, and beans. By about 600 years ago, these tribes had disappeared. It is believed that they may have been assimilated by the Shoshonis, a nomadic

RACER'S DREAM

By the time explorers Jedediah Smith and John C. Frémont arrived in the mid-1800's, the valley was barren. When pioneers bound for California attempted to cross it, they lost horses, wagons, and precious time on the way. But in the 1930's, mining operations began to harvest Great Salt Lake for magnesium, iron, zinc, and dozens of other important minerals, adding significantly to Utah's prosperity. The lake is the largest nonmarine source of salt in the United States. And potash, used mainly as an ingredient in fertilizer, is isolated from lake brines in huge evaporation ponds.

As prosperous as the mining operations are, the ancient lake bed is most famous for its Bonneville Salt Flats, a 30,000-acre tract of unparalleled smoothness. During summer and fall, drivers, their crews, and spectators converge on the 10-mile straightaway to challenge land speed records. The tradition began in 1914, when daredevil Teddy Tetzlaff roared across the flats in a Blitzen Benz at nearly 142 miles an hour. The record was surpassed many times until 1970, when Gary Gabolich set the current mark of just over 622 miles an hour in his three-wheeled rocket car called Blue Flame. Drivers can always count on the Great Basin to provide a good course. Every winter rains cover the valley floor, turning the flats into a vast mire of salty slush. As the flats dry out, spring winds blow standing water across them, buffing the floor, scattering excess salts, and creating the flattest place on the planet. It is so flat that the curvature of the earth is visible to the naked eye. Looking east at sunset, the lights of cars traveling west on the interstate seem to crest a bulge before they descend into Wendover. That bulge is the smooth bottom of Lake Bonneville, planed by water and wind.

ONE OF A KIND

Although Lake Bonneville once covered an area about the size of Lake Michigan, all that remains today of this vast body of water is three lakes: Great Salt Lake, Utah Lake, and Sevier Lake. Great Salt Lake lies in one of a number of the Great Basin's playas, or shallow undrained desert basins. The lake receives about 60 percent of its water supply from the Jordan, Weber, Bear, and Ogden rivers that originate high in the Wasatch and Uinta ranges. Once water from the rivers, which contains a small amount of salt, enters the lake, it is trapped—there is no egress except through evaporation. The warmth of the sun regularly heats the shallow water of the lake to 90°F, providing sufficient energy to evaporate about four feet of water annually. As the water in the lake continues to evaporate, the salt content rises.

A short seven-mile scenic drive from Salt Lake City brings visitors to Little Cottonwood Canyon in the heart of the Wasatch Range. The road climbs between sheer glacier-carved walls and travels through thickets of box elder and aspen. The vacation resorts of Alta and Snowbird lie at the head of the canyon and offer year-round recreational attractions. At Snowbird, an aerial tram lifts visitors to the 11,000-foot summit of Hidden Peak for an unforgettable mountain panorama. To the north, Kessler Peak surges skyward. Directly below lies Little Cottonwood Canyon whose U-shaped walls were created by a Pleistocene glacier.

To the south of the lake, the famed Alpine Scenic Loop drive showcases more Wasatch wonders. At Timpanogos Cave National Monument, water has created a grotto of otherworldly beauty in a mountain face high above American Fork Canyon. After climbing a steep one-and-a-half-mile trail, visitors enter the frigid world of Hansen Cave, the monument's first chamber. Here bizarre shapes, lit by

HARVESTING THE LAKE
Salt evaporation ponds, below, separated by dikes, have been excavated at Stansbury Island and at other locations around Great Salt Lake. The mineral is harvested by chemical companies for industrial uses, much to the dismay of conservationists, who contend that the salt industry is damaging the lake.

SUNRISE REFLECTIONS
The Newfoundland Mountains
cast their reflection on the still
waters of Great Salt Lake, right.

HOME ON THE RANGE
A young pronghorn antelope, above,
displays its two small horns. When
fully mature, the longer horn will
curve backward and the shorter
one will curve forward.

Great Basin. As tectonic forces shoved the immensely thick continental crust upward, creating the Wasatch Range, many layers were fractured by stress, including a limestone layer that was corroded by carbonic acids present in the ancient water table. Rainwater and snowmelt invaded the cracks, hollowing out the caverns.

HEART OF TIMPANOGOS Mineral-rich water continues to seep into the caves. Drops fall from the ceiling and when the water evaporates the minerals accumulate to create stalactites; when water splashes on the floor, the minerals left behind build stalagmites. A steady stream down a cave wall results in a mineral formation called a flowstone. The immense Heart of Timpanogos is a tusk of fused stalactites more than five feet long that branches out like coral or cactus in every direction. The mechanism of this construction is not fully understood, but it is thought that water pressure in the rock pushes moisture through capillaries in the formation's many spindles, needles, and prongs.

Farther along the loop drive at Cascade Springs, visitors can view fanciful fountains of deep bowls and elegant half-shells amid lush ferns shaded by maples and oaks. These natural sculptures were

the stray beam of a flashlight, serpentine up from the floor, corkscrew downward from the ceiling, or lurk in countless alcoves and passageways. Inner chambers are silent but for the steady beat of water dripping into ghostly pools and the occasional flutter of bat wings and chirps of cave crickets. This subterranean sculpture garden owes its origins to the chemical action of water and the geology of the

among other types of rock and ore. At Bingham Canyon, two and a half tons of earth often have to be excavated to obtain a mere 15 pounds of copper. To retrieve enough copper to make the business profitable, Bingham mining companies have had to tear down an entire mountain.

PONY EXPRESS Back in 1860 Pony Express riders set out from Salt Lake City across the Great Basin on the most perilous leg of their service. Besides the ever present threat of ambush, other dangers lurked in the landscape itself: blinding dust storms, blistering sun, and loneliness. The way stations, located at 60-mile intervals, supplied the riders with fresh water and horses, making it possible for them to deliver a letter from Missouri to California in 7 days, 17 hours. Today the trail is a popular byway across the Great Salt Lake Desert.

Fish Springs, a major stop for the riders, is now a national wildlife refuge offering an oasis in the middle of the desert. Water bubbles from five large springs and sustains a flourishing marshland ecosystem that can be viewed from a self-guided road running along a series of dikes. The refuge is a vital stopover for birds migrating along the Pacific Flyway from Canada to Mexico. Ducks arrive by the tens of thousands, a boisterous assemblage of mallards, pintails, and green-winged teal. Canada geese, bald eagles, tundra swans, and white-faced ibis descend on the area during their migrations. The refuge also hosts an astonishingly large and varied resident population of 250 species of birds, including black-crowned night herons, northern harriers, and golden eagles. Muskrats scurry amid the bulrushes and cattails. As the sun sets, mule deer, coyotes, and badgers from the surrounding scrublands and marsh meadows move in to slake their thirst. Below the water's placid surface, Utah chub and mosquito fish move through a world of wigeon grass, pondweed, and algae.

The water at Fish Springs originates beneath the Deep Creek Range, more than 40 miles to the northwest. It flows under the Fish Springs Range, sinks into a fault zone far below the earth's surface, and emerges here, heated to a temperature of 80°F. But in the Great Basin this is not unusual. The surface of this natural phenomenon hides a honeycomb of such mineral-rich aquifers, springs, and seeps that inexorably transforms the character of the land from within.

The powerful forces that shaped the planet are still at work. Ranges rise, the basin stretches. Earthquakes rumble across the Wasatch Front and 1,500 years after bursting through Red Rock Pass, Lake Bonneville continues to sustain life in the communities of the Great Basin.

ALPINE SCENERY
A small lake, below, nestles in a steep-walled canyon in the Raft River Mountains. The range is made of 2.5-billion-year-old rock— the oldest rock in the Great Basin.

created by mineral-rich water, heated underground in alpine faults, that bubbles to the surface. Water slips over the lips of these fragile vessels in a tumult of small waterfalls. The road skirts the crest of Mount Timpanogos before descending through aspen groves into Provo Canyon, where Bridal Veil Falls feathers its way 600 feet down a sheer volcanic cliff in a double plunge. Far below, the Heber Valley Historic Railroad, nicknamed the Heber Creeper, steams along the cliffs of Provo Canyon.

About halfway between Great Salt Lake and Utah Lake lies the Bingham Canyon Copper Mine, the largest man-made excavation in the world. It is over two and a half miles across and more than 2,000 feet deep from its base to the top terrace. Not surprisingly, it is the nation's largest single source of copper. Every year, more than 300,000 tons of ore are mined here.

The copper mine symbolizes the Great Basin's seemingly endless mineral wealth. Here in the Oquirrh Mountains, the faulting and fracturing that gave birth to the basin and range permitted molten ore bodies, especially copper and molybdenum, to intrude into the crust. Along the old continental rift, the rocks fractured in complex ways. The molten copper ore dispersed along these fractures, forming porphyry deposits scattered

NEARBY SITES & ATTRACTIONS

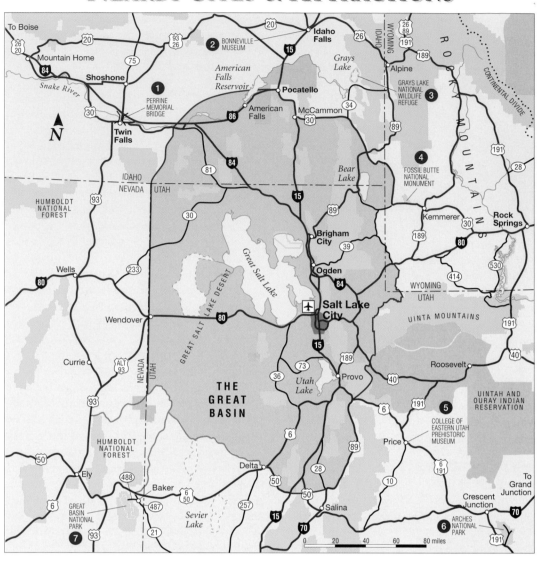

Fiery Furnace, below, is one of the many unusual sandstone formations found in Arches National Park. It can be reached on a ranger-led tour.

① PERRINE MEMORIAL BRIDGE, IDAHO

Completed in 1976 at a cost of $10.5 million, this four-lane bridge spans the Snake River Gorge. It replaced a steel truss bridge that was erected in 1927. The Perrine Memorial Bridge is 1,500 feet in length and rises 486 feet above the Snake River. It is the longest arch-span bridge west of the Mississippi River. Walkways along the bridge allow pedestrians a spectacular view of the sheer cliffs of the gorge and the 212-foot descent of Shoshone Falls. Located in Twin Falls on Hwy. 93.

② BONNEVILLE MUSEUM, IDAHO

This museum in Idaho Falls is housed in the 1916 Andrew Carnegie Library, which was added to the National Register of Historic Places in 1983. Permanent exhibits include displays on Native Americans, explorers, and trappers, as well as on the natural history of the region, its mining industry, agriculture, and more recently, nuclear power. Eagle Rock USA is a walk-through replica of the 19th-

century pioneer town that later became Idaho Falls. Another exhibit contains artifacts from the home of Fred Keefer, an early pioneer. An art gallery features the works of local artists. Located at the junction of Eastern and Elm streets in Idaho Falls.

③ GRAYS LAKE NATIONAL WILDLIFE REFUGE, IDAHO

This marshy area, dotted with cattails and bulrushes, provides a perfect habitat for many species of water birds, including the largest breeding population of sandhill cranes in the world, more than 200 pairs. The birds arrive in spring to breed and nest in the refuge and depart with their offspring in the fall. An observation point atop a 150-foot hill overlooks the refuge and provides visitors with a perch for viewing sandhill cranes as well as whooping cranes, trumpeter swans, Canada geese, eared and western grebes, black terns, and about 15,000 Franklin's gulls, who share their colony with several hundred white-faced ibises. Northern harriers, red-tailed hawks, and peregrine falcons also can be spotted

in the skies overhead. A gravel road borders the refuge, the interior of which is closed to visitors during the summer months. Located 34 miles north of Soda Springs on Hwy. 34.

4 FOSSIL BUTTE NATIONAL MONUMENT, WYOMING

Fifty million years ago Fossil Lake was the smallest of three large lakes that covered parts of Wyoming, Colorado, and Utah. The rock layer in the lake basin, known to geologists as the Green River formation, is composed of limestone, volcanic ash, and mudstone. Many of the fossils embedded in the rock are among the most perfectly preserved in the world and provide a record of the region of some 50 million years ago when the lake was surrounded by a lush green forest. The fossils include more than 20 species of fish, 100 varieties of insects, and innumerable plants. Fossilized animals include primates, birds, turtles, crocodiles, an ancestor of the horse, and the oldest known bat specimen in North America. Many fossils are on display at a museum in the visitor center. Located 10 miles west of Kemmerer on Hwy. 30.

5 COLLEGE OF EASTERN UTAH PREHISTORIC MUSEUM, UTAH

During the Jurassic period, about 147 million years ago, dinosaurs roamed what is now eastern Utah. In 1961 this museum was created to document and preserve the archeological and geological findings in the area. Life-size dinosaur skeletons are on display in the Hall of Dinosaurs. The Hall of Man exhibits some of the tools used by prehistoric man, as well as the Pilling Figurines: unfired clay figures of men and women that are estimated to be 800 to 900 years old. Located in Price.

6 ARCHES NATIONAL PARK, UTAH

Located in the dry Utah desert, this 73,234-acre park has more than 2,000 sandstone arches—the largest known concentration of natural stone arches in the world. An 18-mile scenic drive climbs from Moab Canyon to Devils Garden, passing through the heart of the park. Hiking trails take visitors to many of the arches and towering spires, buttes, and cliffs. These formations were sculpted by wind and rain in the Entrada sandstone over a period of 150 million years. Two of the park's most famous arches are Landscape Arch, which spans 306 feet and is one of the longest natural arches in the world, and Delicate Arch, a salmon-colored formation and one of the park's most famous landmarks. Located 30 miles south of Crescent Junction off Hwy. 191.

7 GREAT BASIN NATIONAL PARK, NEVADA

Established in 1986, the park features flat, arid desert, towering mountains, and subterranean chambers. Bristlecone pines, among the oldest living things in the world, are found on the slopes of the park's 11,000- to 13,000-foot mountains. Several of these trees are estimated to be almost 5,000 years old. Wheeler Peak Scenic Drive, which climbs to an elevation of 10,161 feet, provides visitors with views of the Southern Snake Range. The 12-mile drive passes through piñon-juniper woodlands, travels along a creekbed lined with aspen trees, and through forests of mountain mahogany and manzanita trees, and dense Engelmann spruce and Douglas fir. One of the park's most popular attractions is the Lehman Caves, discovered about 1885 by Absalom Lehman, a local rancher. The cave, which extends a quarter of a mile to the base of the Snake Range, was created 2 to 5 million years ago by rainwater that fell through hairline cracks and dissolved the limestone rock. Along with stalactites, stalagmites, columns, and flowstones, the cave is famous for its shield formations that resemble large, flattened clamshells. Located five miles west of Baker on Hwy. 488.

Grays Lake National Wildlife Refuge, left, is situated in a high valley that is surrounded by the Caribou National Forest and the peaks of the Caribou Mountains.

The vertiginous heights of Perrine Bridge, below, overlook Snake River near Twin Falls, Idaho.

HELLS CANYON

*A sublime monument carved out of rock and watered
by the mighty Snake River, this yawning chasm
tells the story of the birth of North America.*

On a remote section of the Oregon-Idaho border, the earth opens up to reveal the deepest gorge in North America, Hells Canyon. At the bottom of the great black canyon, the Snake River boils over rapids and broods in pools, whispers through chasms, and laughs across the shallows. The canyon is an aria written in rock, and the river intones the melody. Sheer walls resonate with sound as shafts of light illuminate crooked and broken gullies in the shadow of snowcapped peaks.

Hells Canyon is a geological wonder that, because of the demanding terrain surrounding it like a fortress, relatively few travelers have seen. Girded by stalwart mountain ranges and buffeted by daunting weather extremes, the canyon shares its secrets grudgingly. Those who venture within its walls become witnesses to the origins of the Pacific Northwest.

For many, the journey to Hells Canyon begins at Joseph, Oregon. There the road unfurls across a high, grassy plateau, crowned with silvery streams, and slips into the forests of the Imnaha River valley, a narrowing waterway tinged with evidence of recent wildfires. Above, the glaciated granite teeth of the Wallowa Mountains bite into a crisp blue summer sky. The road follows the river through layers of black basalt to the town of Imnaha, one of the most remote settlements in the country. A forest service road claws its way up the sheer face of the Imnaha drainage, and 24 miles later, reaches Hat Point Lookout. The lookout affords an astounding view into the core of Hells Canyon. Here the earth seems to drop its jaw in astonishment.

Deep within the canyon lies a desert world where summer temperatures soar to 100°F or more. At the bottom of the scorching rift, thick-bodied rattlesnakes and black widow spiders search for shaded relief from the sun's unblinking stare, and cacti and hackberry shrubs cling stubbornly to the sparse pockets of topsoil that speckle the arid landscape.

WILDFLOWER DISPLAY
Lush growths of anemones, above, crowd the banks of one of the Bernard Lakes, in the region of the Seven Devils Mountains.

RIVERINE WILDERNESS
Overleaf: Meandering quietly through Hells Canyon, this calm stretch of the Snake River belies the frothing rapids that boaters will face farther downstream. A 106-mile stretch of the river within the canyon is totally undeveloped.

INFORMATION FOR VISITORS

The Wallowa Mountains Visitor Center is one mile west of Enterprise, Oregon, on Hwy. 82. It offers information and displays on Hells Canyon. To reach Enterprise from Lewiston, Idaho, take Hwys. 129 and 3 south; from LaGrande, Oregon, take Hwy. 82. The nearest airport is in Enterprise. Wallowa Mountain Road, Hat Point Road, Imnaha River Road, and Snake River Road give access to the canyon and are part of the National Scenic Byway System. The roads vary from paved two-lane highways to narrow, steep, gravel-covered roads; some are open seasonally. Check at any Forest Service office for information on road conditions before traveling. Within Hells Canyon, the Pittsburg Landing Road (Forest Road 493), one of the gravel roads, leads to the Snake River. Some of the roads are accessible only to vehicles with high clearance.
For more information: Hells Canyon National Recreation Area Headquarters, 88401 Hwy. 82, Enterprise, OR 97828; 541-426-5546.

INQUISITIVE YOUNGSTER
A mountain lion kitten, below, peers through blades of grass. Although Hells Canyon has a healthy mountain lion population, the only sign most visitors see of these shy felines is their paw prints.

The canyon also displays a stark beauty. Warblers and wrens flit through the bluish light, and reflections of sky and canyon walls shimmer on the surface of the Snake as it winds like a platinum-colored boa through the crease in the crusty black rock.

DEEP-DELVED EARTH

Hells Canyon is the deepest river gorge on the continent. For 50 miles of its length, the canyon cuts more than a mile down into the earth; and from the tip of He Devil Peak on the Idaho side to the rushing waters of the Snake, it plunges an incredible 8,043 vertical feet. The Grand Canyon of the Colorado River, by comparison, is 2,000 feet less deep. But the real differences between the two gorges are matters not of numbers but of mood, character, and geological history. The Grand Canyon is a vast and complex sculpture garden of soft sandstone hues, carved over eons by nature's patient artistry. Hells Canyon, on the other hand, is full of hard edges

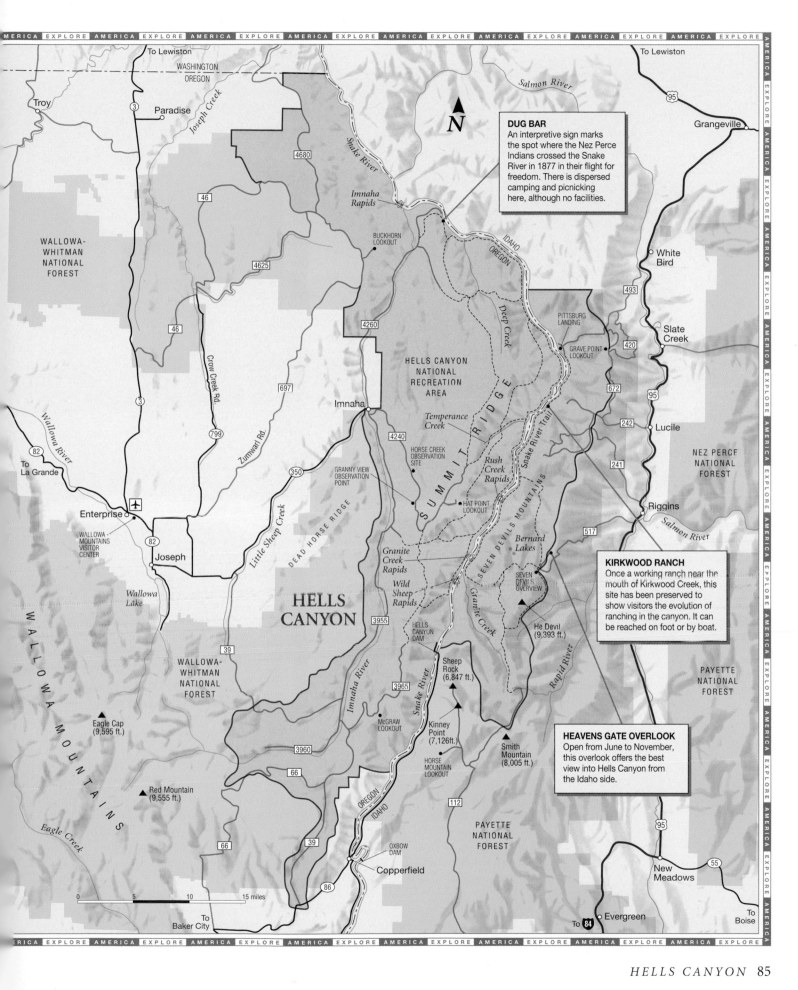

DUG BAR
An interpretive sign marks the spot where the Nez Perce Indians crossed the Snake River in 1877 in their flight for freedom. There is dispersed camping and picnicking here, although no facilities.

KIRKWOOD RANCH
Once a working ranch near the mouth of Kirkwood Creek, this site has been preserved to show visitors the evolution of ranching in the canyon. It can be reached on foot or by boat.

HEAVENS GATE OVERLOOK
Open from June to November, this overlook offers the best view into Hells Canyon from the Idaho side.

To Lewiston
To Lewiston
WASHINGTON
OREGON
Troy
Paradise
Grangeville
Salmon River
Joseph Creek
4680
Snake River
46
White Bird
Imnaha Rapids
WALLOWA-WHITMAN NATIONAL FOREST
BUCKHORN LOOKOUT
4625
IDAHO
OREGON
Slate Creek
493
PITTSBURG LANDING
4260
HELLS CANYON NATIONAL RECREATION AREA
GRAVE POINT LOOKOUT
420
Deep Creek
Crow Creek Rd.
697
SUMMIT RIDGE
46
3
Imnaha
672
95
Temperance Creek
4240
242
Lucile
Wallowa River
799
Zumwalt Rd.
HORSE CREEK OBSERVATION SITE
Rush Creek Rapids
Snake River Trail
NEZ PERCE NATIONAL FOREST
To La Grande
GRANNY VIEW OBSERVATION POINT
350
241
82
Enterprise
HAT POINT LOOKOUT
SEVEN DEVILS MOUNTAINS
Riggins
WALLOWA MOUNTAINS VISITOR CENTER
Little Sheep Creek
DEAD HORSE RIDGE
Bernard Lakes
517
Salmon River
82
Granite Creek Rapids
Joseph
Wild Sheep Rapids
SEVEN DEVILS OVERVIEW
Granite Creek
Wallowa Lake
HELLS CANYON
3955
HELLS CANYON DAM
He Devil (9,393 ft.)
WALLOWA MOUNTAINS
39
WALLOWA-WHITMAN NATIONAL FOREST
Imnaha River
Sheep Rock (6,847 ft.)
Rapid River
PAYETTE NATIONAL FOREST
3965
Eagle Cap (9,595 ft.)
McGRAW LOOKOUT
Kinney Point (7,126ft.)
Smith Mountain (8,005 ft.)
Snake River
3960
HORSE MOUNTAIN LOOKOUT
66
Red Mountain (9,555 ft.)
112
OREGON
IDAHO
Eagle Creek
PAYETTE NATIONAL FOREST
95
66
39
OXBOW DAM
New Meadows
55
0   5   10   15 miles
86
Copperfield
To Baker City
To Boise
To Evergreen
84

VALLEY ROAD
The road from White Bird on the Salmon River, Idaho, to Pittsburg Landing on the Snake River winds through Hells Canyon, above. Pittsburg Landing was once a Native American village site.

and youthful restlessness. Its walls were rammed into place, ground up in faults, and buried in volcanic cataclysms. The impatient Snake River wasted little time in hacking open its mile-deep gorge: the entire process probably took less than 2 million years—a flicker in geological time.

ORIGINS OF THE WEST

Upon first sight, the profundity of Hells Canyon steals a visitor's breath away. But it is what that depth represents that is truly staggering: 200 million years of history lie exposed below Hat Point. This pine-cordoned summit is the perfect vantage point for visitors to view the origins not only of Hells Canyon—but of the entire West Coast.

To the untrained eye, Hells Canyon seems to be little more than a product of erosion: Under the right conditions and with a couple of million years, a river will carve a canyon out of even the most stubborn bedrock. But among geologists, the Snake raises as many questions as it provides answers. For at the bottom of the canyon are found not only rocks originating from the North American continent but also a jumble of foreign materials, such as fossils, that were transported from distant times

and unknown places and deposited in fascinating patterns that defy easy reconstruction.

Hells Canyon holds an important place in the history of the world's plate tectonics, those movements of the earth's crust that produced today's landmasses and oceans. The canyon is an exposed continental suture zone, an area in which widely dispersed pieces of crust came together in the formation of a continent.

The plates float like lily pads on a bubbling pond of molten rock and continually shift in response to currents. During the late Paleozoic era, 250 to 300 million years ago, one such shift brought all the pieces of crust together in a single supercontinent that geologists call Pangaea. North America represented Pangaea's westernmost edge. A stretch of the northwest coast bordered what is now the Salmon River in western Idaho, far to the east of its present location. The coast was backed by the granite massif of central Idaho and fronted by a broad continental shelf buffeted by the waters of the ancestral Pacific Ocean.

Fifty million years after Pangaea was created it began to break up into the continents that exist today, parting to form the Atlantic Ocean and pushing the North American landmass to the west. Thousands of miles away in the Pacific Ocean, an arc of volcanic islands was sprouting from the sea. As the North American continent continued to slide westward, it smashed against the archipelago of volcanoes, compacting them into coastal mountain ranges. In Oregon they formed ranges that include the Klamaths and the Blue Mountains. One group of islands, the Wallowa terrane, became the Seven Devils and the Wallowa mountain ranges—the cradle of Hells Canyon.

Once docked onto the continent, the rocky island debris was grated by faulting in a south–north movement, producing a hodgepodge of volcanic rock and sediments. The faulting also crushed, rotated, tossed, and transported limestone deposits that contained ancient fossils. These formations, known as the Martin Bridge Limestones, are visible from Hat Point, where they appear as large crested rumples halfway down the canyon slopes.

Paleontologists have uncovered mosaic assemblages of fossilized mollusks, corals, and even a rare fish-like reptile, called the ichthyosaur, embedded in the Martin Bridge Limestones. Most of the fossils are tropical in origin, and it is believed that the limestone is the remnant of reefs that once fringed the island arc. Many of Hells Canyon's fossils resemble those found in Europe, the Himalayas, and the eastern Pacific, leading scientists to conclude that when the continents were still huddled together in a single landmass, the terranes were washed by the waters of an ancient ocean that linked the Mediterranean region, Asia, and pieces of land scattered around what is now the Pacific.

Hat Point Lookout is not the only place from which visitors can see the canyon's ancient beauty. On the Oregon side, McGraw Lookout offers spectacular views, as do Kinney Point, Horse Mountain Lookout, and Sheep Rock on the Idaho

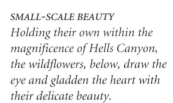

SMALL-SCALE BEAUTY
Holding their own within the magnificence of Hells Canyon, the wildflowers, below, draw the eye and gladden the heart with their delicate beauty.

POWER SOURCE
The introduction of hydroelectric power on the Snake River has stilled this once turbulent stretch of water between the Oxbow and Hells Canyon dams, left.

STEADY GAZE
The wapiti, or American elk, above, roams freely within Hells Canyon. Stags can reach shoulder heights of about five feet and a weight of 1,000 pounds. During the fall season, the canyon echoes with the bugling calls of the males.

side. To get a closer view, visitors can hike or ride along the 1,000 miles of trails that meander through the Hells Canyon National Recreation Area. Years ago paddle wheelers made their way along the Snake and tied up at Pittsburg Landing, near White Bird. Now one of the recreation area's few primitive campgrounds is located there.

ANCIENT LAVA FLOWS Some 17 million years ago, an event occurred that was to have an immeasurable impact on the geology of Hells Canyon, and indeed, the entire Pacific Northwest. For reasons that are still debated by scientists, molten basalt began to pour from an enormous network of vents in northeastern Oregon and southeastern Washington, many of them located along the Grande Ronde River and the Imnaha River, just behind Hat Point.

The extent and impact of the Columbia River lava flows is almost unimaginable. Gushing from the earth in spurts every few thousand years for 5 million years, the flows, some of them up to 200 feet thick and moving as fast as 30 miles an hour, eventually covered an area the size of the state of Washington. When the Columbia flows hardened, northeastern Oregon and southeastern Washington were lacquered with 42,000 cubic miles of dark, shiny basalt and the rolling hills of Oregon and Washington had been flattened into desolate lava plains. Fully one-quarter of all the rock in Oregon is basalt. The lava, in places more than two miles deep, engulfed most of the volcanic islands that

had crashed into the continent. High-altitude basalt deposits on the Idaho side of the Snake indicate that even the Seven Devils were overtaken. The sturdy batholiths of the Wallowas, however, never succumbed entirely to the rising tide of lava.

Hundreds of miles to the south, the lava flows blocked the streams descending from the Rocky Mountains, setting the stage for the Snake River to carve Hells Canyon. The continued tectonic action caused the entire area to rise and the steeper grades gave faster-moving streams added power to cut sharp canyons into the basalt plateau. Then as now, the Salmon River flowed north from its source in the high country of central Idaho to the Columbia basin. One of its smaller tributaries flowed northward following the Oxbow shear zone, an area of faulting along the ancient continental rim. Slowly chewing away at cracks in the rock, this tributary laid the groundwork for the erosive work of the mighty Snake River.

At this time the Snake did not flow through the Hells Canyon region. It began in the young Rocky Mountain range near Yellowstone and coursed through southern Idaho, as it does today. From there it flowed west and emptied into the Pacific Ocean. But another geological event was about to divert the Snake.

In southwestern Idaho, tectonic uplift thrust the Owyhee Mountains into the channel of the Snake River, damming the waterways, which backed up to form Lake Idaho. The lake eventually grew to 200 miles in length. About 1 million years ago, the Snake burst the banks of the lake and began to flow

northward, down the little tributary of the Salmon River. At the same time that the powerful waters of the Snake River were gouging away at the basalt, geological upheaval was raising mountains. With one force cutting downward and another pushing upward, Hells Canyon was born.

A JOURNEY THROUGH THE PAST

A raft trip through the canyon retraces the steps leading up to its emergence. At Hells Canyon Dam, the main site for putting in, the river appears to have been tamed by the yoke of man. But low ripples a quarter mile downstream are a taste of things to come. Once under way, the raft belongs to the river. Wild Sheep, Buck Creek, Imnaha—each set of rapids has its own personality, and the eddies and bars are fickle, always changing their configuration. Some rapids slap the side of the raft without warning. Others suck the bottom out from under the raft, flipping the bow up into the air.

Between rapids, the canyon tells its life story. The Snake has exposed bulbous, rounded basalts where it is joined by the Imnaha River. The lava flows here have descended from their normal place high above the canyon, right down into the river. They are Imnaha basalts from the Columbia lava flow of 17 million years ago. The basalts' green hues are derived from olivine and plagioclase, types of feldspar. Towering chunks of hexagonally fractured basalt look like support columns for the mountains above. The columns were deposited by another lava flow, which erupted from vents north of the Wallowas. In the depths of Hells Canyon at Deep Creek the lava flow has left pinkish gray deposits. Geological upheaval and the slow grinding of rock on rock has also transported granite that is normally associated with the highest crags of the Wallowas and Seven Devils. Here and there the Snake reveals the whitish gray limestone of the ancient coral reefs that were once submerged off the shores of the volcanic island arc. And, along

ANCIENT ETCHINGS
Petroglyphs carved into a piece of granite at Pittsburg Landing, below, suggest that the rock was a Native American fertility site.

NEARBY SITES & ATTRACTIONS

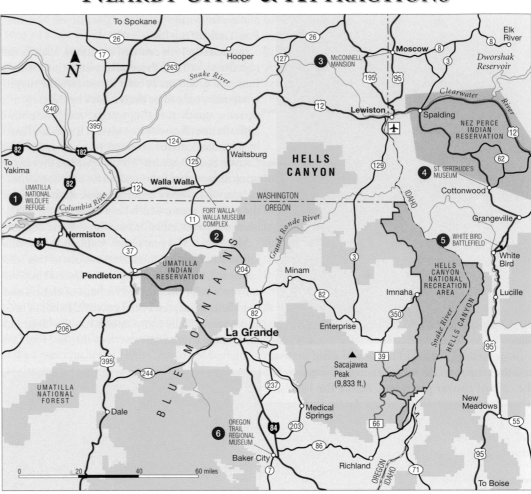

Demonstrations of pioneer handicrafts such as quilting, above, are given at Washington's Fort Walla Walla Museum Complex.

① UMATILLA NATIONAL WILDLIFE REFUGE, OREGON/WASHINGTON

Within the dry desert steppe of the Columbia River Valley lies a 20-mile stretch of islands, riparian areas, and backwater sloughs that is an oasis for waterfowl. The wintering bird population in this 22,885-acre refuge is estimated at 450,000, and includes 12 species of ducks and up to 52,000 Canada geese. The many islands are colonies for double-crested cormorants, great blue herons, Caspian terns, and ring-billed gulls. The shoreline is covered with thickets of willow, cottonwood, and Russian olive, one of which stretches for more than 60 acres and provides a haven for the densest population of small wintering birds in the Northwest. More than 50 pairs of long-billed curlews—noted for their eight-inch-long bills—stay in the refuge from March to June. Among the raptors are five species of owls, northern harriers, and Swainson's and red-tailed hawks. Located two miles west of Irrigon off Hwy. 730.

② FORT WALLA WALLA MUSEUM COMPLEX, WASHINGTON

Covering 15 acres, this re-created pioneer settlement contains 16 buildings of the 19th century, 6 exhibit buildings, and 27,000 artifacts. Included are the 1880 Babcock Railway Station, complete with railroad artifacts, and the 1867 Walla Walla County School House, which contains books and maps, chalkboards, and a potbellied stove of the period. Other pioneer buildings at the site are a blacksmith's shop, a doctor's office, and a blockhouse. Horse-drawn firefighting equipment, a Washington territory prison, a stagecoach, a collection of branding irons, and a 1919 Harris combine harnessed to 33 life-size models of mules are among the fascinating displays in the exhibit buildings. Located at 755 Myra Rd. in Walla Walla.

③ McCONNELL MANSION, IDAHO

Built in 1886, this Victorian mansion's two-story bay windows, steep gables, and narrow doors make it an excellent example of Eastlake architecture. The house is listed on the National Register of Historic Places. Five ground-floor rooms are decorated in styles dating from the turn of the century to the Depression. The upstairs rooms focus specifically on Latah County history. Light filters into the hallway through etched and stained glass, illuminating an oak staircase and banister that was brought from San Francisco. The family parlor is furnished with a phonograph, a Sears-Roebuck piano, and a coal-burning fireplace with marble facing and gold-leaf trim. A live-in servant's room is furnished with objects from 1915. The 1930's kitchen contains a number of utensils that visitors are welcome to handle. A wood-burning stove, a Hoosier cabinet, and an icebox are on display in the kitchen. The house was erected by former Idaho governor William J. McConnell. Located at 110 South Adams in Moscow.

4 ST. GERTRUDE'S MUSEUM, IDAHO

Housed on the grounds of the Priory of Saint Gertrude, the museum was started in 1931 by Sister Alfreda Elsensohn, the author of a two-volume work entitled *Pioneer Days in Idaho County*. While researching the material for her books, she received many historical items from her friends. The museum's eclectic collection includes mining and pioneer items, as well as artifacts that once belonged to personalities from Idaho's past, such as some possessions of a young Chinese woman named Polly Bemis. Although Polly's father called her his 1,000 pieces of gold, he was forced to sell her in exchange for food to Mongolian bandits who brought her to America. Also on display is the Cheyenne saddle that her Yankee husband, Charles Bemis, used to travel the Chisholm Trail, and handcrafted utensils made by Buckskin Bill, a Salmon River mountain man. Located in Cottonwood.

5 WHITE BIRD BATTLEFIELD, IDAHO

The site of the first major battle in the Nez Perce War between the US Army and Nez Perce warriors can best be seen on a 16-mile loop drive. There are seven stops along the loop that mark positions important to the battle, including the Nez Perce Camp, the route used by the advancing US Cavalry, and the main battlefield. Red markers are placed at the sites, and green markers indicate where visitors can enjoy the best views. The battle took place on the morning of June 17, 1877, after hostile US troops approached the Nez Perce camp, situated at the bottom of White Bird Canyon. Nez Perce warriors, alerted to the advancing army, waved a truce flag. The flag was ignored, so the Indians hid in the crevasses of the canyon. Once the troops entered the canyon, the warriors emerged from their hiding places and surrounded them. A Nez Perce warrior shot and killed Trumpeter Jones, and the two remaining trumpeters lost their instruments, depriving the army's captain, David Perry, with a way to communicate with his troops. Despite facing an army superior in number and weaponry, the Nez Perces did not lose a single man; the US Army lost 34 soldiers. The loop tour begins nine and a half miles southwest of Grangeville on Hwy. 95

6 OREGON TRAIL REGIONAL MUSEUM, OREGON

One of the first things visitors see when they enter this museum is Ellen Williams' four-by-eight acrylic painting called "Crossing the Powder," which portrays 19th-century settlers fording the Powder River on the Oregon Trail. The museum houses a collection of 19th-century artifacts recovered from Baker County schools, sawmills, farms, and mines. Also on display are horse-drawn carriages, sleighs, covered wagons, seashells and coral, and the Cavin-Warfel collection of semiprecious stones, minerals, and fossils—considered one of the best in the nation. Located on Campbell St. in Baker City.

The green slopes of White Bird Battlefield, above, look serene today, but in 1877 the US Army lost 34 soldiers here in this first conflict in the Nez Perce War.

The Oregon Trail was an important overland route for settlers heading West during the 19th century. The Oregon Trail Regional Museum in Baker City, left, exhibits many objects relating to the pioneers who settled in Oregon.

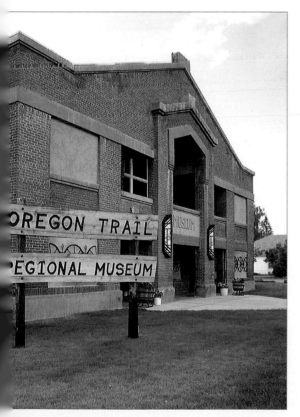

MOUNT ST. HELENS

A violent eruption and its aftermath testify to the destructive and recuperative powers of nature.

Rocks float on water. Lakes are displaced. Acres of trees are struck down in seconds. Mountaintops disintegrate into microscopic particles. Birds drop lifeless out of a black afternoon sky. These things are the impossible, which have been made real by Lawelatla or Loowit, as the Pacific Northwest Indians call Mount St. Helens. The Native names mean "One from Whom Smoke Comes" and "Keeper of the Fire" and were bestowed long ago, during the tribes' 12,000-year acquaintance with the Cascade peak.

For centuries the Cowlitz and Klickitat Indians listened to Loowit speak in eruptions—small or large, beautiful or deadly. During one eruption in 1842, all the fish in the Toutle River were killed, suffocated by Loowit's ash. A few years earlier, another eruption lit the night sky for miles around. The mountain's spectacular explosions seemed to send an urgent message to the Native people who lived in its shadows: Stay away. Consequently, whenever Mount St. Helens was approached it was with a mixture of respect and

BUILDING ANEW
Overleaf: The crumbled north face of Mount St. Helens surveys the scorched remnants of a once thick forest and the wildflowers that have begun to bloom again.

fear. Young Cowlitz men ascended the steep slopes to receive their *tamanawash,* or "guiding spirit," but they ventured no farther than the timberline. Once their quest was completed, they were relieved to make their descent, leaving Lawelatla behind.

When white explorers arrived in the Northwest, the Indians told them about the legend of Keeper of the Fire. One tale, passed down for generations, was recorded by oral historian Ella Clark in her 1953 *Indian Legends of the Pacific Northwest.* The story tells of two quarreling tribes living on opposite sides of the Big River (the Columbia). The discord angered the Great Spirit, who punished the Indians by taking away the sun. The tribes begged for fire to keep them warm, but the only person who possessed fire in her lodge was an old woman named Loowit. Taking pity on the shivering people, the Great Spirit asked Loowit to share her fire. She went to a bridge over the river and offered the fire to people from the north and south. The Great Spirit rewarded Loowit by granting her most fervent wish—to be young and beautiful again. Her transformation caused two suitors, the warriors Wyeast from the south and Klickitat from the north, to fight over Loowit, and soon the tribes were at war again. In anger, the Great Spirit turned the trio of lovers into mountains. Wyeast became

STANDING DEAD
Trees at the blast zone's edge, above, were scorched to death by the 700°F winds that roared out of the volcano.

AFTER THE BLAST
A black-tailed deer, right, who survived the eruption has returned to the blast zone. Some 5,000 black-tailed deer were killed by the blast. Those who survived were in unaffected forest lands just beyond the zone. Now as the deer travel across the pumice, they help break it down, exposing the soil. Plants also benefit, since they are able to use the nutrients contained in deer scat.

INFORMATION FOR VISITORS

From Portland, take I-5 for 49 miles, then head east on Hwy. 504 for 5 miles. The Mount St. Helens Visitor Center provides maps and literature on the volcano, as well as a short film on the 1980 eruption. The Coldwater Ridge Visitor Center, located at the end of Hwy. 504, also dispenses information on the volcano. Summer and fall are the best seasons to tour the area when the main access roads are clear of snow. From late June to early September, park rangers lead nature walks through the monument. Permits must be obtained to hike above 4,800 feet. The crater is closed to the public year-round. Campsites are available outside certain restricted areas. During this delicate period of plant regeneration, visitors are asked to minimize plant damage by staying on marked trails.
For more information: Mount St. Helens National Volcanic Monument, 42218 N.E. Yale Bridge Rd., Amboy, WA 98601; 360-274-2100.

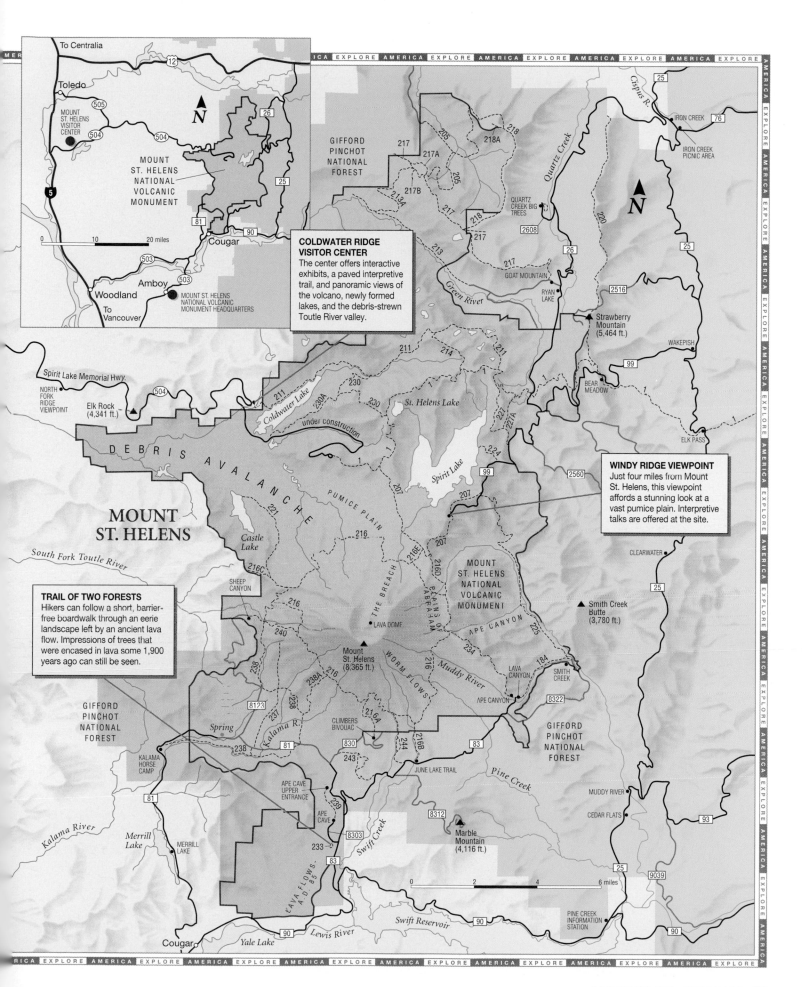

COLDWATER RIDGE VISITOR CENTER
The center offers interactive exhibits, a paved interpretive trail, and panoramic views of the volcano, newly formed lakes, and the debris-strewn Toutle River valley.

WINDY RIDGE VIEWPOINT
Just four miles from Mount St. Helens, this viewpoint affords a stunning look at a vast pumice plain. Interpretive talks are offered at the site.

TRAIL OF TWO FORESTS
Hikers can follow a short, barrier-free boardwalk through an eerie landscape left by an ancient lava flow. Impressions of trees that were encased in lava some 1,900 years ago can still be seen.

MOUNT ST. HELENS

GIFFORD PINCHOT NATIONAL FOREST

GIFFORD PINCHOT NATIONAL FOREST

To Centralia
Toledo

MOUNT ST. HELENS VISITOR CENTER

MOUNT ST. HELENS NATIONAL VOLCANIC MONUMENT

Cougar

Woodland
To Vancouver

Amboy

MOUNT ST. HELENS NATIONAL VOLCANIC MONUMENT HEADQUARTERS

0   10   20 miles

the peak known as Mount Hood, Klickitat became Mount Adams, and Loowit, the lovely Mount St. Helens, who, even in her changed shape, retained the sacred fire of the Great Spirit.

The Indians told explorers other stories about the mountain and of a deep, cold lake on the north side where demons were said to roam. This place was called Spirit Lake because the evil spirits drowned intruders and carried their bodies away. Native people would not go near the lake. In 1848 Paul Kane—a Canadian artist famous for his vivid landscape paintings and depictions of Native American life—tried to hire a Native guide to escort him to Spirit Lake. He was told that the lake was haunted and it was best to stay away.

Prospectors, undaunted by these tales, were the first to stay at Spirit Lake, and from 1892 until 1912 the basin was mined for gold and copper. Shafts were drilled deep into the high ridges, but no ore

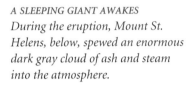

A SLEEPING GIANT AWAKES
During the eruption, Mount St. Helens, below, spewed an enormous dark gray cloud of ash and steam into the atmosphere.

was ever found. Only one miner, Robert Lange, actually settled in the area. After his death in 1933, Lange's family constructed the Spirit Lake Lodge one mile west of the lake. Two other lodges sprang up beside the lake as well, and word of its beauty and of the picture-perfect peak nearby soon spread.

PLACE OF
THE SPIRITS

By 1945 four youth camps and a public campground had been established along the shore. Campers were enchanted by Spirit Lake, whose water was so clear its floor could be seen 50 feet down. Alpine breezes whistled across the surface, carrying a whiff of alder and cotton-wood. Douglas firs and western hemlocks towered 200 feet high near the shore. Wildflowers trailed over moss-covered fallen logs. River otters and mergansers splashed in the shallows. Black bears trundled up to the aroma of steaks sizzling over campfires. And on the horizon, above the trees crowding the south shore, stood the mountain.

Spirit Lake became so popular that thousands of campers went there each summer until 1979 to swim, fish, canoe, and sail. Every so often, unlucky souls were drowned in the lake, and, as foretold in the ancient legends of the Native people, their bodies were never recovered.

On March 20, 1980, shallow earthquakes were detected under the steep 9,677-foot mountain. The fire in Loowit's belly was about to be released. Few

people felt the rumblings. The forest floor was
buried in snow. Creeks needled their way under
the ice. Winter's mantle clung to the conifers.

At Spirit Lake, the caretakers were hunkered
down in their lodges. The lake was frozen. Elk,
mountain goats, cougars, and bears awaited the
arrival of alpine spring. Little did anyone know
what that spring would bring. On March 27 a loud
boom signaled Mount St. Helens' first eruption in
123 years. A small crater was blasted open at the
summit. Over the next month and a half the mountain's north face swelled with gas and magma. One
area near the summit inflated as much as five feet
a day, and geologists with the US Geological Survey
named it the Bulge. Authorities evacuated residents
and forbade thrill seekers from getting within
several miles of the volcano. By the time the lake
had thawed in early May, the mountain's north
face was distended beyond recognition, and ash,
not snow, smothered the forests. By mid-May the
once tranquil peak had become an ash-darkened,
bloated volcano.

One geologist who witnessed the striking changes
at Mount St. Helens was David Johnston, a 30-
year-old volcanologist employed by the United
States Geological Survey (USGS). Johnston was
stationed at Coldwater II, a makeshift camp at the
top of a ridge about six miles away. The site seemed
safe to the agency's seasoned scientists. Johnston,
who specialized in the study of volcanic emissions,

risked his life on May 17 by climbing to the volcano's summit to take gas samples. Less than 24
hours later, he spoke his last words as he watched
Mount St. Helens shake itself apart. "Vancouver!
Vancouver!" he shouted into the radio to the USGS
observatory in Vancouver, Washington. "This is
it!" His next words were garbled, and within
seconds the blast cloud reached him, catapulting his
entire camp hundreds of feet. Johnston's body was
never found.

Back in 1978 two USGS geologists—Dwight Crandell and Donal Mullineaux—had published a bulletin that forecasted an eruption of Mount St. Helens before the end of the century; but they could not predict the direction of the blast. Instead of erupting vertically, the mountain exploded sideways in a 180-degree arc that fanned out to the north, northwest, and northeast. Roaring over mountainsides at more than 500 miles an hour, the stone-hurling clouds of superheated gases toppled nearly everything in their path. The 700°F explosion swept over the land like a fiery, ground-hugging windstorm packed with the force of several megaton bombs. The blast was heard as far away as British Columbia and northern California. Logging trucks were tossed into the air like toys, and trees were mowed down like blades of grass. On the ridgetops closest to the volcano, the topsoil was stripped to the bedrock.

LIVING LAKE
Coldwater Lake, above, was formed when the collapsing mountaintop dammed a valley. The Coldwater Lake Recreation Area offers visitors a chance to picnic, boat, fish, and walk along an interpretive trail.

FROSTED LANDSCAPE
A full moon rises in the early evening sky over a snow-clad Mount St. Helens, right, seen from Coldwater Ridge. From 1980 to 1986 the dome grew in a series of eruptive spurts that appeared to be linked to the lunar cycles.

Within days of the eruption, geologists began to piece together the events of the morning of May 18, 1980. But their calculations defied reason. At 8:32 a.m., a magnitude 5.1 earthquake shook the mountain, initiating the largest landslide ever witnessed in recorded history. Within seconds the unstable north face gave way, avalanching into the Toutle River valley for nearly 15 miles. Blocks of glacial ice the size of houses tumbled to the valley floor. At the same time, the shattered mountain crashed into Spirit Lake so hard that the entire lake sloshed 500 feet up the north slope of its basin. As the water returned to the lake, it swept the surrounding trees along with it, forming a giant raft.

The mountain continued to break apart, releasing pent-up pressure. In the same instant that groundwater inside the volcano flashed to steam, gases in the surging magma hit the steam and exploded in the lateral blast. The blast winds plowed down forests on four major ridges. The winds eventually subsided but remained hot enough to scorch and kill the still upright trees instead of blowing them over. Approximately 10 minutes had passed since the first earthquake shook the area, but the eruption was far from over.

With its summit and north face a gaping hole, the mountain continued to spew vertically for nine straight hours. Lightning cracked over the black sky as a cauliflower cloud shot up some 80,000 feet,

floated east, and showered five states with ash. Scientists estimated that a total of approximately 540 million tons of ash fell over a 22,000-square-mile area. And still the eruption went on. For several hours mudflows roared down rivers draining from the volcano. The Toutle River mudflow deposited so much sediment into the Columbia River that it became unnavigable. For two miles the Columbia's depth was reduced from 39 feet to 15, stranding ships upriver.

THE BLAST ZONE

When the eruption subsided on May 19, search crews flew over the dark, smoldering landscape to try to locate missing people, many of whom would never be found. Visibly shaken, these first investigators of the blast zone spoke with horror of returning from the land of the dead. For roughly 230 square miles, no living thing could be seen. Spirit Lake, once crystal clear, had turned gray, covered from shore to shore with logs and ash. Its water temperature was 91°F—more than 40 degrees higher than normal. There was no sign of its cabins, camps, or lodges. The 100-foot waterfall called Harmony Falls had disappeared, submerged by the lake, which was now 200 feet higher. Fifty-seven people were dead.

Over the next six years Mount St. Helens erupted frequently and violently. In the heart of its crater,

A BURST OF FLOWERS
Along the Coldwater Ridge Nature Trail, above, only six miles northwest of the volcano's crater, grasses and wildflowers seed the fertile soil produced by the eruption. Many trails within the Mount St. Helens National Volcanic Monument lead through the lava caves, devastated forests, and steep canyons of this geologically fascinating terrain.

PEACEFUL AGAIN

One of the youngest of the Cascade peaks, Mount St. Helens has been quiet since 1991; but it remains at the top of the US Geological Survey's list of volcanoes most likely to erupt in the future, possibly within the next generation.

the lava dome ballooned to 1,150 feet in height. Then, in 1986, the dome stopped growing and seismic activity around the volcano slowed. Loowit was quieting down again.

The forests, meanwhile, were rebuilding themselves as dramatically as the volcano had burned and buried them. The land was not dead, it was transformed. Islands of life persisted like desert oases. Tiny Pacific silver firs sprang up from the snowbanks that lay under thick layers of ash. Lakes in the high country, sheltered by ice and snow, had insulated frogs, toads, trout, and other wildlife. On the leeward side of the ridges facing away from the volcano, ferns burst forth. Elsewhere, hardy wildflowers sprouted as early as 1981. Elk wandered in from the blast zone's edges, and pocket gophers tunneled up through the ash. The eruption had generated a rebirth. The forest's cycle—a cycle that dates back 40,000 years to the origins of the volcano—had come around again.

Although Mount St. Helens is a young volcano in geological terms, it belongs to a mountain range that started forming 8 million years ago. Extending from British Columbia to California, the 1,000-mile-long Cascade Range belongs to the Pacific Ocean's Ring of Fire. This ring, containing some of the earth's most active volcanoes, is a living laboratory for what scientists call plate tectonics. In this process, two of the earth's plates—masses of crust that float on the planet's surface—collide and rub against each other. The friction forces one plate under the other, creating magma that erupts aboveground as a volcano. Along the Pacific Northwest coast, the smaller Juan de Fuca Plate is being shoved under the North American Plate to fuel Mount St. Helens and several other Cascade volcanoes.

The 1980 eruption has taught researchers a great deal about the volcano. Early hypotheses have been squelched; predictions have failed to materialize. For example, in one area where scientists had expected plants to be the first living things to return to the barren land, beetles appeared first instead. They fed on dead insect bodies.

Scientists now recognize that the blast zone is incredibly complex. What was once a homogeneous coniferous forest has become an intricate mosaic—desertlike plains, patches of shady forest, and grassy slopes—that eludes easy categorization.

A variety of plants and animals has appeared in the new range of habitats—mudflows, pumice plains, and forested lakeshores. No other landscape resembles this fire-forged, rain-soaked land.

CRATER VIEWS

The blast zone was designated the Mount St. Helens National Volcanic Monument in 1982. Stretching across some 110,000 acres, the monument was established to protect the area for scientific research as well as for the public. More than 200 miles of trails have been etched across the varied terrain by the US Forest Service. The trails offer hikers a challenging adventure that includes several different views of the crater and its cooling lava dome.

The monument contains the second-longest subterranean lava tube in the contiguous 48 states. Named Ape Cave, after a group of youths called the St. Helens Apes, who made an extensive exploration of the cave, it winds under a forest for two miles. The 1,900-year-old cave was unharmed by the 1980 eruption and is open to the public. Visitors can explore part of the tube on foot—the ceiling in some areas is as high as a two-story house—but some sections are much less roomy. Here visitors must resort to crawling on their hands and knees. Interpretative tours by lantern light are offered during the summer. The cave's walls drip water, while a cool wind sneaks up its pitch-black tunnel.

Lava Canyon lies only a few miles from Ape Cave down Highway 83, where a suspension bridge is strung across the gaping chasm. From here hikers can view the southeastern slope of Mount St. Helens and walk across the Pine Creek mudflow, where, during the eruption, millions of gallons of boiling mud stripped bark off trees and tossed huge boulders hundreds of feet.

But perhaps the most rewarding adventure afforded visitors is a scramble up the volcano from the southern side. The steep climb ends at the crater rim, elevation 8,365 feet. On a clear day, climbers watch boulders skip down the crater walls to crash on the floor below. Spirit Lake, slowly clearing of its logs, glistens to the north. The power of volcanic forces is revealed here and at three other potentially active volcanoes—Hood, Rainier, and Adams—that rise like gods from the south, north, and east. Their silent profiles announce who rules the land where rocks float on water and fire sings.

NATURE'S SURPRISE
Within a month of the 1980 eruption scientists were amazed to find that trilliums, such as the one below, were blooming in the sterile, monochromatic ash. Apparently, their underground rootstock had survived the fire.

FLATTENED IN MINUTES
Likened to the force of several megaton bombs, the lateral blast flattened old-growth forests, left, for 230 square miles. Many of the blown-down trees outside the monument were harvested as lumber. Those inside remain as a testimony to the force of nature: As they decay, the trees enrich the soil.

Nearby Sites & Attractions

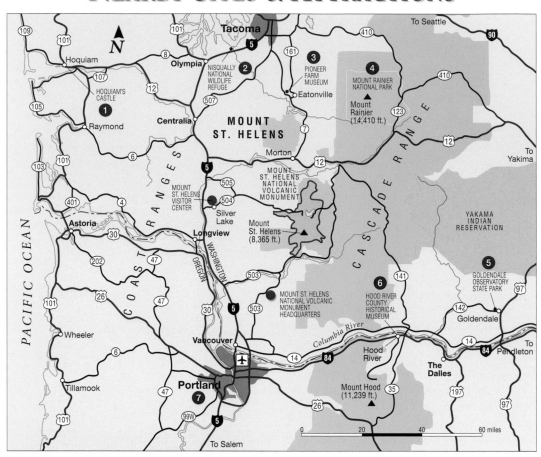

Bathed in sunlight, the face of Mount Rainier, below, is constantly changing as glaciers slowly slide down its slopes.

HOQUIAM'S CASTLE, WASHINGTON

Built by lumber magnate Robert Lytle in 1897, this 19th-century mansion was entirely restored in 1971. The 20-room house is furnished in period style and includes Tiffany lamps and crystal chandeliers. One room has been decorated to resemble a Victorian saloon. Located at 515 Chenault Ave. in Hoquiam.

② NISQUALLY NATIONAL WILDLIFE REFUGE, WASHINGTON

Fed by snowmelt from Mount Rainier, this 2,817-acre refuge on the Nisqually River Delta attracts numerous migratory birds. Some 15,000 wigeons, 6,000 dunlins, Swainson's hawks, and black brants winter here; the raptor population includes northern harriers, bald eagles, and red-tailed hawks. In summer, the refuge offers safety and an abundant supply of food to a colony of 80 nesting great blue herons. Harbor seals, otters, and beavers share the waters of the Nisqually River. Located six miles north of Olympia off Hwy. 5.

③ PIONEER FARM MUSEUM, WASHINGTON

Educational displays, focusing on Native American and pioneer history, and authentic structures from the 1880's revive the spirit of the Oregon frontier at this unique hands-on museum. Visitors can milk a cow, card wool, churn butter, and grind wheat. A Native American tour, available on summer weekends only, offers visitors the opportunity to use a bow and arrow, grind corn, and identify animal tracks and furs. The Pioneer Folklore/Craft Tour shows visitors how to make cornhusk dolls and candles; and a unique overnight program lets participants relive the days of the pioneers as they cook over an open fire and perform morning chores in the barn. Located three miles north of Eatonville on Ohop Valley Rd.

4 MOUNT RAINIER NATIONAL PARK, WASHINGTON

A 1-million-year-old volcano that was born of fiery explosions, Mount Rainier is 14,410 feet in height. Some 26 glaciers, all originating from Mount Rainier, span 34 square miles, making this the largest single-peak glacial system in the United States outside Alaska. Scattered throughout the 235,404-acre park, ancient lava flows and outcrops are chilling reminders that Washington State's highest mountain is a dormant volcano. Below 5,000 feet the slopes are blanketed in thick forests of western hemlock and Douglas fir, and dissected by more than 300 miles of trails. Black bears, deer, mountain goats, golden-mantled ground squirrels, and hares are among the park's denizens. The area between the forest and the glaciers is dotted with colorful wildflowers, including lupines, paintbrushes, and heather. Hiking trails range from easy to difficult, and rock and glacier climbing should be attempted by experienced climbers only. Located 65 miles southeast of Tacoma on Hwy. 410.

5 GOLDENDALE OBSERVATORY STATE PARK, WASHINGTON

This unique state park offers videos, displays, and educational demonstrations on astronomy. The highlight is the 24.5-inch Cassegrain telescope—one of the largest amateur-built telescopes in the nation—which is available for public inspection. Also on display is an eight-inch Celestron telescope, designed to observe the sun. Use of the telescopes is on a first-come, first-served basis. Visitors are introduced to star gazing, and a reference library and meeting room are also on the premises. Located one mile north of downtown Goldendale off Hwy. 142.

6 HOOD RIVER COUNTY HISTORICAL MUSEUM, OREGON

The museum is devoted to the cultural history of the Hood River valley. Some displays focus on the valley's Native inhabitants and others on the arrival of the first white settlers in 1854 and the valley's development as a major fruit producer in the 20th century. Main floor exhibits include Native baskets and beadwork and articles from the local Finnish and Japanese communities. Upstairs there are samples of pioneer schoolwork, a jeweler's workbench, and traditional dolls and toys. There is also an atrium with native plants and flowers. Located in Hood River.

7 PORTLAND, OREGON

Located at the confluence of the Willamette and Columbia rivers, Portland was established as a city in 1844. It was nicknamed Stumptown because of the numerous tree stumps left behind by early traders in the region. The city became an important commercial hub in the latter half of the 19th century following the Indian wars and the gold rushes in California and Oregon. Today Portland is renowned for its clean air and water, as well as for its many magnificent parks. Washington Park encompasses 404 acres of hills, valleys, and streams, and Leach Botanical Park displays more than 600 flower species.Trails wind through the Portland Audubon Society's 265-acre wildlife refuge that cares for injured animals. Located on Hwy. 5.

With Mount Hood as a backdrop, downtown Portland, above, lights up at nightfall. The city retains its magnificent vistas by restricting buildings to 40 stories.

Turreted Hoquiam's Castle, left, affords a spectacular view of Grays Harbor and the Pacific Ocean from its hillside perch.

GLACIER BAY

As colossal glaciers retreat from this icy vastness, they reshape the land, creating new habitats.

The amber sunlight dances off the snow-capped mountains, and sleek porpoises silently break the ocean surface as a cruise ship turns north in Alaska's Icy Strait and enters the world of Glacier Bay. Flocks of sea ducks wing across the bow. The haunting calls of humpback whales sound in the distance. Hermit thrushes fill the shoreline forest with their liquid song.

The cruise ship has entered a landscape of mountains, forests, sea, and shore that did not exist 200 years before. Glacier Bay is a living laboratory of change, an unfinished symphony, a place only recently released from the frozen grip of the Ice Age.

When George Vancouver, captain of the H.M.S. *Discovery,* dropped anchor in nearby Port Althorp in 1794, there was no Glacier Bay. His lieutenants explored Icy Strait by longboats in their hunt for a northwest passage to Hudson Bay. They found instead a barren indentation, its tides and currents powerful, its waters thick with castles of icebergs. At its back was a single imposing tidewater glacier 2,300 feet high, from which towers of ice broke free and crashed into the sea.

Little did Captain Vancouver and his crew realize that their visit would be a benchmark for the most dramatic and rapid glacial retreat on record. In the next 170 years the great glacier witnessed by his men would retreat 65 miles to reveal one of the most dynamic landscapes in North America.

A JOURNEY THROUGH TIME

A journey to Glacier Bay is like traveling back in time. The visit begins in the present—in the forested world of the lower bay—and culminates in the past—in the upper bay, where visitors come face to face with the tidewater termini of the Margerie, Grand Pacific, Johns Hopkins, and Reid glaciers, each sequestered at the head of an inlet.

Passengers gather on the deck of the ship and drink in the scenery as though it were an elixir. They crowd the rail waiting for a great blue shard of ice, called a serac, to fall from the luminous, deeply crevassed face of Margerie Glacier. Their one- to two-week cruise through the Inside Passage of Alaska has taken in the nautical and historical ports of call of Ketchikan and Skagway, as well as Juneau—Alaska's capital city.

Black-legged kittiwakes, a species of small gull, nest on the neighboring cliffs, their eggs laid securely in crevices on the ledges. Harbor seals rest on icebergs and watch the ship with their obsidian eyes. The ship noses to within a quarter mile of the giant glacier, which flows into the bay.

The park naturalists do not utter a word—it is time to let the glacier speak, time to hear the voice of the ice. Suddenly a small piece breaks free and hits the sea with a sharp report, like cannon fire. This is a preamble. Another piece of ice breaks away, and another; then, with accelerated motion and finally breakneck speed, the entire serac, nearly 200 feet tall and weighing countless tons, plunges into the sea, shooting up a tremendous plume of water. The passengers whoop and applaud with delight as the captain wheels the ship's bow into the oncoming swell. The kittiwakes fly off their ledges and scream in the air; the harbor seals wrinkle their whiskered noses and slip into the sea.

The ship's passengers have witnessed what Tlingit Indians refer to as "white thunder." The huge blocks of glacial ice that awe visitors today as they crash into the bay were formed from snow that fell in the mountains only 200 years ago. The passengers' exhilaration was shared by the American naturalist John Muir who, 85 years before, wrote: "The sound they make is like heavy thunder, with a prolonged roar after deep thudding sounds—a perpetual thunderstorm easily heard three or four miles away. The roar . . . and the shaking of the ground one or two miles distant from points of discharge seems startlingly near."

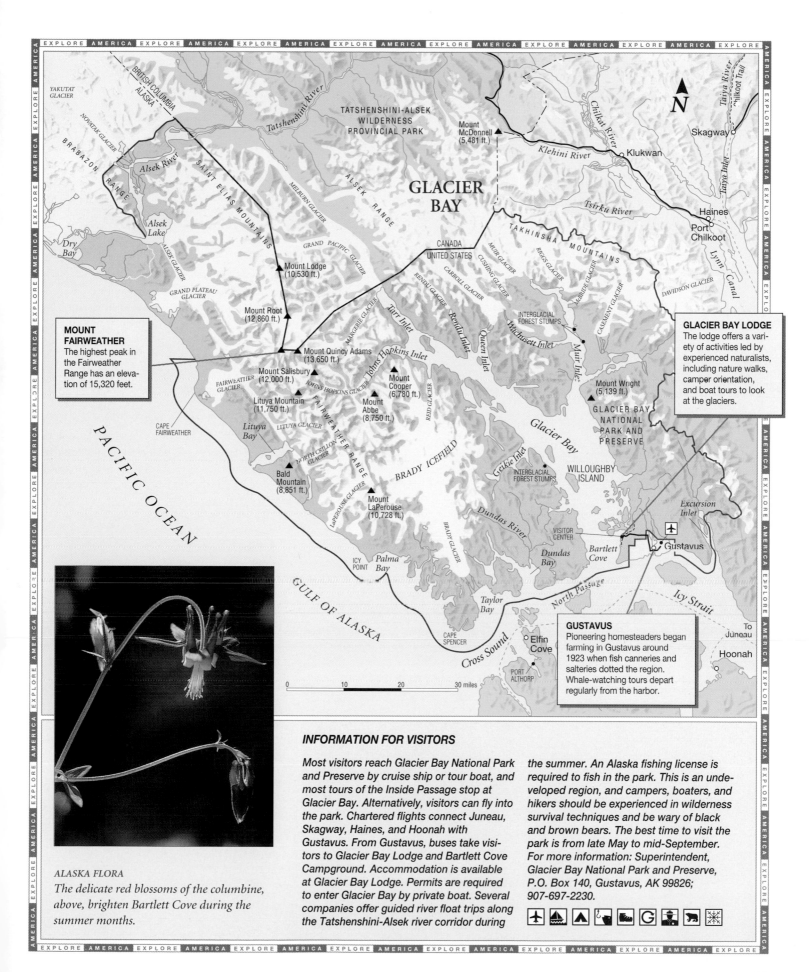

N

YAKUTAT GLACIER

BRITISH COLUMBIA / ALASKA

Tatshenshini River

TATSHENSHINI-ALSEK WILDERNESS PROVINCIAL PARK

Mount McDonnell (5,481 ft.)

Chilkat River

Taiya River
Chilkoot Trail

Skagway

Klehini River

Klukwan

NOVATAK GLACIER

BRABAZON RANGE

Alsek River

SAINT ELIAS MOUNTAINS

MELBURN GLACIER

ALSEK RANGE

GLACIER BAY

Tsirku River

TAKHINSHA MOUNTAINS

Haines

Port Chilkoot

Alsek Lake

ALSEK GLACIER

Dry Bay

GRAND PACIFIC GLACIER

CANADA
UNITED STATES

MUIR GLACIER

CUSHING GLACIER

RIGGS GLACIER

McBRIDE GLACIER

CASEMENT GLACIER

DAVIDSON GLACIER

Taiya Inlet

Lynn Canal

GRAND PLATEAU GLACIER

Mount Lodge (10,530 ft.)

CARROLL GLACIER

Mount Root (12,860 ft.)

RENDU GLACIER

MARGERIE GLACIER

Tarr Inlet

Rendu Inlet

Queen Inlet

Wachusett Inlet

INTERGLACIAL FOREST STUMPS

Muir Inlet

MOUNT FAIRWEATHER
The highest peak in the Fairweather Range has an elevation of 15,320 feet.

Mount Quincy Adams (13,650 ft.)

Johns Hopkins Inlet

GLACIER BAY LODGE
The lodge offers a variety of activities led by experienced naturalists, including nature walks, camper orientation, and boat tours to look at the glaciers.

FAIRWEATHER GLACIER

Mount Salisbury (12,000 ft.)

JOHNS HOPKINS GLACIER

Mount Cooper (6,780 ft.)

Mount Wright (5,139 ft.)

CAPE FAIRWEATHER

Lituya Mountain (11,750 ft.)

Mount Abbe (8,750 ft.)

FAIRWEATHER RANGE

REID GLACIER

Glacier Bay

GLACIER BAY NATIONAL PARK AND PRESERVE

Lituya Bay

LITUYA GLACIER

NORTH CRILLON GLACIER

BRADY ICEFIELD

Geikie Inlet

INTERGLACIAL FOREST STUMPS

WILLOUGHBY ISLAND

Bald Mountain (8,851 ft.)

PACIFIC OCEAN

LAPEROUSE GLACIER

Mount LaPerouse (10,728 ft.)

BRADY GLACIER

Dundas River

Excursion Inlet

VISITOR CENTER

Bartlett Cove

Gustavus

ICY POINT

Palma Bay

Dundas Bay

GULF OF ALASKA

Taylor Bay

North Passage

Icy Strait

CAPE SPENCER

Cross Sound

Elfin Cove

PORT ALTHORP

GUSTAVUS
Pioneering homesteaders began farming in Gustavus around 1923 when fish canneries and salteries dotted the region. Whale-watching tours depart regularly from the harbor.

To Juneau

Hoonah

0   10   20   30 miles

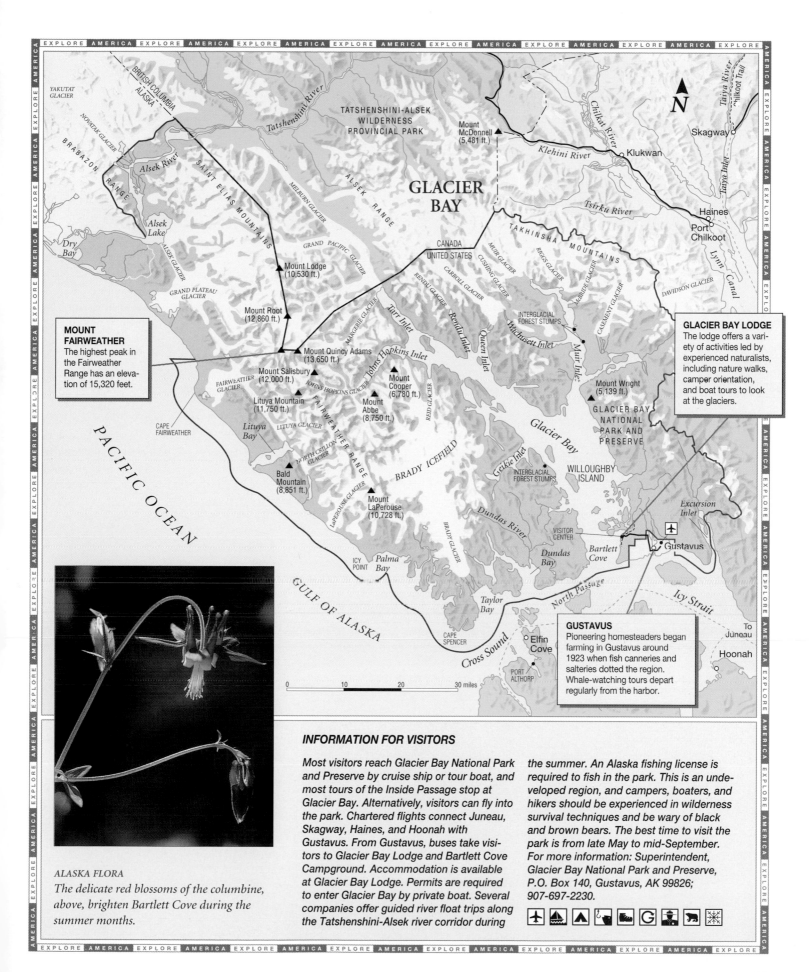

ALASKA FLORA
The delicate red blossoms of the columbine, above, brighten Bartlett Cove during the summer months.

INFORMATION FOR VISITORS

Most visitors reach Glacier Bay National Park and Preserve by cruise ship or tour boat, and most tours of the Inside Passage stop at Glacier Bay. Alternatively, visitors can fly into the park. Chartered flights connect Juneau, Skagway, Haines, and Hoonah with Gustavus. From Gustavus, buses take visitors to Glacier Bay Lodge and Bartlett Cove Campground. Accommodation is available at Glacier Bay Lodge. Permits are required to enter Glacier Bay by private boat. Several companies offer guided river float trips along the Tatshenshini-Alsek river corridor during the summer. An Alaska fishing license is required to fish in the park. This is an undeveloped region, and campers, boaters, and hikers should be experienced in wilderness survival techniques and be wary of black and brown bears. The best time to visit the park is from late May to mid-September. For more information: Superintendent, Glacier Bay National Park and Preserve, P.O. Box 140, Gustavus, AK 99826; 907-697-2230.

BALD MOUNTAIN
Bald Mountain, right, in the Fairweather Range, casts its reflection on Lituya Bay. Boulders left behind by retreating glaciers lie scattered along the shoreline.

WHALE WATCHING
A trio of humpback whales breaches the waters of Glacier Bay, below. Humpbacks feed on krill, shrimp, capelin, and other fish along the shorelines and in the bays and fjords of the region.

When John Muir first entered Glacier Bay in October 1879, he was using maps made by Captain Vancouver. Muir had traveled by canoe from Fort Wrangell in search of corroboration for the theory that continental glaciation had created California's Yosemite. His guides were Tlingit Indians, descendants of the hunters and gatherers who had been forced to leave their ancestral home in the bay because of encroaching glaciers. The glaciers reached their maximum extent here about 1750. This Little Ice Age—which in no way approached the extent of the glaciation that stretched south to Wisconsin during the Pleistocene epoch 2 million years ago—is responsible for the glaciers that visitors see today in Glacier Bay.

From the slopes above his camp near Geikie Glacier, Muir observed a landscape that "was smothered in clouds. . . . But at length the clouds lifted a little, and beneath their gray fringes I saw the berg-filled expanse of the bay, and the imposing fronts of five huge glaciers, the nearest being immediately beneath me. This was my first general view of Glacier Bay, a solitude of ice and snow and new-born rocks, dim, dreary, mysterious."

THE GLACIER BEATS A RETREAT

The glacier that almost filled Glacier Bay at the time of Vancouver's visit had retreated another 40 miles and split into smaller, still magnificent tributary glaciers. Muir returned the next year, and again in 1890, each time noting tremendous changes as the great glacier continued to withdraw, branching into the Grand Pacific, Margerie, and Johns Hopkins glaciers in the bay's West Arm, and the Muir Glacier in the east. Muir's poetic descriptions and love of the wilderness sparked nationwide interest in the area. Steamships began touring the bay, carrying wide-eyed passengers to the ice front and sometimes disembarking them where they could climb onto Muir Glacier by a boardwalk. The journalist Eliza Ruhamah Scidmore was among these early visitors. She wrote, "The great buttresses of ice that rose first from the water and touched the moraine were as solidly white as marble, veined and streaked with rocks and mud, but further on . . . the color deepened to turquoise and sapphire blues. The crashes of falling ice were magnificent at that point, and in the face of a keen wind that blew over the icefield we sat on the rocks and watched the wondrous scene."

Tourism in Glacier Bay was abruptly terminated in 1899, when a massive earthquake rocked the area. Muir Glacier shattered and filled the bay with such thick quantities of floating ice that ships could not approach the glacier for years. Thereafter, what was left of Muir Glacier retreated at great speed, and by the 1980's the glacier was nearly 25 miles from its position a century before.

By advancing and retreating, glaciers have shaped and reshaped every waterway and land formation in Glacier Bay, creating rich and ever changing

ORNAMENTED EVERGREEN
Yellow cinquefoils, named after their five-petal blooms, mingle with the boughs of a young Sitka spruce tree, above.

PORT OF CALL
A cruise ship rides the waters of Tarr Inlet near Margerie Glacier, left, giving passengers a close up view of the glacier.

INVITING TRAIL
A boardwalk winds through the spruce and hemlock temperate rain forest in Bartlett Cove, right.

STRIKING A POSE
A tufted puffin, below, shows off its parrotlike profile and signature plumes, which curve forward around its head.

marine and terrestrial habitats. Their advance or retreat is determined by the rate of snowfall, the topography, and climatic trends. Muir Glacier and other glaciers on the bay's western side are slowly advancing, whereas glaciers on the bay's eastern side are retreating. As these glaciers erode faster than they are built, they leave behind a canvas for nature's artistry as plants, followed by animals, regain their foothold on the land.

PLANT SUCCESSION

At the lower end of Glacier Bay, which was deglaciated in Captain Vancouver's time, grows a forest of Sitka spruce and western hemlock. The upper bay, deglaciated mere decades ago, supports mosses and flowers: The irony is that by altering the conditions in which they thrive, these pioneering plants make the soil hospitable for the rival species that eventually displace them. The smaller plant life surrenders to alders and willow trees. In time the theme repeats itself as thickets of alder pump nitrogen into the soil and provide the shade needed by Sitka spruce, which then displaces the alder. In turn, spruces make conditions suitable for hemlocks.

At the lower end of the bay, in Bartlett Cove, guests at the Glacier Bay Lodge quietly walk a loop boardwalk trail beneath the dark canopy of hemlock and spruce forest. A ranger/naturalist accompanies them and describes the vegetation that dapples the land in a dozen shades of green—the textured mosses and resplendent ferns on the forest floor, the tasty blueberries and spiky devil's

club that create an understory. Visitors listen intently to the sounds of the forest as a red squirrel chatters, a bald eagle calls, and a male blue grouse drums his basso profundo song. The woods are alive with the vibrant pulse of life, where two centuries before only glaciers lay.

| ANIMAL MIGRATION | Blue ice sculpts this land, and green forests quilt it. Each new pocket of vegetation quickly becomes a new habitat for |

wildlife. Brown bears roam the sparse upper bay, while black bears occupy the forest of the lower bay. Both have been seen swimming across inlets and climbing crevassed glaciers. Wolves howl in the night and hunt everything from meadow voles to mountain goats, taking down the old, sick, and infirm. Moose, which were rarely seen in the bay until recently, seem to migrate to a different inlet every year in search of their favorite browse: willow. Even these powerful animals fall victim to predators: In 1992 two moose seen swimming across Icy Strait near the entrance to Glacier Bay were attacked by orca whales. The orcas got one of them and the other unfortunate moose became entangled in a bed of kelp and slowly drowned.

The waters of Glacier Bay are no less bountiful than the land. The summer sun arcs into 19 hours of daylight; tides regularly flood and ebb an average of 15 vertical feet. Nutrients flush through the water column, and the sea blooms with life. Vast schools of small fish—herring, capelin, sandlance—provide food for terns, gulls, puffins, and countless other birds, and for two species of baleen whales: humpback and minke. The humpbacks, having wintered in Hawaii and Mexico, where they give birth and eat little if any food, arrive hungry in Alaska. Daily tour boats from Bartlett Cove to view the glaciers, pause to watch the whales spout and rise, lob their tails, slap their flippers, even leap completely from the sea.

Of the five species of Pacific salmon—silver, sockeye, pink, chum, and king—all but the king inhabit streams and rivers of Glacier Bay. Sea otters, once nearly exterminated for their furs, have begun repopulating Glacier Bay and can sometimes be

SNACK TIME
A black bear, below, feeds on the soft-stemmed grasses of an open meadow. Most of the bear's diet consists of grasses and berries.

RIVER OF ICE
An aerial view reveals the enormity of Riggs Glacier, left, which flows from the Takhinsha Mountains into Muir Inlet.

seen in rafts of 50 males or more, floating on their backs as they feed on sea urchins and crab. Other newcomers, Steller's sea lions, have established a stronghold in southeastern Alaska; at the same time their numbers plummet in the Gulf of Alaska and the Bering Sea, probably from overfishing.

Kayakers disembark the tour boats and paddle into the Glacier Bay wilderness to camp. They may stay for one night or more, alone but never lonely. When they return, they see the modern, mechanized world in a new light, having awakened in their tents to the sounds of thundering glaciers, howling wolves, and the comical calls of oystercatchers, the dark red-billed shorebirds that nest on nameless islands in hidden coves. The kayaker and the luxury cruise ship passenger experience different Glacier Bays, as does the sightseer who gets a bird's-eye view of the vast land of ice and snow from a plane thousands of feet overhead.

Established as a national monument in 1925 and a national park and preserve in 1980, Glacier Bay is in danger of being loved to death. Every year cruise ships, tour boats, and kayaks course through its waters in greater numbers, and more planes buzz overhead. A few areas have been set aside as motorless waters, although some are still open to commercial fishing. And while some wildlife species migrate to the bay, others disappear from it. The boreal toad, for example, once abundant, has declined sharply, perhaps because its skin is hypersensitive to the thinning ozone layer and the resulting increase in ultraviolet light.

If the past is prologue, the glaciers will re-advance and bury this land, as they have many times before. Until they do, however, Glacier Bay National Park and Preserve will be the setting not only for continued geological and ecological change but also for an alteration in human thinking that respects the wilderness and keeps it wild.

GLACIAL DEBRIS
A granite boulder left behind by a retreating glacier, opposite page, sits on a promontory above the ice-strewn waters of Alsek River.

LIFE IN THE WILD
A group of hikers set up camp on a grassy plain looking up at the rugged snowcapped peaks of Glacier Bay, left.

VERSATILE MAMMAL
A female Pacific harbor seal and her pup recline on an iceberg, left. A thick layer of fat insulates seals from the cold, keeps them buoyant, and provides them with a source of energy to go for long periods without food.

NEARBY SITES & ATTRACTIONS

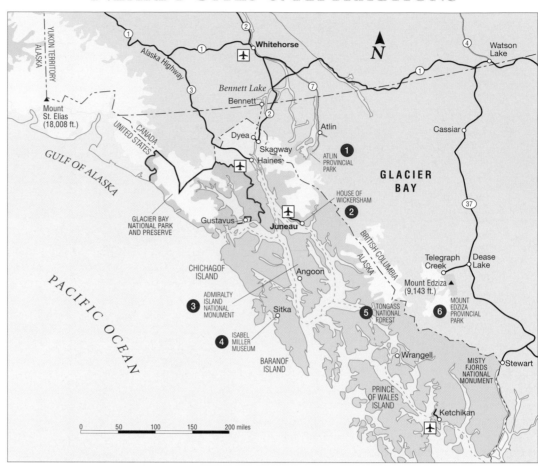

The House of Wickersham, below, belonged to Congressman James Wickersham, who, as Alaska's delegate in 1917, introduced the first bill proposing Alaska's statehood—43 years before it became a reality.

① ATLIN PROVINCIAL PARK, BRITISH COLUMBIA

One-third of this park's 669,700 acres, which encompass two mountain ranges, is covered by glaciers. The park's centerpiece is Atlin Lake, the largest natural body of water in the province. Teresa Island, one of 80 islands in the lake, rises 6,758 feet above the brilliant blue waters. There are three distinct vegetation zones in the park. Lodgepole pine and white spruce dominate the boreal forests of the river valleys and lakeshores, Engelmann spruce and subalpine fir are found on the mountain slopes of the middle elevation zone, and sparse vegetation exists above the timberline in the alpine tundra zone. Grizzlies, black bears, moose, caribou, and wolves roam the park. Located 16 miles south of Atlin.

② HOUSE OF WICKERSHAM, ALASKA

Built in 1898, this Victorian house was named after James Wickersham, an Alaskan judge, lawyer, and delegate to Congress, who lived in the house from 1928 until his death in 1939. He was also the first

A fishing fleet is moored in the harbor of Mitchell Bay near Angoon, right, located adjacent to Admiralty Island National Monument.

non-Native to attempt the ascent of Mount McKinley. Wickersham began his career by settling mining claim disputes and collecting saloon license fees. He played an important role in gaining congressional legislation to create Mount McKinley National Park, which was later named Denali National Park. His home contains displays of Alaskan artifacts and photographs. Located at 213 7th St. in Juneau.

3 ADMIRALTY ISLAND NATIONAL MONUMENT, ALASKA

About 1,700 Alaskan brown bears range freely across this 1-million-acre national monument, called Xootsnoowu, or Bear Island, by the Tlingit Natives. These massive animals can be spotted foraging in the monument's forests or on the shores of Admiralty Island. A system of canoe and portage trails connect nine interior lakes. Nesting on the island is a huge population of bald eagles that exceeds the entire bald eagle population of the contiguous United States. More than 800 eagle nests, some of which measure 12 feet high and 6 feet deep, are found in the old-growth hemlock trees. The island's geographical features include snow-capped mountains, thick forests, meadows, bogs, streams, and saltwater bays. The island can be reached by floatplane or ferry from Juneau.

4 ISABEL MILLER MUSEUM, ALASKA

The museum boasts fine examples of wood carvings and baskets made by the area's first settlers, the Tlingit Natives. A large diorama depicts the city of Sitka in 1867 when the territory of Alaska was transferred from Russia to the United States. American and Russian artifacts, including paintings, furniture, antique dolls, photographs, and a journal by naval officer George Foster Emmons, illustrate the contributions the two cultures made to the building of this historic city. Located on Harbor Dr. in Sitka.

5 TONGASS NATIONAL FOREST, ALASKA

Covering almost 17 million acres, this national forest, which was created in 1907, is the largest in the nation. It stretches across most of the Alaska

Panhandle and encompasses bays, fjords, alpine meadows, mountains, rivers, and lakes. The imposing landscape has been, and continues to be, carved by hundreds of glaciers, the most famous being the Mendenhall Glacier. Measuring 12 miles long and more than 1 mile wide, this enormous mountain of ice feeds into Mendenhall Lake. Massive blocks of ice break from the forest's southernmost tidewater glacier, Le Conte Glacier, and plunge into Le Conte Bay. The high level of moisture in the rain forest nourishes stands of cottonwood, Sitka spruce, and western hemlock trees. This temperate rain forest is home to bald eagles, moose, mountain goats, and brown bears. The area's rivers, streams, and lakes are renowned for their abundant supply of salmon and trout. Forest headquarters are located in Ketchikan, Petersburg, and Sitka.

6 MOUNT EDZIZA PROVINCIAL PARK, BRITISH COLUMBIA

Covering 568,000 acres of highlands, the park's landscape was shaped by ancient volcanic activity. The main attractions here include lava flows, basalt plateaus, and cinder cones. Mount Edziza, a 9,143-foot volcano, has been dormant for the past 10,000 years; however, small eruptions have taken place around it, creating numerous cinder cones that have been given fanciful names such as Coffee and Cocoa craters. The yellow, red, white, and purple rock of the Spectrum Mountains was created by lava flows from Mount Edziza. Water has also helped to shape the landscape. The Klastline River cuts through the park, and five significant lakes contain rainbow trout. Animals that inhabit the region include moose, Stone sheep, arctic ground squirrels, caribou, black bears, and grizzlies. Although there are numerous hiking trails, the park has no facilities and is suitable only for those with advanced wilderness experience. The park may be accessed from the town of Telegraph Creek, or Kinaskan Provincial Park on Hwy. 37 near Iskut.

Splashes of paintbrush, cinquefoil, and shooting star flowers color the rugged terrain of Tongass National Forest, above.

GAZETTEER: *Traveler's Guide to Natural Wonders*

Miner Castle monolith at Pictured Rocks National Lakeshore, Michigan.

ALASKA
Lake Clark National Park
and Preserve   119

ARIZONA
Grand Canyon National Park   120

ARKANSAS
Ozark National Forest   121

CALIFORNIA
Lava Beds National Monument   122

COLORADO
Florissant Fossil Beds National
Monument   123

FLORIDA
Corkscrew Swamp Sanctuary   124

HAWAII
Waimea Canyon   125

IDAHO
Craters of the Moon National
Monument   126

ILLINOIS
Cache River Wetlands   127

KANSAS
Flint Hills   128

LOUISIANA
Mississippi Delta   129

MICHIGAN
Pictured Rocks National
Lakeshore   130

MISSISSIPPI
Mississippi Petrified Forest   131

NEW JERSEY
Pine Barrens   132

NEW MEXICO
White Sands National
Monument   133

NEW YORK
Adirondack Park   134
Letchworth State Park   135

OREGON
Crater Lake National Park   136

SOUTH DAKOTA
Badlands National Park   137

TENNESSEE
Cumberland Caverns   138

UTAH
Capitol Reef National Park   139

WYOMING
Devils Tower National Monument 140
Old Faithful   141

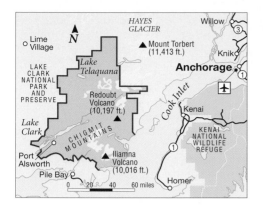

The huge rock spire, called The Tusk, left, is one of the dramatic geological formations in Lake Clark National Park and Preserve.

Often called the Alaskan Alps because of the formidable Alaska and Aleutian ranges that meet within its boundaries, Lake Clark National Park and Preserve is a rugged and varied landscape. The jagged peaks of the Chigmit Mountains run down the spine of the region. Towering granite spires, two active volcanoes, glaciers, and 50-mile-long Lake Clark (from which the area gets its name) also are found within the park and preserve's more than 4 million acres.

The mountains were formed during millions of years of geological activity that included uplifts, earthquakes, volcanic activity, and glacial and tectonic plate movements. The Pacific Plate, located along the Aleutian Trench, has become wedged under its North American counterpart. This tectonic plate movement under southern Alaska has given rise to the Chigmits, which lie on the edge of the North American Plate. The area's two active volcanoes show that the continental plates are settled. The snowcapped peaks of Iliamna and Redoubt volcanoes rise more than

10,000 feet above sea level. Redoubt Volcano erupted as recently as December 14, 1989, and Iliamna frequently vents steam gases. Both of these volcanoes are links in the Pacific Ring of Fire, which circles the Pacific Ocean.

DIVERSE LANDSCAPES

Along with its geological wonders, the park and preserve also contains diverse vegetation zones. The uppermost layer of arctic tundra—a marshy area that supports mosses, lichens, and low-growing shrubs—is located on the Turquoise-Telaquana Plateau. Below that is a permanently frozen subsoil known as the permafrost. During the summer the springy tundra floor is carpeted with flowering fireweeds, lupines, and other alpine plants.

The eastern flank of the Chigmit Mountains descends to Cook Inlet. This wet coastal plain is covered with dense stands of Sitka and white spruce, balsam, poplar, and alder. Fossils of fish, shells, and other sea life dating back 150 million years have been uncovered in the coastal cliffs. Puffins, kittiwakes, cormorants, and other seabirds nest in the crevices of cliffs. Seals and whales swim offshore.

More than a score of glacially carved lakes mark the park's western boundaries. Canada geese alight on the vivid blue waters, which are rimmed by stands of balsam, poplar, cottonwood, paper birch, and black spruce. The lakes and the myriad streams that flow into Bristol Bay are prime waters for anglers. Lake Clark, fed by waterfalls that spill from bordering mountains, is the headwaters for red salmon during their annual spawning. All five species of salmon, plus arctic char, grayling, Dolly Varden, northern pike, lake trout, and rainbow trout are found in the park and preserve.

Arctic ground squirrels scramble through the alpine meadows—plump prey for bald eagles, gyrfalcons, ospreys, and peregrine falcons. Dall sheep trot up the sheer cliffs to graze in the tundra, and lynx, wolves, and foxes prowl the foothills. Both black and brown bears are frequently sighted here. For many travelers, the sight of a herd of caribou crossing the tundra is the high point of their visit to this untamed land.

Located 150 air miles southwest of Anchorage, the park and preserve is accessible only by aircraft. There are no maintained campsites and only one maintained hiking trail, which starts near the ranger station at Port Alsworth and leads to Tanalian Falls and Kontrashibuna Lake.

FOR MORE INFORMATION:

Superintendent, Lake Clark National Park and Preserve, 4230 University Dr., Suite 311, Anchorage, AK 99508; 907-271-3751.

Arctic tundra, richly tinged by the autumn chill, borders Lower Twin Lake in Lake Clark National Park, left.

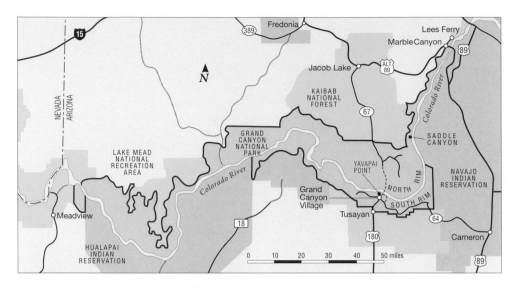

different ecological zones as they would encounter on a trip from British Columbia, Canada, to the Mexican border.

The higher regions of the Kaibab Plateau are covered with forests of spruce, fir, and quaking aspen. The lower plateau and rim areas are cloaked in pygmy forests of piñon pine and Utah juniper. Spotted skunks, Grand Canyon rattlesnakes, and chuckwalla lizards skulk among the cacti, agaves, and blackbrushes that thrive at the lowest elevation of the canyon.

EXPLORING THE RIVER

River trips leave from Lees Ferry. The motorized or oar-powered excursions, led by experienced guides, last from three days to two weeks. John Wesley Powell headed the first major river expedition through the canyon in 1869. River-running remained a daring feat until 1963, when the Glen Canyon Dam controlled the waters.

The dam also stanched the annual spring floods that had replenished the shoreline and maintained the spawning grounds of endangered fish such as the humpback chub. In 1996 the US Department of the Interior initiated a system of controlled flooding of the canyon. Floodgates were opened for seven days, allowing more than 117 billion gallons of water to deluge the canyon. The artificial flood, which broadened the canyon's beaches by up to three feet, was hailed as a success.

W hen sunlight illuminates the rainbow-hued walls of the Grand Canyon, this, one of nature's greatest masterpieces, earns all its superlatives. The chasm's slopes, gorges, cliffs, and river rapids have challenged explorers, inspired artists, thrilled adventurers, and fascinated geologists for years.

The Grand Canyon's vital statistics are astounding. The canyon is 277 miles in length; its two rims are, at points, separated by 18 miles; and the walls plunge down one vertical mile, reaching layers of rock that are 2 billion years old. At the lowest depths of the canyon the mighty Colorado River is still eating away at the Kaibab Upwarp—a raised plateau covering a section of north-western Arizona.

Nine trails make their way from the South Rim to river level, while four others meander down the North Rim. As visitors descend, they travel through as many

FOR MORE INFORMATION:

Superintendent, Grand Canyon National Park, P.O. Box 129, Grand Canyon, AZ 86023; 520-638-7888.

A miniature waterfall, above, pools in secret within the sand-colored rocks of Saddle Canyon.

The sun rises behind the South Rim of Grand Canyon National Park, right, which is viewed from Yavapai Point.

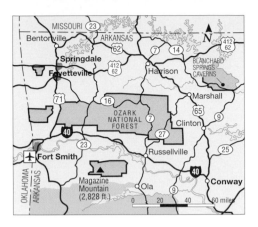

A seemingly endless forest of hardwood trees can be seen from the top of Magazine Mountain, above.

Ozark National Forest unfolds across northwestern Arkansas like a vast green quilt. Patched with five wilderness areas and threaded with streams, the 1-million-acre national forest encompasses crystal-clear lakes, six wild and scenic rivers, limestone bluffs, and hardwood forests. Its many geological wonders include natural bridges, waterfalls, a maze of caverns, and 2,828-foot Magazine Mountain, the highest peak in the state.

The rivers and streams are bordered by sandstone bluffs, the most spectacular of which are located along Shoal Creek and at Deep Hollow, Devil's Canyon, Blanchard Springs, and Bee Rock. These dramatic rock faces are colored in rich earth tones of brown, tan, rust, and amber.

Where wind and water have eroded the bluffs, a few pedestal formations are all that remain of the original cliffs. Hikers can view pedestals at Three Rocks, Standstone, Sam's Throne, and Pedestal Rocks. Sometimes the action of water on rock produces natural bridges such as those found in the Hurricane Creek Wilderness Area and at Alum Cove Natural Bridge, a stunning 130-foot rock span.

Within the national forest area there are open grasslands, bushy thickets, oak-hickory woods, pine forests, and mixed forests. Birding trips offer sightings of scarlet tanagers, indigo buntings, red-eyed vireos, pileated woodpeckers, belted kingfishers, and yellow-breasted chats. More rarely, birders may glimpse a red crossbill, a yellow-headed blackbird, a Cape May warbler, or a rough-legged hawk.

Hunters can obtain permits to hunt and trap game, including white-tailed deer, black bears, gray squirrels, fox squirrels, cottontail rabbits, wild turkeys, mourning doves, bobwhites, and various waterfowl. Permits are also needed to fish the deep lakes and mountain streams where largemouth bass, spotted bass, smallmouth bass, crappie, sunfish, catfish, and trout flourish.

The Ozark Highlands Trail takes cross-country hikers on a climb up and over the mountaintops for 160 miles. Starting at Lake Fort Smith, the trail runs in an easterly direction through some of the forest's most scenic areas, including the Boston Mountain, Pleasant Hill, and Buffalo Ranger districts. Shorter trails are provided for activities such as bicycling, horseback riding, and all-terrain-vehicle driving.

For those who seek solitude, plenty can be found in the forest's 65,826 acres of wilderness areas, where backpackers camp, fish, and hunt in the valleys, bluffs, and fern-cloaked hollows of Upper Buffalo, Hurricane Creek, Richland Creek, East Fork, and Leatherwood.

SPELUNKERS' HEAVEN

At Blanchard Springs Caverns beneath the verdant northeastern part of the Ozark National Forest, spelunkers descend into a mysterious underworld of corridors and chambers. Spelunkers, exploring these caverns in the 1950's, discovered the bones of a prehistoric Native American man and the remains of a bundle of reeds he might have used to light his way. No other evidence of exploration before the 20th century exists. Six miles of rooms and passageways have since been discovered, although only a mile and a half of trails have been developed and are open to the public.

On the cavern's upper level, the Dripstone Trail leads through a fantasyland of flowstone, pillars, stalactites, stalagmites, and popcorn crystals. These formations, called speleothems, are deposits of calcite, the mineral found in the limestone layers that form the bedrock of the Ozark Mountains. Other speleothems, called draperies, are suspended in delicate folds of translucent sheets of calcite. Hollow soda straws on the ceiling were formed as water ran down inside them and deposited rings of calcite at their tips.

The highlight of the trail is the Cathedral Room, which measures 1,150 feet long—almost the length of four football fields—and 180 feet at its widest. This chamber features a giant 65-foot-tall column.

Discovery Trail, which retraces the journey of the 1950's spelunkers, winds through lower and younger sections of the caverns. Pale, sightless creatures, such as blind crayfish, blind isopods, blind amphipods, and four-inch-long Ozark blind salamanders, dwell in this twilight world. Visitors can see an underground stream, and look up through the 70-foot-long natural entrance to the caves, where the decaying bones of that first intrepid explorer, dating from about A.D. 900, were discovered.

FOR MORE INFORMATION:
Ozark/St. Francis National Forests, 605 W. Main St., Russellville, AR 72801-3614; 501-968-2354.

121

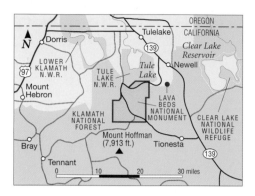

Lava Beds National Monument preserves a vast 47,000 acres of basalt landscape, where craters, cinder cones, chimneys, and fumeroles are the material reminders of a million years of volcanic eruptions. The windswept plateau south of Tulelake contains globular rocks, coils of lava, pumice, and cinder cones—formed when the vented lava of volcanoes cooled in the air.

Plant communities in the monument range from grasslands and sagebrush to juniper and ponderosa pine, varying with the elevation, which rises from 4,000 feet in the north to 5,493 feet in the south. Various rodents, such as kangaroo rats, yellow-bellied marmots, and mountain voles scurry in the underbrush to keep out of sight of the two dozen species of raptors that fly overhead. Bald eagles winter here in greater numbers than can be found any place outside Alaska.

Underground, 346 lava tubes form a maze of caves and grottoes that snake for thousands of feet. The most recent lava tubes were formed about 30,000 years ago by a volcanic eruption that reached temperatures of 1,800°F. As the surface of the lava cooled, fiery rivers underneath continued to flow hot and fast, leaving hollow tunnels after the flow subsided. Lava tubes such as Big Painted Cave and Symbol Bridge are underground galleries of Modoc Indian rock art. Petroglyphs carved and pecked into the rock here and on cliff faces along Tule Lake date from 380 to 1,480 years ago, and consist of wavy or zigzag lines, dots, stars, moons, and human figures.

Cave Loop Road winds past a cluster of lava tube caves, many of which were first explored and named by J. D. Howard, a local miller. Among the dozen-odd caves off this road are Labyrinth and Lava Brook caves, featuring lava pillars and lavacicles; Blue Grotto, its ceiling covered in powder blue bacteria; Golden Dome Cave, gilded with yellowish bacteria; and Catacombs Cave, a complex puzzle of passages. An ideal site for novice spelunkers is Mushpot Cave, which is equipped with interpretive signs explaining the phenomena.

TURBULENT PAST

Modoc Indians inhabited the area until the 19th century. They fished Tule Lake and Lost River and used the tule, a kind of large bulrush, to make their dome huts and their woven boats. They gathered edible plants and hunted deer, bighorn sheep, and pronghorns on the sagebrush-covered plateaus. Many pronghorns still survive in the eastern portion of the monument. Wildlife watchers may glimpse the skittish animals foraging in the sagebrush or racing across the plateau. Pronghorns regularly sprint at a speed of 30 miles an hour, but it is believed that they can sustain cruising speeds of more than 50 miles an hour

An early morning fog hovers over frosted rabbit-brush in Lava Beds National Monument, above. The area is often hazy in winter, when temperatures frequently drop to 20°F.

when traveling over a distance of three-quarters of a mile or more.

The Modocs were a tenacious people who rebelled against incursions on their land. Tensions between whites and Indians escalated into a conflict of cultures with the US Army between 1872 and 1873. The Modoc Indian War ended with the Modocs being exiled to Oklahoma where disease accomplished what bullets had not.

Most of the fighting took place in the lava beds in the northern part of the monument near Captain Jacks Stronghold. Visitors can see the place where 52 warriors, under their leader, Captain Jack, held the American troops at bay for almost five months.

FOR MORE INFORMATION:
Lava Beds National Monument, Box 867, Tulelake, CA 96134; 916-667-2282.

A lava tube, left, in Lava Beds National Monument was exposed when its roof collapsed.

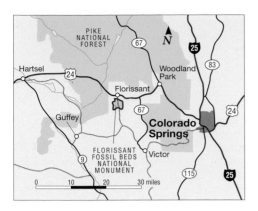

In the mountains of central Colorado is the dried-up bed of an ancient lake that has proved to be a paleontologist's dream. The first fossils were discovered in the Lake Florissant bed in 1871. Since then paleontologists have gathered tens of thousands of specimens of prehistoric plants and animals from Florissant that create a fascinating portrait of Colorado during the late Eocene epoch—some 30 million years after the age of dinosaurs and at least 33 million years before humans appeared.

Animal finds from Lake Florissant reveal the presence of mollusks, fish, birds, and opossums, as well as extinct mammals such as the mesohippus, an ancestor of the horse, and the oreodont, a piglike mammal. The leaves, twigs, seeds, flowers, and pollen grains of 120 plant species have been uncovered, as has an astonishing number of petrified spiders and insects including more than 1,100 species of dragonflies, ants, butterflies, and beetles.

The lake bed was designated a national monument in 1969. Visitors to the Florissant Fossil Beds discover a land of meadow and forest located at an elevation of 8,350 feet in the Rocky Mountain high country. Mule deer, coyotes, and bobcats roam through the ponderosa pine, spruce, fir, and aspen that cover the rolling hills of the 6,000-acre monument. In the winter herds of elk can be seen, and in spring and summer the meadows are brightened by a colorful palette of Indian paintbrush, locoweed, wild iris, senecio, columbine, scarlet gilia, and shooting star. The profusion of blossoms inspired the name of the lake bed and the town that is located nearby: Florissant comes from the French word for "flowering."

Thirty-five million years ago, however, the region was a water land. Lush ferns and shrubs grew in the shadows of massive redwoods, cedars, and oaks that surrounded a lake measuring 12 miles long and 3 miles wide. A community of rich wildlife flourished in the warm, humid climate until a series of violent volcanic eruptions transformed the landscape. Tons of ash, dust, and pumice spewed out over the countryside, smothering plants, birds, insects, and mammals in a deadly cloud. Many of the organisms fell into the lake and sank to the bottom. Caught in the lake sediment, they eventually became fossilized as the sediments turned into shale.

EXTRAORDINARY FIND

Many specimens, uncovered during the time when Florissant ran a lively trade in fossils, belong to museum and university collections around the world. Some fossils have disappeared into private collections and are lost forever to public view. However, there are more than 250 specimens now on display in the monument's visitor center. Visitors can examine pieces of prehistoric fern, pine cone, hickory nut, and giant sequoia embedded in the paper-thin, gray shale fragments.

But many visitors consider the insect display the highlight of the collection: the fossil beds of Lake Florissant are one of the world's richest sources of insect fossils. Insects are rarely preserved as fossils because they are so delicate, but the volcanic ash that showered over the lake was so fine it preserved even the most fragile of creatures intact. Careful inspection of the specimens reveals insect antennae, legs, hairs, and wings, colored brown or black by a thin residue of organic material. Many of the fossils are so detailed and complete they look as though they could spread their wings and flutter away. Studies show that many of the insects of the epoch are still found here, such as caterpillars and butterflies; other species, such as the tsetse fly, common to sub-Saharan Africa, have vanished from Colorado.

Specimens of petrified wood are on display outside the visitor center. Eons ago volcanic mudflows flooded the area, burying the trees. Over time minerals from the mud penetrated the living tissue of the trees and gradually crystallized the tissue. This process turned tree stumps into rock-hard petrified wood. The grotesquely shaped fossilized trees still stand around the ancient lake bed. Redwood trees, which underwent the petrification process, no longer grow in Colorado.

Petrified sequoia stumps can be seen on the Walk Through Time and Petrified Forest trails, the latter of which leads to Big Stump. This giant sequoia has a circumference of 76 feet at its base. All together, 12 miles of hiking trails loop through the meadows and trees of the monument. Here and there along the paths visitors can spot fossil-bearing shale. One trail goes to the Hornbek Homestead, built in 1878 by Adeline Hornbek, who came here to farm and ranch with her children. The pioneer farm consists of the original main cabin and reconstructed hired hands' quarters, stable and barn, and a root cellar built into the side of a hill.

There are regularly scheduled interpretive walks, talks, and weekend seminars held by park rangers in the summer when visitors can also go horseback riding and picnic in the monument. Wintertime visitors can snowshoe or cross-country ski on trails through the hills and forests.

FOR MORE INFORMATION:
Florissant Fossil Beds National Monument, P.O. Box 185, Florissant, CO 80816; 719-748-3253.

Visitors pause to look at the petrified remains of a sequoia tree, below, that measures 38 feet at its greatest circumference.

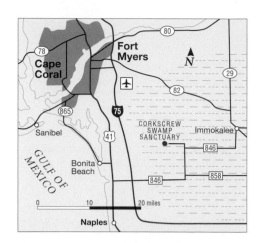

The sex of a baby alligator, above, is determined by the incubating temperature of the eggs. If the eggs stay at temperatures below 85°F, they hatch as females, and males develop at temperatures above 91°F.

When visitors to Corkscrew Swamp Sanctuary enter the preserve, they are often surprised to be greeted by rows of stately pines, cabbage palms, and fields of wildflowers. Further exploration reveals that the 10,560-acre sanctuary does indeed encompass swampland, along with a variety of other habitats such as pine flatlands, wet prairie, pond cypress, and willow wetland. The sanctuary also shelters 700 acres of virgin bald cypress, the world's largest remaining old-growth bald cypress forest.

The sanctuary is located in the heart of one of south Florida's last remaining intact watersheds and typifies a kind of wetland ecosystem that is unique to the state. In the summer months, when the sanctuary is lush and green, water levels rise by as much as two and a half feet, providing fish and other small aquatic creatures with a perfect breeding habitat. During the dry winter months water levels decrease and the fish get trapped in small pools of water.

This results in a high concentration of fish that provides a critical food source for many species of birds and other animals, including herons, egrets, wood storks, alligators, and otters.

The wetland is a delicately balanced ecosystem that requires management and protection to hold out against the rapidly growing human population. Fortunately the National Audubon Society funds and protects the sanctuary. Each year more than 100,000 people can visit and learn about this important natural environment. Corkscrew's staff offers educational programs on nature interpretation and habitat management, so that the public can learn more about the efforts to manage the nonnative plant and animal species that threaten to invade the area.

BRIDGE OF DISCOVERY

The high point of any trip to the sanctuary is a self-guided tour along an almost two-mile-long elevated boardwalk, overhung with Spanish moss. The tour along the boardwalk trail begins at the Corkscrew Visitor Center and penetrates deep into the old-growth forest, past lettuce lakes, floating tussocks, water hemlocks, ropes of strangler fig, brilliant hibiscus, royal palms, and bald cypresses. Many of the cypress trees here reach heights of 130 feet and have girths measuring more than 25 feet. Core samples indicate that some of the trees date back 600 years, making them a century old when Columbus arrived in the New World and putting them among the oldest trees in eastern North America. The cypresses anchor an impressive array of plant life, such as tree-growing butterfly, cigar, and clamshell orchids. The trees' gnarled branches spread over wild pines and a rich mixture of mosses and ferns, and their bark is patched with pink, white, and green lichens. The sweet fragrance in the air of flowering orchids and clear-flowing, shallow pools dispel the notion that all swamps are foul and stagnant places.

A cacophony of bird squawks, honks, and clucking sounds assails visitors from every direction. In the shadow of these 130-foot cypress trees lives a multitude of wading birds, including slender-legged egrets, herons, and the largest colony of endangered wood storks left in the United States. In springtime the sounds of the sanctuary are augmented by the plaintive cries of hungry baby wood storks calling from their nests hundreds of feet off the ground in the lofty canopy.

As visitors stroll along the boardwalk, they may be rewarded by glimpses of some of the shyest creatures in the Corkscrew

Swamp Sanctuary—bears and bobcats. Sharp-eyed hikers might spot a limpkin, a reclusive bird that is found only in Florida, or a shiny black racer snake slithering into the grass. Occasionally a skink may be seen sunning on a log or a red-shouldered hawk resting on a branch. The impressive forms of snowy egrets are hard to miss, poised as they often are only a few feet from the boardwalk.

Cool early summer mornings are usually the best time to explore the sanctuary. The piney uplands are favorite nesting sites for active red-bellied woodpeckers; the wet prairie attracts white-tailed deer; and the freshwater ponds—the deepest and wettest sections of the cypress forest—are the domain of the wily alligator.

The Corkscrew Swamp Sanctuary is entirely dependent on rainfall to feed its numerous ponds, wet prairie, and piney uplands; there are no hidden springs or branching river system to feed the flowing wilderness. Instead, the sanctuary and surrounding watershed require careful and sustained management to ensure that the water is kept pure and clean, so that this age-old habitat will continue to prosper for future generations to enjoy.

FOR MORE INFORMATION:
Corkscrew Swamp Sanctuary, 375 Sanctuary Road, Naples, FL 34120; 941-657-3771.

The bald cypress, below, forms buttresses at its base that help support the tall tree. These trees host a great variety of plant life.

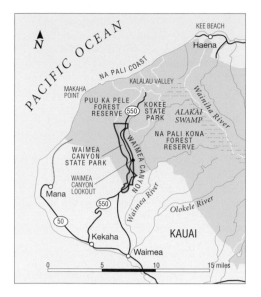

Though Waimea Canyon, above, is often shrouded in a mist at midday, the view of it in the morning or in the afternoon is usually crystal clear.

Aptly compared to a knife slash through the Kokee Plateau on Kauai, Waimea Canyon is a vast gorge, sometimes dubbed the Grand Canyon of the Pacific. The canyon is 10 miles long, 1 mile in breadth at its widest point, and up to 3,600 feet deep. Initially created by the force of water runoff in Kauai's interior highlands, the canyon was etched deeper into the landscape by swelling streams and waterfalls that cascaded down to the Pacific Ocean.

Visitors can reach Waimea Canyon either from Kekaha or Waimea. From Kekaha the drive along Route 550, otherwise known as Kokee Road, travels 12 miles up the dry scrub-covered hills above the canyon to the main lookout.

Waimea Canyon Road, which starts in Waimea—where Capt. James Cook made landfall looking for food and water in 1778—zigzags up into the cool, misty forests that crown Kauai, Hawaii's oldest island. Before heading out, many visitors to the region pause to visit the monument in Waimea's town plaza that commemorates Cook's arrival.

Not far outside Waimea, the road passes the ancient remains of what was once a great aqueduct, called Menehune Ditch. According to local legend the aqueduct was built by the Menehunes, a race of diminutive people with supernatural powers, who inhabited Kauai when the first Hawaiians arrived from the Marquesas archipelago and Tahiti around A.D. 1000.

Waimea Canyon Road travels the canyon rim before joining Route 550. The road is a tribute to modern engineering that combines heart-stopping switchbacks with lookouts of the canyon and river below. Twenty minutes from the sweltering cane fields of the low coastal rim near the town of Waimea, the canyon opens up to the blues and mossy greens of lush vegetation and the umber, ocher, and gray of the canyon walls.

WAIMEA CANYON STATE PARK
Flanking the road about seven miles from Waimea is the 1,866-acre Waimea Canyon State Park. One and a half miles into the state park is the Iliau Nature Trail, a quarter-mile loop named after the plant of the same name. The iliau plant has sword-shaped leaves and produces stalks of cream-colored flower sprays two to three feet high, with 500 flowers per spray. A member of the sunflower family, it is unique to the western mountains of Kauai, although it is closely related to the bizarre-looking and better-known silverswords of Maui. Interpretive signs along the trail describe the plants of the region. Near the middle of this trail, the Kukui Trail begins, which descends some 2,000 feet for more than two miles along the west wall to the Waimea River. A fine mist often rises from the river, and from the path visitors can see the cathedral-like appearance of the canyon walls. The shadows of clouds skitter across the wind-sculpted surface, intensifying the vastness. In the distance, waterfalls tumble in slow-motion grace. At the head of the canyon, the waters of the famous Waialae Falls plunge from a mountain ridge.

As the road leaves the park and reaches the spine of Waimea Canyon, visitors will be struck by the palpable difference between the cool air of the mountains and the torpor of the lowlands. Gnarled and twisted trees cling to the red bare earth. From Waimea Canyon Lookout, 3,400 feet above sea level, there is a magnificent vista of the side canyons, sculpted gorges, and clefts of Waimea Canyon State Park. Looking down, visitors can see the opalescent Waimea River as it snakes its way to the ocean. The river looks far too insignificant to have carved the awesome chasm. It drains from Alakai Swamp, at the foot of Mount Waialeale, a mountain that receives the most precipitation of any place in the world. From Pookapele Lookout visitors are rewarded with stunning views of Waipoo Waterfall. Kalalau Lookout—perched 4,000 feet above the pounding surf—provides visitors with panoramic vistas of Kalalau Valley.

FOR MORE INFORMATION:
Kauai Visitors Bureau, 3016 Umi St., Suite 207, Lihue, HI 96766; 808-245-3971.

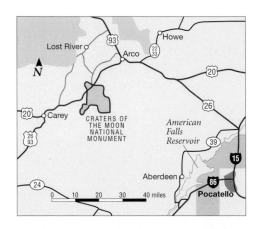

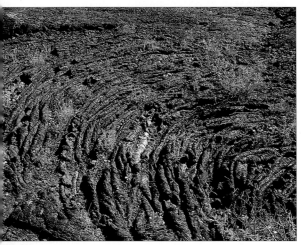

The ropy lava found at the North Crater Lava Flow, above, is a distinctive feature of other sites within the monument.

Marked by deep craters, mangled rock, and terrain sharp enough to shred a visitor's shoes, Craters of the Moon National Monument looks more like a setting for a science fiction movie than a part of south-central Idaho. This pitted field of black basalt encompasses some 54,000 acres of a 643-square-mile lava flow. It is an outdoor museum of volcanic activity, where visitors can explore cinder cones, lava tubes, spatter cones, and tree molds.

While weird rock formations give the volcanic garden a primeval appearance, the area is young in geological terms. About 15,000 years ago molten rock began to gush through vents along a series of fissures called the Great Rift. During eight eruptive periods, 60 lava flows emerged, the last occurring only 2,000 years ago.

Among the more distinctive formations in the monument are *aa* lava, a Hawaiian term meaning "hard on the feet." This treacherous landscape was formed when masses of subterranean rubble were slowly pushed out by volcanic pressure. Also in

evidence is the lava is known as *pahoehoe*, the Hawaiian name for "ropy." It was formed when fluid rock bubbled to the surface and was squeezed out in ropelike coils.

Networks of natural tunnels, called lava tubes, run for great distances beneath the surface of the monument and range in diameter from as little as a half-inch to 50 feet. As the lava flows cooled, molten material continued to propel its way beneath the surface, draining to the front of the flows and leaving empty tubes behind. Above ground, upright tubes called tree molds were formed when liquid rock coated the vegetation. Travelers will learn more about the region's geological history at the exhibits and video presentation housed in the visitor center.

TOURING THE MOONSCAPE

A seven-mile loop drive affords visitors a good sense of the range and textures of this landscape, described by an early traveler as "the strangest 75 square miles on the North American continent."

The first stop is North Crater Lava Flow, a broad *pahoehoe* lava field edged with *aa* lava. Farther along, a side trail leads to Devil's Orchard, a magnificent garden of flowers, trees, and rock formations. Inferno Cone offers travelers panoramic views of the charcoal-and-rust-colored lava fields. From this vantage point, visitors can see a string of cinder cones along the horizon. Big Cinder Butte is the tallest purely basaltic cinder cone in the world, rising 700 feet from the ground.

Hikers should have their flashlights handy to navigate the Cave Area, where dark, cool lava tubes—some of them enormous—bear such fanciful names as Beauty, Surprise, and Dewdrop, and invite exploration. Indian Tunnel, which measures 50 feet wide and 30 feet high, runs for more than 830 feet. Other caves offer hidden surprises: the Boy Scout Cave, for instance, has a floor of ice year-round.

This gust-swept territory supports some 300 species of plants. Pruned and sculpted by the shearing winds, the stunted limber pines resemble Japanese bonsai trees. Shrubs such as big sagebrush, rubber rabbit brush, and tansy bush thrive in deeper deposits of volcanic soil, while plants such as desert parsley, scabland penstemon, and Indian paintbrush grow in the sparser soil that collects in the crevices.

During the summer months, the black color of the lava is offset by splashy blossoms of buckwheat, blazing star, larkspur, scorpionweed, paintbrush, bitterroot, arrowleaf balsamroot, monkey flower, and prickly pear cactus.

The terrain might look desolate, but Craters of the Moon supports a surprising number of animals. Mule deer, red squirrels, marmots, pikas, and ground squirrels survive on the sparse vegetation, attracting predators such as coyotes and bobcats. Great horned owls sleep by day in the dark caves, while falcons and other raptors take to the sky, scanning the lava flows in search of rodents and small birds.

Visitors are welcome to hike in the backcountry; permits are required to camp overnight. It is easy to see why NASA astronauts bound for the moon have walked the rough terrain of the monument.

FOR MORE INFORMATION:
Craters of the Moon National Monument, P.O. Box 29, Arco, ID 83213; 208-527-3257.

The gnarled form of a lifeless limber pine, above, lies sprawled amid the wildflowers in Craters of the Moon National Monument.

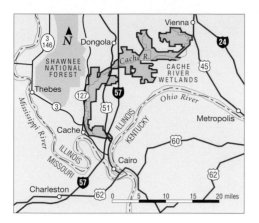

A cluster of cypress trees rises from the bright duckweed that fills Heron Pond, left, in the Cache River Wetlands.

The Cache River Wetlands, in all its unspoiled splendor, is located at the southern tip of Illinois. This 60,000-acre expanse of prairie glade, forest, swamp, marsh, and limestone bluff is the northernmost example of a southern swamp ecosystem. It represents what the Illinois landscape looked like before it was irrevocably changed with the arrival of European settlers in the 1700's.

This natural drainage system originated some 10,000 years ago after the last great ice sheets of the Pleistocene epoch had receded. Glaciers left behind a vast wetland covering some 480,000 acres above the confluence of the Mississippi and Ohio rivers. Designated a Wetland of International Importance in 1996, the area offers a unique setting for hiking, birdwatching, canoeing, and fishing.

The marshes, swamps, and unhurried waters of the Cache River provide flood control and pollutant filtration for the Ozark, Shawnee, and Cretaceous hills. At the juncture of four major ecological environments, the wetlands are also home to a broad range of plants and wildlife.

Sadly, this pristine showcase is under extreme threat due to silt accumulation, a problem compounded by the surrounding erosion-causing farmland. Overcutting of lowland forest has also contributed to soil depletion and resulted in excessive drainage and flooding. Fortunately, a collaborative land acquisition and restoration effort by The Nature Conservancy, the US Fish & Wildlife Service, the Illinois Department of Natural Resources, and Ducks Unlimited is working to reclaim disturbed parts of the 60,000 acres by reconverting them to marsh and swamp.

Some 56 endangered animal species find refuge here, and scores of rare plants thrive in the fertile habitats of the Cache River's meandering waterways and cool, old-growth forests. Shorebirds and waterfowl use the area as a nesting and feeding haven. Bobcats, river otters, and mink abound, as

do Cooper's hawks, orange-footed pearly mussels, and dusky salamanders. Sinuous cottonmouth snakes glide into sun-dappled pools where bullfrogs sit half-submerged and motionless. Pileated woodpeckers, black and turkey vultures, ospreys, and bald eagles can also be sighted. Reintroduced to the region in 1989, wild turkeys can occasionally be spotted foraging for food. The many fish varieties found in the waters include such rare species as the banded pygmy sunfish and the cypress minnow.

Newcomers to the region may be surprised by the symphony of sounds that greets them. Peeping tree frogs and sweet-voiced warblers and other songbirds make traveling through the swampy glades an extraordinary auditory experience. The Cache, a renowned paradise for birdsong, is a place of mystery far removed from the modern urban world.

ANCIENT CYPRESS

Some nine miles of hiking trails dissect the wetlands today, with more of them in the planning stage. The highlight of

the one-and-a-half-mile Heron Pond Trail is the floating boardwalk that zigzags to the heart of the bald cypress and tupelo gum swamps. Here, visitors stand before cypress trees that are among the oldest living things east of the Mississippi. The area's largest specimen towers 75 feet high and boasts a 34-foot circumference.

Located at the northern end of the wetlands, Look Out Point Trail is an easy one-mile walk up to the summit of Wildcat Bluff, which provides an impressive vista of the entire Cache region. Scanning the prairie barren and lowlands swamp, visitors will see ancient relics of the massive hardwood trees that once populated the area, jutting skyward from low ridges. Elsewhere, steep-sided glades are covered with a dazzling carpet of purple cone flowers and blazing stars.

Little Black Slough Trail, a moderately difficult six-and-a-half-mile hike, crosses swampland and low floodplain forests, and winds through sandstone bluffs, hillside glens, and remnants of open grassy terrain. Cutting through the Black Slough Preserve, this trail is known for its birding and other wildlife-watching opportunities. Herons, including the great blue and the yellow-crowned night heron, feed in the marshes.

Waterfowl can also be spotted in the spring-fed slough on the two-mile Limekiln Springs Trail. By following a wooden walkway through stands of maple, oak, hickory, and black walnut, hikers can learn about the surrounding plant and animal life with the aid of an interpretive trail brochure.

Buttonland Swamp lines both sides of the Lower Cache River and is best explored by canoe. Guided tours and canoe rentals for self-guided excursions are available. To fully experience the mystery of the swamp, visitors should remain until sundown, when the mist curls over the limpid green pools and fragrances intensify in the moist air. A night canoe trip in the spring is especially pleasurable. The swamp air vibrates with the sound of some 19 species of toads and frogs—a strange but thrilling concert that has played on spring evenings in the wetlands for generations.

FOR MORE INFORMATION:
The Nature Conservancy, Rte. 1, Box 53E, Ullin, IL 62992; 618-634-2524.

An abandoned farm, right, near Junction City in the Flint Hills, is slowly being reclaimed by the land its owners once cultivated.

S tretching through east-central Kansas from Nebraska to Oklahoma, Flint Hills represents the last unbroken stand of original tallgrass prairie in North America. The 5-million-acre oasis of native grassland and prairie wildflowers, spared from the farmer's plow by its rocky soil and sharp escarpments, remains virtually unchanged since the days of the Oregon Trail and is a favorite stop for nature lovers, artists, and sightseers. This distinctive terrain is formed from sediment that was deposited by inland seas some 200 million years ago. Over the course of centuries, wind and water erosion have sculpted the exposed rock into a masterpiece of gently sloping hills and steep cliffs.

A mix of flora thrives in the velvety uplands. Stretching uninterrupted for more than 200 miles, Indian bluestem and switch grass lay a thick carpet over the smoothly rolling landscape. In early summer a rich tapestry of plant life reveals its glorious color beneath the glowing sun. More than 500 species of wildflowers, shrubs, and trees grow in this untamed environment, which is also home to animals ranging from domestic cattle and llamas, to badgers, bobcats, coyotes, and antelope. By summer's end, the tallgrass can reach heights close to eight feet, providing camouflage for the wild bison that roam the habitat.

PRESERVING THE LAND

Located just south of the city of Manhattan, the 8,600-acre Konza Prairie Research Natural Area is dedicated to protecting the Flint Hills' unique ecosystem. This outdoor laboratory, managed by the Division of Biology of Kansas State University, provides naturalists with an opportunity to study and learn about the tallgrass environment. The conditions of the prairie, such as wildfires and grazing, are simulated in controlled experiments that demonstrate their effects on plant life. The research station is open to the public on specially designated days; tour guides make presentations on topics such as how planned burning, an agricultural technique practiced by Native Americans and white settlers, eliminates weeds and encourages new growth.

Open from dawn to dusk, three public hiking trails located near the entrance of the research station allow visitors to experience this natural wonder firsthand. Interpretive hikes as well as hayrides are available.

Visitors who yearn to experience the pioneer days can explore the expansive tallgrass prairie on two-day treks by covered wagon. Departing just south of Cassoday, the Flint Hills Overland Wagon Train Trip follows the path of the settlers who opened the West in the 1870's. After a day spent catching glimpses of the elusive pronghorn and white-tailed deer along the trail, modern pioneers will enjoy hearty chuck wagon cooking, a blazing campfire, and a glorious night under a blanket of stars in the open prairie.

Located at the confluence of the Smoky Hill and Republican rivers, Fort Riley was established in 1852 to guard the vulnerable wagon trains traveling on the Santa Fe Trail. Later the fort became the headquarters of the US Cavalry. The soldiers and wagon caravans are gone, but the prairie still beckons, inviting visitors to enter its vast and soothing embrace.

FOR MORE INFORMATION:

The Kansas Department of Commerce, Travel and Tourism Division, 700 SW Harrison St., Suite 1300, Topeka, KS 66603; 913-296-2009.

An old gate, left, stands lonely sentinel over the Kansas prairie in Flint Hills. The region owes its name to famed soldier and explorer Zebulon Pike, who passed through the area in 1806 and was the first to describe it.

wildlife refuge. The lush delta environment of the sanctuary is covered by marshes and forested uplands, and crisscrossed by freshwater channels. This carefully managed refuge offers visitors easy access to the area while preserving the natural beauty of the unique habitat.

Jutting into Lake Pontchartrain, the refuge's perimeter is awash in the salty waters of the Gulf of Mexico. The mix of saltwater and draining freshwater creates ideal conditions for spawning fish. It is also the preferred feeding ground for several species of egrets, terns, and herons.

oak woodlands, palmetto fronds, and red maple with populations of alligators and crawfish and squadrons of bright-colored butterflies. Barataria's easily accessible hikes range from the Bayou Coquille Trail, which begins at the site of a prehistoric Native American village and descends through several vegetation zones, to the Ring Levee Trail, with its raised boardwalk suspended safely above the swamp.

A WATERFOWL WONDERLAND

Following an ever-narrowing strip of land 70 miles to the southeast, the river suddenly develops an artery of channels that break in the direction of Breton Sound. These small channels, or passes, form the delicate veins of the 48,000-acre Delta National Wildlife Refuge. In winter, as the North suffers under the lash of windswept snow, the channels of the delta are a welcome refuge for close to 100,000 snow geese. Another 150,000 birds, including 22 species of ducks and 25 of warblers arrive in the winter. A major stop along the Mississippi Flyway, the Delta National Wildlife Refuge attracts more than 239 species of birds, making it a must-see for bird-watchers.

To the west of Breton Sound, crossing back over the Mississippi at the head of Barataria Bay, lies an eight-mile stretch of sandy beach facing the Gulf of Mexico that seems far removed from the Mississippi marshland. But it too is associated with the mighty river. As a barrier island, Grand Isle acts as a breakwater, protecting the low-lying bayous and channels that flow from the Mississippi River. Grand Isle East State Park, a one-mile strip of the island, contains the only public beach on the Louisiana Gulf and boasts some of the best deep-sea fishing in the entire country. The park is also an excellent place to surf fish for speckled trout. More than 280 species of fish thrive in the nutrient-rich waters. A 400-foot-long pier on Grand Isle allows for both day and night fishing, attracting ardent fishermen year-round.

Encompassing some 150 square miles of brackish marsh, cypress swamps, bayous, clear lakes, tiny islands, and moss-draped trees, the Mississippi Delta is a natural treasure trove. With every flood and the generation of new waterways, the region reinvents itself, changing from day to day and from visitor to visitor.

Sprouting amid the bald cypress trees are clusters of giant blue irises, above, adding an elegant touch of lavender to the predominantly green landscape.

Like a gigantic twisted rope, the Mississippi River winds its way south from its origins in northern Minnesota's Lake Itasca. By the time it reaches the frayed edges of the Mississippi Delta some 2,500 miles away, its waters are laden with runoff that contains half a billion tons of rich, alluvial silt and sediment collected from more than 20 states. As it deposits its sandy cargo in the Gulf of Mexico, this gargantuan drainage system re-creates and extends the delta and its accompanying strands of streams and bayous by some 200 feet a year.

Just 18 miles east of downtown New Orleans, within the city limits, the 22,770-acre Bayou Sauvage National Wildlife Refuge is the nation's largest urban national

Canoe trips are a popular way to explore the waterways that bisect Bayou Sauvage. On a slow, steady paddle through the twisting bayous, visitors might chance upon the bulbous eyes of an alligator as it slowly surfaces, or a colorful southern leopard frog lingering in the duckweed. Whatever the season, visitors should bring long pants, sunscreen, and insect repellent.

Just south of New Orleans is another delta nature refuge, the Barataria Preserve Unit, which is situated on the southern tip of the Jean Lafitte National Historical Park and Preserve. Hugging Lake Salvador, this small 10,000-acre wilderness teems with life. Mammals as varied as the nine-banded armadillo and the nutria, a 15-pound aquatic rodent, share their lush terrain of

FOR MORE INFORMATION:
Louisiana Office of Tourism, P.O. Box 94291, Baton Rouge, LA 70804-9291; 504-342-8100.

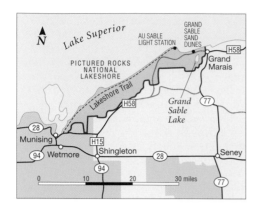

The park follows the shore of Lake Superior for 42 miles and consists of two zones: the lakeshore zone, owned and managed by the National Park Service, and the Inland Buffer Zone, ownership of which is shared by a partnership of federal, state, and private interests. Together the zones protect a total of 72,903 acres of Lake Superior's shoreline and watershed.

GEOLOGICAL HISTORY

The advance and retreat of massive glaciers some 500 to 800 million years ago began the carving of the land here, enlarging the river valleys that ultimately became the basins of the Great Lakes. Meltwater from the glaciers fed powerful rivers that coursed over the plains and dumped millions of tons of pulverized rubble, collected from the northern highlands. As the glaciers shrank, the exposed bedrock of sandstone was left at the mercy of eroding wind, waves, and ice. Small kettle hole lakes, steep-sided hollows that have no surface drainage, pockmark the terrain.

Today this park offers visitors spectacular sightseeing opportunities throughout the year. In summer hikers can tackle the 42-mile-long Lakeshore Trail, which takes in the entire shoreline and offers extraordinary vistas of the lake, cliff formations, sand dunes, and Munising Falls, which cascades some 50 feet over a sandstone bluff into a thundering natural amphitheater.

Farther along the trail, the ramparts of the cliffs descend to Twelvemile Beach, an unspoiled stretch of sand and pebbles bordered by a 20-foot-high sand bluff. At the eastern tip of the beach, travelers can explore the Au Sable Light Station, a superb, late-1800's vintage masonry lighthouse. When the lake waters are still, visitors might spot the wrecks of the *Sitka* and the *Gale Staples*, two ships that sank offshore in the early 1900's, lurking below the surface. Other sections of the ships can be seen on the beach half-buried in the sand.

A few miles down the trail, 85-foot-high sand dunes tower above the 200-foot-tall banks of an ancient glacial deposit. After a challenging climb to the top of a dune, adventurers can reward themselves with a refreshing plunge into the waters of Grand Sable Lake, bordered by a dune field that covers four square miles. Visitors who are not up to the lengthy hike on the Lakeshore Trail can gain access to park sites by following any in a series of shorter trails through the lakeshore area.

Black bears, porcupines, minks, white-tailed deer, and the occasional timber wolf roam the forest habitat near the shore. A large variety of water- and shorebirds gather along Lake Superior and the many streams and rivers in the region, where fish such as trout and coho salmon abound.

Equipped with three campgrounds and miles of well-marked trails, Pictured Rocks National Lakeshore promises wildlife enthusiasts a unique encounter with natural beauty, wilderness, and seclusion—a pledge that is never broken.

FOR MORE INFORMATION:
Superintendent, Pictured Rocks National Lakeshore, P.O. Box 40, Munising, MI 49862-0040; 906-387-3700.

Dwarfed by the imposing cliffs of Pictured Rocks National Lakeshore, a sailboat, above, skims the waters of Lake Superior.

Sculpted over time into extraordinary formations of caves, pillars, and arches that rise dramatically from Lake Superior, the exquisitely colored sandstone cliffs of Pictured Rocks National Lakeshore, in Michigan's Upper Peninsula, create one of the most spectacular shorelines in the nation. The massive wall of jagged rock and precipices extends for almost 15 miles along the lakeshore, with some cliffs towering as high as 200 feet above the deep blue lake. Tinted by mineral-laden groundwater, the cliffs glisten in shades of ocher, brown, white, gray, and pink, and are interspersed with cascading waterfalls and dense forests of maple and balsam fir.

The forest floor in the national lakeshore, right, is blanketed with the warm colors of autumn.

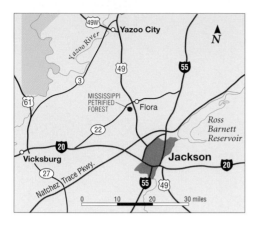

Nestled in the rolling hills near the historic city of Jackson, amid flourishing stands of green cedar and pine, an extraordinarily different kind of forest has stood for millions of years. Here in the Mississippi Petrified Forest, established in 1963, crumbling sandy cliffs reveal the fossilized remains of trees that are more than 36 million years old. The forest preserves one of the nation's richest sources of petrified wood—and is the only petrified forest found east of the Rocky Mountains. A stroll through this National Natural Landmark takes visitors past the sparkling beauty of these jeweled logs of stone and invokes their fascinating story.

The trees have been snapped into logs, 3 to 20 feet in length, by the force of the earth that had buried them. Varying in diameter from three to seven feet, the lichen encrusted logs are the remains of prehistoric maples and firs that once towered more than 100 feet above the earth's floor. Uprooted by a powerful river millions of years ago, the giant trees were stripped of their branches and sent on an epic journey. Roaring currents swept the trees approximately 1,000 miles south to this lowland area, where they were caught in a massive logjam. With each fresh flood from the north, the massive logs sank deeper into the riverbed and were buried by layers of sand and silt.

As the logs sat submerged in the primeval mud, dissolved minerals penetrated them. Rotting areas of the wood were filled with types of silica known as chalcedony and common opal, and tiny quartz crystals formed within the actual wood tissue. As the silica slowly changed the trees into stone, the wood was imbued with sparkling shades of yellow, red, tan, and orange. Over eons, the wood fiber was replaced entirely by minerals and the miraculous transformation completed.

Encased within thick layers of red sand and silt deposits, the petrified trees, now called the Forest Hill formation, were buried still deeper by successive layers of wind-blown glacial debris. The logs remained hidden until a few hundred years ago, when erosive forces gradually began to unearth these ancient relics.

STEPPING BACK IN TIME

A fenced trail, part concrete and part packed sand, winds through the site. Called the Nature Trail, the path is dotted with markers that interpret the history of these prehistoric rarities. Among the highlights are Caveman's Bench, a huge log partially embedded in the wall of a cliff that offers visitors a closeup view of its grain, and the Frog, so named because of its distinctly amphibian shape. This massive specimen, weighing 166 pounds per cubic foot, tips the scales at an estimated 14,940 pounds.

Also on the trail, a cross section of a modern sequoia tree, brought here from California, suggests how some of the logs in the ancient forest may have looked before petrification. Almost 1,000 years old when it was felled in 1960, the tree had lived through every major event in American history. Nearby is a large petrified trunk of a coniferous tree similar to the modern sequoia. To identify a petrified tree variety, scientists cut into it with a diamond saw and shave the stone to less-than-paper thinness. The sample is studied under a microscope and identified by its well-preserved cell structures. By this method scientists have identified a cone-bearing tree whose nearest counterpart grows in northwest Africa and a broad leafed tree that resembles varieties now found in the Amazon basin and in the West Indies.

Much of the area's prehistoric wood lies untouched in the sands at the base of the modern forest. The lower red-and-pink portion of the deeply eroded cliffs resembles a miniature badlands. This section is composed of layers of sediment in which the trees were buried while they crystallized from wood into stone.

Wildlife abounds amid the ancient forest. Scampering through the branches of the living trees are comical flying squirrels, raccoons, and opossums. Visitors who walk through the pine-scented forest may also happen across deer, cardinals, red-headed woodpeckers, tiny lizards, foxes, badgers, armadillos, and numerous insect species.

Not all the region's history is ancient. Tunica and Marksville Indians lived here as early as the 16th century. During the Civil War, Confederate and Union forces camped in the forest more than once, among them some 20,000 troops under Gen. William Sherman in March 1864.

Leafy greenery provides a living backdrop for an ancient stump-turned-stone, above, in the Mississippi Petrified Forest.

A 40-minute walking tour ends at a small museum that features more than 500 specimens of petrified wood, vertebrate fossils, gems, and minerals from Mississippi and around the world.

Travelers can lunch at the picnic area or, in the summertime, spend the night at a campground within the landmark. There, beneath the twinkling stars in the still of the petrified forest, the visitor may ponder the sublime forces that created this timeless natural masterpiece.

FOR MORE INFORMATION:
Mississippi Petrified Forest, P.O. Box 37, Flora, MS 39071-0037; 601-879-8189.

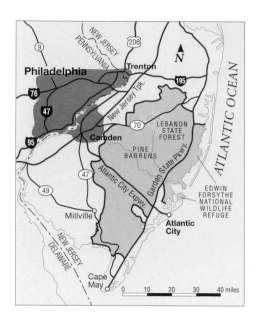

Autumn colors light up the shores of Harrisville Lake, above, in the Pine Barrens. Visitors to the area can wander through the ghost town of Harrisville at the southern end of the lake.

Wedged between the sprawling metropolitan areas of New York City and Philadelphia, the New Jersey Pine Barrens are a 1-million-acre expanse of pine and oak woods and cedar swamps that testify to nature's resilience. Shaped millions of years ago by retreating glaciers, this landscape of flatlands, deep sandy soil, and forests was for the most part ignored by settlers in the 17th and 18th centuries because its porous ground and acidic water were not conducive to farming.

The Pine Barrens, designated a US Biosphere Reserve by UNESCO in 1983, actually conceal some of the world's purest water. Scientists estimate that close to 17 trillion gallons of pristine water—enough to flood the entire state of New Jersey to a depth of 10 feet—lie as little as 3 feet below the sandy surface.

The barrens are home to more than 1,200 species of plants and animals. The northern part of the reserve, known as Pine Plains, is the site of the country's largest pygmy pine forest. Sprawling across some 12,000 acres, these stands of stunted pitch pine and blackjack oak reach heights no greater than four feet.

Receiving some 45 inches of rain on average each year, the region's wetlands, white cedar swamps, and smooth flowing streams are ideal places for amateur naturalists to explore. Minks, otters, deer, raccoons, opossums, tree frogs, and gray foxes thrive in this soggy environment, as do a number of snake species.

Twenty species of orchids flourish here, along with other wondrous plants such as the rare curlygrass fern. Swarms of buzzing insects make a feast for the area's numerous carnivorous plants, such as the sundew and

pitcher plants. In July the lush landscape blooms with the largest stand of bog asphodel in the world, carpeting the sandy floor in a thick pile of yellow.

CANOEING THE WATERWAYS

Since the barrens are ringed in many places by moist, sandy flats and white cedar swamps, an excursion by canoe is an excellent way for intrepid adventurers to gain access to the hidden waterway treasures of the interior. Canoes can be rented at several points along the Oswego and Mullica rivers. Paddling gently along the narrow banks, visitors may come upon a turtle basking in the sun, delicate fisher-spiders skating across the water, or thread-leafed sundew plants nestled on the side of a stream, waiting to trap unsuspecting insects in their snare of sticky leaves.

The Pine Barrens encompass within their limits many villages, public hunting and fishing grounds, and state forests. The thick forests serve as shielding curtains for the timeless pines that spring from the porous sand. Sites such as the Lebanon State Forest offer visitors swimming and various other outdoor activities. Cabins and numerous campsite facilities are also available. Visitors to the Edwin Forsythe National Wildlife Refuge will be thrilled by the spectacle of tens of thousands of waterfowl passing through the wetlands during the spring and fall migration periods.

FOR MORE INFORMATION:
The Pinelands Commission, P.O. Box 7, New Lisbon, NJ 08064; 609-894-9342.

A weathered boardwalk, below, zigzags through a shaded trail in the Lebanon State Forest.

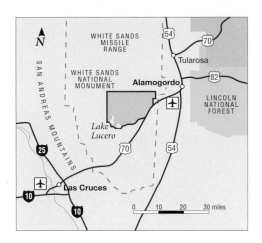

A sheer wall of white gypsum sand casts its shadow on a lone stand of Indian rice grass, above, clinging tenaciously to life in the White Sands National Monument.

Southwest of Alamogordo, plaster-white sand ripples across sunbaked Tularosa Basin and forms the largest gypsum dune field in the world. In this ghostly wonderland, dunes rise in crests, domes, and ridges, and eerie shadows modulate the endless expanse of white.

At the end of the last ice age some 10,000 to 15,000 years ago, gypsum began leaching from the San Andreas and Sacramento mountains and was pulverized into fine particles by the continual action of rain and wind. Today the desert valley contains approximately 8 billion tons of the mineral. Spread over 500 square miles, this gentle landscape is often perfumed with the sweet lilaclike scent of sand verbena, a plant that grows in the dune field.

Approximately half of the blanched desert is contained within the 230-square-mile White Sands National Monument. Here geological exhibits housed in a historic adobe building explain the area's history and describe how dunes are formed. The visitor center includes a garden display of the desert plants that endure in this harsh environment, including skunkbush sumac, Indian rice grass, Rio Grande cottonwood, and yucca.

Visitors can set off on a 16-mile round-trip tour along Dunes Drive to observe the landscape's features firsthand. Travelers will learn to distinguish between U-shaped parabolic dunes, crescent-shaped barchan dunes, and transverse ridges. The scenic road travels past a small playa and several gypsum pedestals. The pedestals are formed when the stems of buried plants push their way up through the sand and bind grains of gypsum together. Once exposed by wind, the roots resemble sandy pedestals.

Five miles into the drive, a trail leads to a primitive campsite where backpackers can view the glistening desert by moonlight. Backcountry hikers should take compasses with them to avoid becoming disoriented among the shifting dunes. Other trails lead to sites for sand surfing and serve as nature walks along which hikers might spot white mice, white lizards, and light-colored insects in the bleached environment.

Thirteen times a year, car caravans head to Lake Lucero, a low playa in the basin that occasionally fills with water. As the pool evaporates, beds of yellow gypsum crystals—some three feet long—form on the lakeshore. The elements grind the crystals into fine particles then, carried by the wind, the powder is added to sand drifts.

TESTING GROUNDS

White Sands National Monument lies within the White Sands Missile Range and Holloman Air Force Base, a 4,000-square-mile area reserved since the 1940's for testing weaponry and space technology.

The first atomic bomb was detonated near the upper edge of the range on July 16, 1945. The massive blast left a crater 400 yards in diameter and fused the sand into a solid glasslike sheet. This dramatic jade-colored mineral was named trinitite after the project's code name, Trinity.

While the range is usually off-limits, two days each year the public is allowed to tour the Trinity Site, where a lava rock obelisk marks the site of the atomic bomb test. Nearby is the MacDonald Ranch, the adobe building where the bomb was assembled. Visitors can walk through the empty rooms, which have been reconstructed to look as they did in 1945.

FOR MORE INFORMATION:
Superintendent, White Sands National Monument, P.O. Box 1086, Holloman Air Force Base, NM 88330; 505-479-6124.

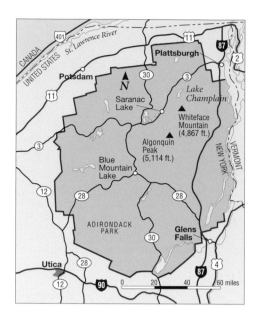

Spectacular fall colors are mirrored by the waters of Heart Lake, above. Each year thousands of sightseers visit the region to admire autumn's vibrant palette.

What sets Adirondack Park apart from most nature preserves is sheer size. Encompassing some 10,000 square miles, this immense patchwork of public and private lands is roughly the size of the state of New Hampshire. At the heart of the park is the Forest Preserve, belonging to the people of New York State and amounting to more than 2.5 million acres. From the rolling hills and crystal-clear lakes of the west and south to the mountainous zone of the northeast, the park supports some 73 species of trees, including vast stands of spruce, fir, beech, and maple. Wildflowers add color to the landscape, and a multitude of shrubs and grasses provides an ideal habitat for hundreds of animal species, including white-tailed deer, martens, and black bears.

MOUNTAIN MARVEL

With 42 peaks that reach heights over 4,000 feet, the High Peaks area is a veritable city skyline of mountains. At 5,114 feet, Algonquin Peak is the second-highest summit. It is accessible via the Heart Lake Trail, which starts in a hardwood forest at the base of the mountain and leads past sweet-smelling spruce and balsam before going up to the stunted trees that hug the rugged rock face. Higher still, the alpine zone shelters a carpet of Arctic lichen and moss. The park's fifth-highest peak, Whiteface Mountain, can be accessed by car; other summits can be reached on foot.

As a watershed for the Hudson River and Lake Champlain, the Adirondacks are webbed by thousands of miles of rivers, brooks, and more than 3,000 lakes and ponds. Fishing, canoeing, and island camping are offered throughout the park. Early morning canoeists are often serenaded by the haunting cries of loons.

Perhaps the awesome beauty of the Adirondack Park was best summed up by a young surveyor named Verplanck Colvin in 1873, who declared the wilderness "the wonder and glory of New York."

FOR MORE INFORMATION:
Adirondack Park Visitor Interpretative Center, Box 3000, Paul Smiths, NY 12970; 518-327-3000.

Cascade Mountain, left, and the surrounding hills in Adirondack Park are dusted with a light powdering of snow.

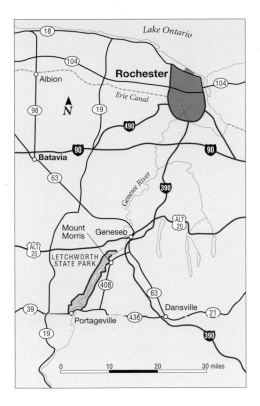

C arved out of shale and sandstone bedrock by the powerful Genesee River, the 17 miles of spectacular gorge, 500-foot cliffs, and three main churning waterfalls in Letchworth State Park comprise as dramatic a landscape as a traveler could hope to find. The region has been revered by humans for centuries. The ancient Seneca Indians believed that during its daily journey across the sky, the sun paused midway to take in the magical spectacle of the falls.

William P. Letchworth, a 19th-century hardware merchant and conservationist, also revered the impressive landscape. He fell in love with the land when he watched a translucent rainbow take shape in the mist of the 107-foot-tall Middle Falls. He purchased several hundred acres and an existing tavern that overlooked the falls. Letchworth restored the abandoned structure and named it Glen Iris for Iris, the goddess of the rainbow in Greek mythology. Much of the land had been ravaged by timber cutters, so Letchworth replanted it with thousands of new trees. When he died in 1910, he left his property to the state of New York.

The 14,350-acre Letchworth State Park preserves this magnificent area, giving visitors an opportunity to explore an idyllic setting of upland forest, deep gorges, and mighty waterfalls that show why the region is sometimes referred to as the Grand Canyon of the East.

From the south entrance at Portageville, hikers can choose from more than 60 miles of trails. They range from moderate half-mile trails to the spectacular seven-mile Gorge Trail. A well-marked path departs from the Erie Highbridge parking lot at the southern end of the park and rims the gorge, offering stunning views of the churning waters. Plumes of mist waft through the pine-scented woods from the roaring river below. As the trail rises through shadowy woodlands of oak and birch, the thunderous crash of waterfalls can be heard ahead.

Spanning some 300 feet, Middle Falls plunges more than 100 feet down the rugged shale face. On sunny days, a rainbow—like the one that captivated Letchworth—can be seen dancing in the soft, diffused light. The colonnaded Glen Iris Inn is still open for business and offers travelers comfortable accommodations in the style of an old-fashioned country bed-and-breakfast.

Tramping downstream, hikers wander through a shady forest that conceals misty glens where, according to Seneca legend, a race of tiny beings lived. The trail leads past the smaller cascades of the Lower Falls and slowly winds around Big Bend to end at St. Helena, where visitors can catch their breath at one of several picnic areas.

Although backpacking is forbidden in the park, there are more than 270 camping sites located five miles north of St. Helena. The park also rents 82 cabins ranging from secluded, rustic one-room cabins hidden among sycamores, to more commodious

The thick trunk of a red pine in Letchworth State Park, above, is dappled as if by an Impressionist painter.

three-room cabins furnished with fireplaces, flush toilets, and electric heat.

Beyond Big Bend, the Genesee River meanders through hills and forest into open Appalachian plains. Off the park road to the north, explorers can follow trails into the dense wilderness or they can continue along the main path through the Mount Morris Dam area to the northern entrance to the park at Mount Morris.

RIVER COUNTRY

Letchworth State Park also offers 17 miles of bucolic country roads suitable for cycling, and trails that are reserved for horseback riding. However, created and dominated by water, the region is perhaps best seen by boat. Waterways below the Lower Falls can be explored by canoe or kayak. A day's fishing in the stocked trout ponds in the southern section of the park can yield foot-long rainbow trout and brown trout. Swimming in the Genesee River or gorge is off-limits to visitors, but the park has two swimming pools that are open in the summer. For a bird's-eye view of the foaming, glacial gorges, a chartered hot air balloon ride is recommended.

Deer, foxes, beavers, woodchucks, rabbits, and raccoons abound in the park, especially in the early morning when they rustle among the pinecones as they forage for food. Bird-watching offers its own rich rewards. More than 200 species of birds inhabit the park, including 140 nesting species, such as wild turkeys. At the southern end of the park, huge turkey vultures ride the updrafts over the gorge, and an occasional bald eagle can be sighted.

People interested in the human history of the area should pay a visit to the Pioneer and Indian Museum. The museum focuses on the cultural development of western New York with displays of Native American artifacts, including tools made of stone and bone, weapons, pottery, clothing, and woven baskets. Other exhibits depict the daily life of the first white settlers to come to the Genesee Valley in the early 1800's.

Letchworth State Park offers activities for visitors such as nature tours, summer lectures, even performing arts programs. Cross-country skiing, skating, snowmobiling, and tube-sledding at several locations in this magnificent park are available to visitors during the winter months.

FOR MORE INFORMATION:
Park Manager, 1 Letchworth State Park, Castile, NY 14427; 716-493-3600.

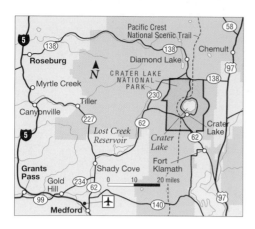

Phantom Ship, above, pierces the still waters of Crater Lake. The 167-foot-high formation is composed of lava flows that date back 400,000 years.

Crater Lake tends to elicit a rhapsodic response. It has been called the Gem of the Cascades and was declared "Oregon's Greatest Asset" by the writer Jack London. Set among the peaks of south-central Oregon, the lake is the centerpiece of Crater Lake National Park. It is six miles wide and plunges to a depth of 1,932 feet, making it the deepest lake in the nation. A fortress of cliffs, rising as high as 1,900 feet above the rocky shore, ring its 26-mile circumference.

The huge basin is the legacy of Mount Mazama, a 12,000-foot-tall volcano in the Cascade Range that blew its top some 7,700 years ago, leaving a vast pit known as a caldera. Cracks in the caldera floor created by pressure from underground magma were sealed off by lava, and rain and melted snow filled the basin. No rivers or streams feed the lake, but evaporation and precipitation keep the water level fairly constant.

Thrusting from the terrain like giant daggers, the Pinnacles, below, are formed of hardened volcanic ash and reach heights of 200 feet.

VOLCANIC FORMATIONS

Travelers can circle the caldera along the 33-mile-long Rim Drive. Among the most popular lookouts are the Watchman, an 8,013-foot peak on the lake's western side; Hillman Peak, at 8,151 feet the highest point along the rim; and Kerr Notch, from which travelers can peer down at the "sails" of Phantom Ship, a jagged lava formation that resembles a schooner.

The only access to the lake itself is by a steep mile-long trail on the northeastern side. Guided boat tours leave from Cleetwood Cove, where anglers can plumb the clear blue waters for rainbow trout and kokanee salmon, which were introduced to the lake from 1888 to 1941.

The cruise takes visitors past Devil's Backbone, a 50-foot-thick ridge extending down the caldera wall. The spine was formed thousands of years ago when lava oozed through the cracks in the caldera. Shaped like a sorcerer's hat, Wizard Island grew out of the volcano's collapse. A steep 700-foot climb up the cinder cone leads to a place one early explorer called "one of the rockiest and most utterly desolate in all the world."

Elsewhere in the park, the ravages of relentless eruptions and lava flows are scarcely visible. Once a gutted wasteland of ash, pumice, and pungent sulfur deposits, the caldera rim is fringed now with mountain hemlock and Shasta red firs. Ponderosa and sugar pines and white and Douglas firs occupy the lower regions of the park.

The more than 140 miles of trails that crisscross the park include a section of the Pacific Crest Trail, which runs from Mexico to Canada. This route follows the caldera rim along the western side of Crater Lake and affords several magnificent views of the water. Castle Crest Wildflower Trail leads to a lush meadow that blooms throughout the summer with violets, shooting stars, and monkey flowers. From Rim Drive, hikers climb a switchback trail up 8,926-foot Mount Scott, the highest point in the park. Here above the mountaintops, where falcons and eagles soar, visitors meet the gaze of the clear indigo eye of Crater Lake.

FOR MORE INFORMATION:
Superintendent, Crater Lake National Park, P.O. Box 7, Crater Lake, OR 97604; 541-594-2211.

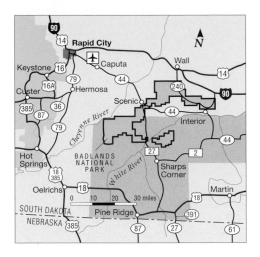

This arid region of clay pinnacles, saw-toothed ridges, and steep-walled canyons that stretches across South Dakota was called *mako sica* by the Sioux Indians, or "bad land." French Canadian trappers found the topography inhospitable too—especially when violent thunderstorms turned the hills into treacherous mounds of mud. They described the area as *les mauvaises terres à traverser,* or "bad lands to travel across."

Spanning thousands of square miles in South Dakota and the Nebraska panhandle, these are considered the most spectacular badlands in North America. Badlands National Park encompasses more than 243,500 acres of this formidable wasteland, including a massive section of its most breathtaking natural feature—an imposing jumble of ridges, pillars, overhangs, shelves, and chimneys called the Badlands Wall.

Chiseled by the foaming waters of the White River and its tributaries, this otherworldly land is a work in progress: heavy rains cleave chunks of clay from its walls, and dust and grit carried by the wind act as natural sandpaper. The annual rainfall of 13 to 15 inches is concentrated in a few heavy downpours that funnel clay and silt into streams. Much of the clay ends up in White River, which is named for its chalky color.

Eroding in places at a rate of one inch per year, the Badlands are a dissolving landscape of shales, clays, and sandstones. Weathering transforms the landscape so rapidly that some places are unrecognizable from what they were 50 years ago.

Eighty million years ago the bottom layer of black rock, called Pierre Shale, was the bed of an ancient sea. When the Rocky Mountains and the Black Hills were formed about 60 million years ago, the slope in the land east of the mountains gradually forced the inland sea to drain away, leaving a wet, marshy plain. Periodic floods alternated with dry intervals during the Oligocene epoch, resulting in layers of sediments being added to the terrain.

MOUNTAIN MARVEL

The Badlands' beds are among the world's finest sources of Oligocene epoch fossils, many of which can be seen from the trail. The quarter-mile-long Fossil Exhibit Trail allows visitors to peer into transparent domes and examine the fossilized remains of ancient sea turtles, horses, giant pigs, saber-toothed cats, and camels. Among the most unusual fossils is that of the protoceras—a sheeplike mammal that had three pairs of horns sticking out of its head.

Cliff Shelf Nature Trail explores another of the region's hidden treasures: a tiny oasis of junipers, prairie grass, and cattails fed by a series of water-filled sinkholes. Offering hikers shaded relief from the parched Badlands, this pocket of vegetation is a sanctuary for birds, including the black-billed magpie and mountain bluebird.

Other jaunts include the Door Trail, a fairly level path that enters the eroded landscape through a natural breach in Badlands Wall. It is just over a half-mile-long round-trip. Notch Trail, which begins near the Windows Overlook, demands a challenging climb up a sheer claystone cliff via a wooden ladder. Along the ledge, a hole in the side of the gully offers a stunning view of the Badlands and the White River.

Visitors who want to explore the Badlands on bikes may choose from a variety of roads. The 22-mile stretch of the Loop Road from Pinnacles Overlook to the Ben Reifel Visitor Center is particularly beautiful, passing several scenic areas and including the Homestead and Ranches Overlook.

While the rocky sections of the Badlands are inhospitable to most vegetation, the grassy plains to the north and south support more than 300 varieties of plants, including prairie golden-pea, scarlet globe-mallow, prickly pear, yucca, and sagebrush. Boasting 70 varieties of prairie grasses, the Badlands have the largest concentration of native grassland of any US national park.

Numerous prairie dog colonies are burrowed in the grasslands. Bison, mule deer, Rocky Mountain bighorn sheep, chipmunks, and eastern cottontails also inhabit the region. Coyotes are more often heard than seen, but hikers sometimes catch glimpses of pronghorn antelopes as they race across this wondrous land at speeds of up to 50 miles an hour.

FOR MORE INFORMATION:

Superintendent, Badlands National Park, P.O. Box 6, Interior, SD 57750; 605-433-5361.

South Dakota's Badlands, right, are a desolate landscape of cracked mud, dry buffalo grass, and jagged outcrops.

Visitors to the Cumberland Caverns are greeted by a sight they won't soon forget. Flickering in blue and red, from the rocky ceiling of a 600-foot-long subterranean limestone gallery hangs a massive crystal and brass chandelier that tips the scales at three-quarters of a ton. The chandelier's dim red and blue lights illuminate the Volcano Room, one of the many enormous chambers found in this vast labyrinth. A national landmark and the second largest U.S. cave system open to the public, Cumberland Caverns boasts larger rooms and an even greater variety of formations than its more extensive Kentucky cousin, Mammoth Cave.

Situated near the town of McMinnville, at the western edge of the Cumberland Mountains, the caverns were discovered in 1810 by Aaron Higginbotham, a young surveyor who entered the cave with only a torch to light his way. Legend has it that his torch was extinguished by a rush of air in one of the immense vaulted chambers,

and he was found four days later clinging to a ledge. His hair was said to have turned completely white from terror.

During the War of 1812 and the Civil War, the caves were mined extensively for saltpeter, an essential ingredient in gunpowder. Visitors to the caverns can see the remains of these mines, including leaching vats, tools, and the wooden tobacco pipes smoked by miners.

In 1946 members of the National Speleological Society began to probe deeper into the unexplored recesses of the caverns. Some 32 miles of subterranean passageways have been mapped all together, with many more passageways yet to be discovered. The caves remained a secret spelunkers' paradise until 1956 when they were opened for public viewing.

BIRTH OF THE CAVERNS

The caverns' honeycomb passages were formed over thousands of centuries by acidic underground water that circulated through the joints and faults of the limestone. The corrosive water ate away at the limestone, slowly turning small cracks into twisting tunnels.

The caverns reveal an eerie landscape dominated by stalactites and stalagmites, stony pendants and pillars that formed when calcium carbonate precipitated out of dripping water. Many of the stalactites and stalagmites have fused together in spectacular towering columns. In fact, the largest formation in the cave is a gigantic tan-colored column resembling a pipe organ.

The enormous galleries are replete with other bizarre and exquisite features. Spectacular limestone draperies made of

thin sheets of rock hang from the cavern ceilings. Flowstone deposits, smoothed over by a constant trickle of water, look like massive frozen waterfalls against the cavern wall. In parts of the cave that are not open to visitors, delicate crystal spirals of gypsum flowers sprout alongside strange twisted cylinders on the walls, ceilings, and floors.

Salamanders lay their eggs in cool ponds inhabited by blind fish. Crickets, lizards, raccoons, spiders, beetles, millipedes, and flatworms travel in and out of the caves.

The most impressive chamber in the Cumberland Caverns is the Hall of the Mountain King. The largest single cave room in the eastern United States, the hall is 600 feet long, 150 feet wide, and 140 feet high. It serves as a magnificent setting for a spectacular sound-and-light presentation. The Volcano Room, which gets its name from its craterlike shape, is set up as an underground dining room that seats 500 and is available for group rental.

The Cathedral Room is decorated with gigantic stalactites and stalagmites, and soaring columns. At the lower levels of the cave visitors can walk across the ancient riverbed that carved Devil's Quarry, an eerie chamber in which the tour guide often takes visitors to the lower depths of the cave, extinguishes the lights, and tells ghost stories to a hushed audience in the total darkness.

The splendor and majesty of the caverns are enhanced by carefully placed soft lighting. The lights illuminate the variety and color of the ethereal limestone formations and cast eerie shadows on the damp walls. Here, hundreds of feet below the earth's surface, as light and dark dance across the bizarre terrain, travelers can experience the otherworldly effect of this place.

This is an everchanging world in which deposits of calcium carbonate, called travertine, will, over the millennia, seal off existing passages and chambers, while corrosive water gnaws new tunnels and caverns into the soft rock.

FOR MORE INFORMATION:
Cumberland Caverns, 1437 Cumberland Caverns Rd., McMinnville, TN 37110; 615-668-4396.

A stalactite and a stalagmite grow toward each other in Cumberland Caverns, left. In time the formations will meet in a single column.

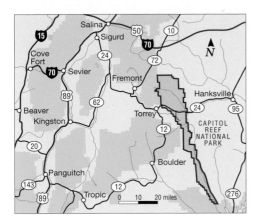

Ash, cottonwood, and willows line the Fremont River, left, that meanders across desertlike Capitol Reef National Park.

The upswept walls of Capitol Reef look like nothing less than huge, crashing waves. Stretching for 100 miles across south-central Utah, this multicolored escarpment forms a barrier as daunting as a coral reef.

Red, white, and chocolate brown rock formations, layered like Neapolitan ice cream, tell an ancient story of collision, upheaval, and erosion. These events took place some 60 million years ago when the massive plate beneath the Pacific Ocean wedged under the North American plate, forcing the Rocky Mountains upward and raising the Colorado Plateau.

While the uplift was generally uniform, a wrinkle formed in the earth's crust beneath south-central Utah in the shape of a huge curved ridge, now known as the Waterpocket Fold. Time and the elements carved this rocky outcrop into the sheer cliffs, pointed spires, and solitary monoliths of the Capitol Reef.

The 241,671-acre Capitol Reef National Park preserves this geological masterpiece. Visitors come to the park to explore the bizarre rock formations. They hike through steep canyons and graceful arches or drive the scenic road that skirts the reef. They learn about the fascinating people who lived in this stark terrain, where names such as Paradise Flats, Cow Dung Wash, Bloody Hands Gap, and Dirty Devil River hint at a many storied past.

At the base of the reef's western facade, dark brown shale bears ripples left by the tides of ancient seas. East of the reef, the badlands of the Morrison Formation are colored by layers of volcanic ash.

Three dry valleys lie in the park's northern end: South Desert, the Harnet Desert, and Cathedral Valley, accessible by a high-clearance road. Here 400- to 500-foot-tall towers of red stone jut from the earth like magnificent steeples. The huge monoliths, made of soft Entrada sandstone, are capped by hard Curtis rock that protects them from erosion.

Life in Capitol Reef relies heavily on water. Shortly after a rare downpour or flash flood, potholes in the rock turn into thriving aquatic communities. Shriveled gnat larvae are revived, fairy shrimp eggs burst into life, and spadefoot toads emerge from the clay. The wriggling creatures set the food chain in motion, attracting snakes, birds, salamanders, badgers, and coyotes.

EARLY INHABITANTS

Travelers can hike the backcountry or visit the dwellings of the area's early inhabitants. A small patch of green along the banks of the Fremont River—one of only three streams that flow through the arid land—drew Fremont Indians to the area, who farmed it from about A.D. 700 to 1300. While the fate of these Native Americans is unknown, their pictographs and petroglyphs, which are scattered throughout the park, reflect a sophisticated culture. Rock art found off Capitol Gorge Trail depicts animals, particularly bighorn sheep, and human figures wearing ornate headdresses, necklaces, earrings, and sashes. Visitors can examine artifacts at the visitor center and view the remains of an Indian pit house along Hickman Bridge Trail, which ends at a 133-foot-long natural bridge, hollowed out of rock by flowing water.

FOR MORE INFORMATION:

Superintendent, Capitol Reef National Park, H.C. 70, P.O. Box 15, Torrey, UT 84775-9602; 801-425-3791.

The Strike Valley Overlook, left, is a vision of stark beauty in one of the most spectacular vistas in the park.

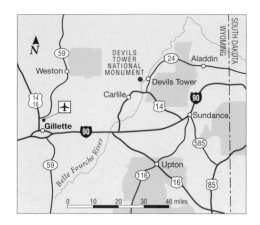

Against the sheer bulk of Devils Tower, a juniper tree, right, stretches toward the sun.

Devils Tower has long inspired the imagination. Native American legends recount the story of how a group of maidens who were out gathering flowers escaped the attack of some giant bears by climbing up on a rocky mound. As the bears clawed their way toward the women, the gods sent the mound shooting up into the sky, and the beasts slid to earth, gouging deep grooves into the rock. Centuries later, the stark gray tower of stone that soars 1,250 feet above the Black Hills became an American movie icon as the fateful meeting place between humans and extraterrestrials in the 1977 film *Close Encounters of the Third Kind*.

This unique outcrop was created some 50 million years ago, when molten rock oozed from the earth's crust and was trapped by overlying layers of sedimentary rock. The molten material then hardened into a dome-shaped mass of igneous rock called phonolite porphyry. When the rock cooled it contracted and fractured into fluted columns. As the combined forces of rain, wind, and snow gradually wore away at the outer layers of shale, gypsum, sandstone, and limestone, the dramatic monolith emerged. In 1906 Pres. Theodore Roosevelt designated Devils Tower as the nation's first national monument.

ROCK CLIMBERS' PARADISE

The sheer face of Devils Tower was first opened to rock climbers in 1937. Currently more than 5,000 climbers a year go there looking for a challenge. Climbers must register with a park ranger before attempting the arduous ascent, which takes an average of six hours. William Rogers and Willard Ripley blazed the first route to the top as a publicity stunt on July 4, 1893, but climbers can now choose from among 120 routes to the summit.

The self-guiding Tower Trail circles the monument. At the base, hikers pass through a large boulder field, created when sections of columns began to split away from the tower more than 10,000 years ago. Some fallen columns reach lengths of 25 feet and measure 8 feet in diameter.

Other paths in the 1,347-acre monument take travelers through woodlands, pine forests, and grasslands. The dark forest of ponderosa pines and junipers around the tower is alive with the activity of red squirrels, mice, cottontail rabbits, and porcupines. White-tailed deer graze along the banks of the Belle Fourche River, which is edged with plains cottonwood, Wyoming's state tree. Other mammals drawn to the water's edge include muskrats and beavers; nearby woodlands harbor red-headed woodpeckers and black-capped chickadees.

Along the monument's southernmost trail, prairie dogs bark, warning one another of the approach of hikers. The small mammals burrow intricate underground colonies. The prairie dog is the most prevalent animal in the park. Its numbers are kept in check by predators such as hawks, eagles, bull snakes, coyotes, and minks.

The barren-looking tower is actually blanketed in lichen. At its summit a cover of grasses, prickly pear cactus, gooseberry bushes, and native big sage hide prairie rattlesnakes, wood rats, and chipmunks, which climb to the top along cracks and fissures in the rock. Prairie falcons, white-throated swifts, and rock doves nest on the tower's uppermost columns. Giant bears, however, haven't been seen in these parts for years.

FOR MORE INFORMATION:
Superintendent, Devils Tower National Monument, P.O. Box 10, Devils Tower, WY 82714-0010; 307-467-5283.

The Belle Fourche River, left, winds past Devils Tower. On a clear day, five states—Wyoming, North Dakota, South Dakota, Montana, and Nebraska—can be seen from the summit.

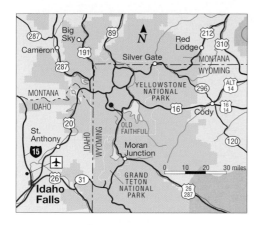

Although Yellowstone National Park has more geysers, hot springs, mud pots, and fumaroles than the rest of the world combined, visitors travel from far and wide to see one phenomenon in particular: Old Faithful. But the geyser isn't a top attraction because it is the largest or most powerful fountain in the park—rather Old Faithful's reputation rests on its refusal to change its ways.

Seldom diverging from its schedule, Old Faithful erupts 20 times a day, averaging an hour to one and a half hours apart. Its age-old regularity sets the illustrious fountain apart from the park's 200 to 250 other active geysers, some of which lie dormant for weeks, months, and even years before making their appearances.

Yellowstone's 1,300-square-mile hotbed of hydrothermal activity is fueled by an underground magma chamber made of molten rock that accumulated during a volcanic period some 50 million years ago. Acting like a massive furnace, the chamber heats the overlying rocks to temperatures above 400°F. Rainwater percolates through cracks in the rocks above the magma chamber, where it is compressed and superheated as if in a giant pressure cooker. When enough pressure builds up, steam and scalding water shoot up through any outlet.

The form an eruption takes depends upon its plumbing system. Hot springs occur when the water is released into a surface pool. A constant gusher requires a large smooth route. Mud pots develop when thin but steady trickles of steam reach the surface and decompose the earth until it bubbles like hot porridge. A geyser is created when the surge of water is delayed by cavities and constrictions; as cavities empty and fill up, water and steam are ejected as geysers. If all the water boils off underground, steam alone hisses from a fumarole.

Old Faithful's reliability can be traced to the composition of its duct system, which is made of virtually insoluble minerals. As water gushes through the rock, it neither picks up nor deposits much material, thus the water's course through the channel remains for the most part unaltered.

Most of Yellowstone's 10,000 hydrothermal phenomena lie near Grand Loop Road, a 142-mile figure eight through the lodgepole pine wilderness. Visitors will see the best eruptions and burbles along the Lower Loop section. En route to Old Faithful, a sampler of springs is colorfully named Fountain Paint Pot. Among them are small basins of pink mud, fumeroles venting hot steam, geysers, and Excelsior Geyser Crater, a powerful geyser that blew up, leaving a deep basin of ethereal blue water.

A broad valley of volcanic ash called Upper Geyser Basin surrounds Old Faithful and Yellowstone's other geysers. The Giantess Geyser erupts up to 41 times a year in 200-foot-tall spouts of water that last from 3 to 43 hours. Contorted cones mark other fountains, including Beehive, Castle, and Grand geysers.

CROWD PLEASER

Although Old Faithful has yet to learn new tricks, it never fails to delight a constant throng of spectators. Sending up an alert with a few squirts of water, Old Faithful follows up by shooting from 3,700 to 8,400 gallons of boiling water an average 135 feet into the air. The towering column of water maintains this intensity for up to five minutes, before slowly ebbing and disappearing until the next show.

Visitors can obtain schedules of eruptions from the Old Faithful Visitor Center. Benches around the famous geyser offer choice seats, but views from the boardwalk circling the attraction are equally good.

Located in the middle of the basin, the 1903 Old Faithful Inn is as much of an institution as its namesake. The inn claims to be the largest native-log structure in the world. It boasts a massive stone fireplace, a seven-story lobby, hand-hewn staircases, and three tiers of balconies. Flags and pennants adorn the gabled and dormered roof. Resembling a massive Swiss chalet, the rustic hotel is the perfect match for the regular displays of Old Faithful.

FOR MORE INFORMATION:
Superintendent, National Park Service, P.O. Box 168, Yellowstone National Park, WY 82190; 307-344-7381.

A lodgepole pine stands unbowed near the edge of spouting Old Faithful, above. When the water is underground, it can reach temperatures three times as hot as the boiling point.

INDEX

Bold numerals indicate map reference.
Italic numerals indicate an illustration.
State abbreviations are in parentheses.

NCA = National Conservation Area
NF = National Forest
NHP = National Historical Park
NHS = National Historic Site
NM = National Monument
N MEM = National Memorial
NP = National Park
N PRES = National Preserve
NP & PRES = National Park & Preserve
NRA = National Recreation Area
NWR = National Wildlife Refuge
SF = State Forest
SHP = State Historic Park
SHS = State Historic Site
SP = State Park

A-B-C

Abraham Lincoln Birthplace NHS (KY), **46**, *47*
Acadia National Park (ME), **16**, *17*
Adirondack Park (NY), **134**, *134*
Admiralty Island NM (AK), **116**, *116-117*
Aguereberry Point (CA), **61**
Alaska
  Admiralty Island NM, **116**, *116-117*
  Alsek River, **109**, *114*
  Bald Mountain, **109**, *110*
  Bartlett Cove, **109**, *109*, **112**, 113
  Cape Spencer, **109**, *108*
  Glacier Bay Lodge, **109**, 112
  Glacier Bay NP & PRES, **109**, *106-115*, **116-117**
  Glaciers, **109**, 108, *111, 112-113*
  Gustavus, **109**
  House of Wickersham, **116**, *116-117*
  Isabel Miller Museum, **116**, 117
  Johns Hopkins Inlet, **109**, *106-107*, Juneau, **116**, 117
  Lake Clark NP & PRES, **119**, *119*
  Lituya Bay, **109**, *110*
  Mount Fairweather, **109**
  Muir Inlet, **109**, *112-113*
  Takhinsha Mountains, **109**, *112-113*
  Tarr Inlet, **109**, *111*
  Tongass NF, **116**, *117*
  Whales, **109**, *110*, 113
Alpine Scenic Loop (UT), **73**, 77
Alsek River (AK), **109**, *114*
Alta (UT), **73**, 77
American Falls (NY), **21**, *18-20*
American Funeral Service Museum (TX), **56**, 57
Ancient Bristlecone Pine Forest (CA), **68**, 68-69
Antelope Island (UT), **73**, 74
Antelope Island SP (UT), **73**, 70, *72*
Ape Cave (WA), **97**, 103
Arches NP (UT), **80**, *80*, 81
Arizona
  Grand Canyon NP, **120**, *120*
Arkansas
  Blanchard Springs Caverns, **121**, 121
  Ozark NF, **121**, 121
Artists Palette (CA), **61**, 64, *64-65*
Ashford Mill (CA), **61**
Atlin Provincial Park (British Columbia), **116**, 116
Badlands NP (SD), **137**, *137*
Badwater Basin (CA), *58-59*, 60
Bald Mountain (AK), **109**, *110*
Bartlett Cove (AK), **109**, *109*, **112**, 113
Bayou Sauvage NWR (LA), **129**, 129
Beals Island (ME), **11**, 12
Bear River Migratory Bird Refuge (UT), **73**
Bears, *113*, 117
Beech Woods Trail (TX), **51**
Bernard Lakes (ID), **85**, *84*

Big Thicket N PRES (TX), **51**, *48-55*, 56-57
Big Tree Trail (PR), **31**, 35
Birds, *13, 67, 75, 76, 112*
Black Duck Cove (ME), **11**, *15*
Blanchard Springs Caverns (AR), **121**, 121
Bonneville Museum (ID), **80**, 80
Bonneville Salt Flats (UT), **73**, *72*, 76
Bridal Veil Falls (NY), **21**, *25*
British Columbia
  Atlin Provincial Park, **116**, 116
  Mount Edziza Provincial Park, **116**, 117
Buffalo (NY), **26**, 26
Burnham Tavern (ME), **16**, *16*, 17
Cabo Rojo NWR (PR), **36**, 36
Cache River Wetlands (IL), **127**, *127*
Caimitillo Picnic Area (PR), **31**
California
  Aguereberry Point, **61**
  Ancient Bristlecone Pine Forest, **68**, 68-69
  Artists Palette, **61**, 64, *64-65*
  Ashford Mill, **61**
  Badwater Basin, *58-59*, 60
  Caves, 122
  Colonel Allensworth SHP, **68**, 69
  Cottonwood Canyon, **61**, *66*
  Dantes View, **61**, 62
  Death Valley NP, **61**, *58-67*, 68-69
  Devils Golf Course, **61**, *62*, 65
  Devils Postpile NM, **68**, 68, *69*
  Eureka Dunes, 63
  Furnace Creek Visitor Center, **61**, 60, 62
  Harmony Borax Works, **61**, 67
  Inyo Mine, **61**, *63*
  Lava Beds NM, **122**, *122*
  Laws Railroad Museum and Historical Site, **68**, 68
  Lowest elevation, **61**, 62
  Manly Peak, **61**, *67*
  Maturango Museum, **68**, 69
  Mosaic Canyon, **61**, 62
  Pupfish, 64, 65-66
  Racetrack Valley, **61**, *63*
  Salt Creek, **61**, *62*
  Saratoga Spring, **61**, *64*, 66
  Scottys Castle, **61**, *66*, 67
  Stovepipe Wells Village, **61**, 62, 63
  Telescope Peak, **61**, *58-59*,
  Ubehebe Crater, **61**, 63
  Wildrose Canyon, **61**, *60*, 66
  Zalud House, **68**, 69
Cape Cove (ME), **11**, *14*
Cape Spencer (AK), **109**, *108*
Capitol Reef NP (UT), **139**, *139*
Caribbean NF (PR), **31**, *28-29, 33-34*, 35
Casa Roig (PR), **36**, 37
Cave of the Winds (NY), **21**, 25
Caves, *39-45, 81, 103, 121, 122, 126, 138*
Coldwater Lake (WA), **97**, *100*
Coldwater Ridge Visitor Center (WA), **97**, 96
College of Eastern Utah Prehistoric Museum (UT), **80**, 81
Colonel Allensworth SHP (CA), **68**, 69
Colorado
  Florissant Fossil Beds NM, **123**, *123*
Corkscrew Swamp Sanctuary (FL), **124**, 124
Cottonwood Canyon (CA), **61**, *66*
Crater Lake NP (OR), **136**, *136*
Craters of the Moon NM (ID), **126**, *126*
Cumberland Caverns (TN), **138**, *138*
Cypress trees, *50, 124, 127*

D-E-F-G

Danger Cave (UT), **73**, 76
Dantes View (CA), **61**, 62
Davy Crockett NF (TX), **56**, *56, 57*
Death Valley NP (CA), **61**, *58-67*, 68-69
Deer, *17, 96*
Delta NWR (LA), **129**, 129
Dennison Ferry Campground (KY), 41

Devils Golf Course (CA), **61**, *62*, 65
Devils Postpile NM (CA), **68**, 68, *69*
Devils Tower NM (WY), **140**, *140*
Dug Bar (OR), **85**
Dunkirk Historical Lighthouse and Veterans Park Museum (NY), **26**, 26
Edwin Forsythe NWR (NJ), **132**, 132
El Yunque (PR), **31**, *28-35, 36-37*
El Yunque NRA (PR), **31**, 35
Enterprise (OR), **85**, 84
Eureka (UT), **73**
Eureka Dunes (CA), 63
Fish Springs NWR (UT), **73**, *72, 75, 76*, 79
Flint Hills (KS), **128**, *128*
Florida
  Corkscrew Swamp Sanctuary, **124**, 124
  Florissant Fossil Beds NM (CO), **123**, *123*
Fort Knox SHS (ME), **16**, 17
Fort Walla Walla Museum Complex (WA), **92**, *92*
Fossil Butte NM (WY), **80**, 81
Furnace Creek Visitor Center (CA), **61**, 60, 62
Ganter Cave (KY), 41
George Eastman House (NY), **26**, 27
Glacier Bay Lodge (AK), **109**, 112
Glacier Bay NP & PRES (AK), **109**, *106-115*, **116-117**
Glaciers, **109**, 108, 111, *112-113*
Goat Island (NY), **21**, *20*, 25
Goldendale Observatory SP (WA), **104**, 105
Golden Spike NHS (UT), **73**
Grand Canyon NP (AZ), **120**, *120*
Grand Isle East SP (LA), **129**, 129
Granite Creek Rapids (OR/ID), **85**, 90, *91*
Grays Lake NWR (ID), **80**, *80-81*
Great Basin (UT/ID), **73**, *70-79*, 80-81
Great Basin NP (NV), **80**, 81
Great Salt Lake (UT), **73**, 70, 76, *78*
Great Salt Lake Desert (UT), **73**, *76*
Great Salt Lake SP (UT), **73**, 70
Great Wass Archipelago (ME), **11**, *8-15*, 16-17
Great Wass Island (ME), **11**, *8-9*
Gustavus (AK), **109**

H-I-J-K

Hacienda Buena Vista (PR), **36**, *37*
Harmony Borax Works (CA), **61**, 67
Hat Point Lookout (OR), **85**, 83, 86, 87
Hawaii
  Waimea Canyon, **125**, *125*
Head Harbor Island (ME), **11**, 8
Heavens Gate Overlook (ID), **85**
He Devil Peak (ID), **85**, 84
Hells Canyon (OR/ID), **85**, *82-91*, 92-93
Hells Canyon NRA (OR/ID), **85**, 84, *88-89*
Heritage Trail (KY), 41
Hickory Creek Savannah Unit (TX), **51**, *54*
Holloman Air Force Base (NM), 133
Hood River County Historical Museum (OR), **104**, 105
Hoquiam's Castle (WA), **104**, 104, *105*
Horseshoe Falls (Ontario), **21**, *20*, 22-23, *24-25*
House of Wickersham (AK), **116**, *116-117*
Houston (TX), **56**, 57
Idaho
  Bernard Lakes, **85**, *84*
  Bonneville Museum, **80**, 80
  Caves, 126
  Craters of the Moon NM, **126**, *126*
  Granite Creek Rapids, **85**, 90, *91*
  Grays Lake NWR, **80**, *80-81*
  Great Basin, **73**, *70-79*, 80-81
  Heaven's Gate Overlook, **85**
  He Devil Peak, **85**, 84
  Hells Canyon, **85**, *82-91*, 92-93
  Hells Canyon NRA, **85**, 84, *88-89*
  Kirkwood Ranch, **85**
  Massacre Rocks SP, **73**, 75
  McConnell Mansion, **92**, 92-93

Perrine Memorial Bridge, **80**, 80, *81*
Pittsburg Landing, **85**, 88, *89*, 90
Rafting, 89, 90, *91*
Seven Devils Mountains, **85**, *84*
Snake River, **85**, *82-91*
Snake River Trail, **85**, *91*
St. Gertrude's Museum, **92**, 93
White Bird Battlefield, **92**, *93*
Illinois
  Cache River Wetlands, **127**, *127*
IMAX Theatre (Ontario), **21**, 25
Imnaha (OR), **85**, *83*
Inyo Mine (CA), **61**, *63*
Isabel Miller Museum (AK), **116**, 117
Jack Gore Baygall Unit (TX), **51**, 53
Jefferson Davis SHS (KY), **46**, *46*, 47
John James Audubon SP (KY), **46**, 46
John Jay French Historic House (TX), **56**, 57
Johns Hopkins Inlet (AK), **109**, *106-107*
Jonesport (ME), **11**, 8
Juneau (AK), **116**, 117
Kansas
  Flint Hills, **128**, *128*
  Konza Prairie Research Natural Area, **128**, 128
Kentucky
  Abraham Lincoln Birthplace NHS, **46**, *47*
  Dennison Ferry Campground, 41
  Ganter Cave, 41
  Heritage Trail, 41
  Jefferson Davis SHS, **46**, *46*, 47
  John James Audubon SP, **46**, 46
  Mammoth Cave NP, **41**, *38-45*, 46-47
  Oscar Getz Museum of Whiskey History, **46**, *47*
  Owensboro Area Museum of Science & History, **46**, 46
  Patton Museum of Cavalry & Armor, **46**, 46-47
  Schmidt's Coca-Cola Museum, **46**, 47
  Sloans Crossing Pond, **41**, *42*
Kirkwood Ranch (ID), **85**
Konza Prairie Research Natural Area (KS), **128**, 128

L-M

Lake Clark NP & PRES (AK), **119**, *119*
Lakeview Sand Bar (TX), **51**
Lance Rosier Unit (TX), **51**, 53, *54*
Las Cabezas de San Juan Nature Reserve (PR), **36**, *36*, 37
Lava Beds NM (CA), **122**, *122*
Lava Canyon (WA), **97**, 103
Laws Railroad Museum and Historical Site (CA), **68**, 68
Lebanon SF (NJ), **132**, *132*
Lehman Caves (NV), 81
Letchworth SP (NY), **135**, 135
Little Cape Point Trail (ME), **11**, *10*, 13
Little Cottonwood Canyon (UT), **73**, 77
Little Hardwood Island (ME), **11**, 12
Little Sahara Recreation Area (UT), **73**, *72*, 74
Lituya Bay (AK), **109**, *110*
Louisiana
  Bayou Sauvage NWR, **129**, 129
  Delta NWR, **129**, 129
  Grand Isle East SP, **129**, 129
  Mississippi Delta, **129**, 129
Lowest elevation, **61**, 62
Maid of the Mist (NY/Ontario), **21**, 18, 20, 22, 23
Maine
  Acadia National Park, **16**, 17
  Beals Island, **11**, 12
  Black Duck Cove, **11**, *15*
  Burnham Tavern, **16**, *16*, 17
  Cape Cove, **11**, *14*
  Fort Knox SHS, **16**, 17
  Great Wass Archipelago, **11**, *8-15*, 16-17
  Great Wass Island, **11**, *8-9*

Head Harbor Island, 11, 8
Jonesport, 11, 8
Little Cape Point Trail, 11, 10, 13
    Little Hardwood Island, 11, 12
Maine Forest and Logging Museum, 16, 16
Man Islands, 11
Mark Island, 11
Mistake Island, 11, 12
Moosabec Reach, 11, 12-13
Moose Peak Lighthouse, 11, 12
Petit Manan NWR, 16, 17
St. Croix Island International Historic Site, 16, 16-17
Whales, 10, 17
Mammoth Cave NP (KY), 41, 38-45, 46-47
Man Islands (ME), 11
Manly Peak (CA), 61, 67
Mark Island (ME), 11
Martin Bridge Limestones (OR), 87
Massacre Rocks SP (ID), 73, 75
Maturango Museum (CA), 68, 69
Mayagüez (PR), 36, 36
McConnell Mansion (ID), 92, 92-93
Michigan
    Pictured Rocks National Lakeshore, 130, 118, 130
Mississippi
    Mississippi Petrified Forest, 131, 131
    Mississippi Delta (LA), 129, 129
Mistake Island (ME), 11, 12
Moosabec Reach (ME), 11, 12-13
Moose Peak Lighthouse (ME), 11, 12
Mosaic Canyon (CA), 61, 62
Mount Edziza Provincial Park (British Columbia), 116, 117
Mount Fairweather (AK), 109
Mount Hood (OR), 104, 105
Mount Ranier NP (WA), 104, 104, 105
Mount St. Helens (WA), 97, 94-103, 104-105
Mount Timpanogos (UT), 73, 79
Muir Inlet (AK), 109, 112-113

N-O

Nacogdoches (TX), 56, 56, 57
Neches River (TX), 51, 48, 50, 52-53
Nevada
    Great Basin NP, 80, 81
    Lehman Caves, 81
    Red Rock Canyon NCA, 68, 69
    Rhyolite, 61
New Brunswick
    Roosevelt-Campobello International Park, 16, 17
Newfoundland Mountains (UT), 73, 78
New Jersey
    Edwin Forsythe NWR, 132, 132
    Lebanon SF, 132, 132
    Pine Barrens, 132, 132
New Mexico
    Holloman Air Force Base, 133
    Trinity Site, 133
    White Sands NM, 133, 133
New York (state)
    Adirondack Park, 134, 134
    American Falls, 21, 18-20
    Bridal Veil Falls, 21, 25
    Buffalo, 26, 26
    Cave of the Winds, 21, 25
    Dunkirk Historical Lighthouse and Veterans Park Museum, 26, 26
    George Eastman House, 26, 27
    Goat Island, 21, 20, 25
    Letchworth SP, 135, 135
    Maid of the Mist, 21, 18, 20, 22, 23
    New York SP, 21, 25
    Niagara Falls, 21, 18-25, 26-27
    Niagara River, 21, 18, 20, 27
    Old Fort Niagara, 26, 25, 26, 27
    Rainbow Bridge, 21, 23
    Rochester, 26, 27

Schoellkopf Geological Museum, 21
    Three Sisters Islands, 21
    Tifft Nature Preserve, 26, 26
    Whirlpool SP, 21, 22, 24
Niagara Falls (NY/Ontario), 21, 18-25, 26-27
Niagara-on-the-Lake (Ontario), 26, 27
Niagara River (NY/Ontario), 21, 18, 20, 27
Niagara Spanish Aero Car (Ontario), 21, 24
Nisqually NWR (WA), 104, 104
Old Faithful (WY), 141, 141
Old Fort Niagara (NY), 26, 25, 26, 27
Old San Juan (PR), 36, 37
Ontario
    Horseshoe Falls, 21, 20, 22-23, 24-25
    IMAX Theatre, 21, 25
    Maid of the Mist, 21, 18, 20, 22, 23
    Niagara Falls, 21, 18-25, 26-27
    Niagara-on-the-Lake, 26, 27
    Niagara River, 21, 18, 20, 27
    Niagara Spanish Aero Car, 21, 24
    Queenston Heights Park, 26, 27
    Rainbow Bridge, 21, 23
    Skylon Tower, 21
    The Whirlpool, 21, 24
Oregon
    Crater Lake NP, 136, 136
    Dug Bar, 85
    Enterprise, 85, 84
    Granite Creek Rapids, 85, 90, 91
    Hat Point Lookout, 85, 83, 86, 87
    Hells Canyon, 85, 82-91, 92-93
    Hells Canyon NRA, 85, 84, 88-89
    Hood River County Historical Museum, 104, 105
    Imnaha, 85, 83
    Martin Bridge Limestones, 87
    Mount Hood, 104, 105
    Oregon Trail Regional Museum, 92, 93
    Portland, 104, 105
    Rafting, 89, 90, 91
    Snake River, 85, 82-91
    Umatilla NWR, 92, 92
    Wallowa Mountains, 85, 83
Oscar Getz Museum of Whiskey History (KY), 46, 47
Owensboro Area Museum of Science & History (KY), 46, 46
Ozark NF (AR), 121, 121

P-Q-R

Patton Museum of Cavalry & Armor (KY), 46, 46-47
Perrine Memorial Bridge (ID), 80, 80, 81
Petit Manan NWR (ME), 16, 17
Pictured Rocks National Lakeshore (MI), 130, 118, 130
Pine Barrens (NJ), 132, 132
Pioneer Farm Museum (WA), 104, 104-105
Pittsburg Landing (ID), 85, 88, 89, 90
Portland (OR), 104, 105
Pronghorn antelope, 78, 122
Provo Canyon (UT), 73, 79
Puerto Rico
    Big Tree Trail, 31, 35
    Cabo Rojo NWR, 36, 36
    Caimitillo Picnic Area, 31
    Caribbean NF, 31, 28-29, 33-34, 35
    Casa Roig, 36, 37
    Castillo San Felipe del Morro, 37
    El Yunque, 31, 28-35, 36-37
    El Yunque NRA, 31, 35
    Hacienda Buena Vista, 36, 37
    Las Cabezas de San Juan Nature Reserve, 36, 37
    Mayagüez, 36, 36
    Old San Juan, 36, 37
    Rio de la Mina, 31, 35
    San Juan, 36, 37
    Sierra de Luquillo, 31, 30, 32

Sierra Palm Visitor Center, 31
    Yokahu Tower, 31, 35
Pupfish, 64, 65-66
Queenston Heights Park (Ontario), 26, 27
Racetrack Valley (CA), 61, 63
Rafting, 89, 90, 91
Raft River Mountains (UT), 73, 79
Rainbow Bridge (NY/Ontario), 21, 23
Red Rock Canyon NCA (NV), 68, 69
Rhyolite (NV), 61
Rio de la Mina (PR), 31, 35
Rochester (NY), 26, 27
Roosevelt-Campobello International Park (New Brunswick), 16, 17
Roy E. Larsen Sandyland Sanctuary (TX), 51, 55

S-T

Salt Creek (CA), 61, 62
Salt Lake City (UT), 73, 80
Sam Houston Memorial Museum Complex (TX), 56, 56, 57
San Juan (PR), 36, 37
Saratoga Spring (CA), 61, 64, 66
Schmidt's Coca-Cola Museum (KY), 46, 47
Schoellkopf Geological Museum (NY), 21
Scottys Castle (CA), 61, 66, 67
Seals, 10, 14, 115
Seven Devils Mountains (ID), 85, 84
Sierra de Luquillo (PR), 31, 30, 32
Sierra Palm Visitor Center (PR), 31
Skylon Tower (Ontario), 21
Sloans Crossing Pond (KY), 41, 42
Snake River (OR/ID), 85, 82-91
Snake River Trail (ID), 85, 91
Snowbird (UT), 73, 77
South Dakota
    Badlands NP, 137, 137
    Spirit Lake (WA), 97, 98
St. Croix Island International Historic Site (ME), 16, 16-17
St. Gertrude's Museum (ID), 92, 93
Stansbury Island (UT), 73, 74
Stansbury Mountains (UT), 73, 70-71
Steamboat House (TX), 57
Stovepipe Wells Village (CA), 61, 62, 63
Takhinsha Mountains (AK), 109, 112-113
Tarr Inlet (AK), 109, 111
Telescope Peak (CA), 61, 58-59
Tennessee
    Cumberland Caverns, 138, 138
Texas
    American Funeral Service Museum, 56, 57
    Beech Woods Trail, 51
    Big Thicket N PRES, 51, 48-55, 56-57
    Davy Crockett NF, 56, 56, 57
    Hickory Creek Savannah Unit, 51, 54
    Houston, 56, 57
    Jack Gore Baygall Unit, 51, 53
    John Jay French Historic House, 56, 57
    Lakeview Sand Bar, 51
    Lance Rosier Unit, 51, 53, 54
    Nacogdoches, 56, 56, 57
    Neches River, 51, 48, 50, 52-53
    Roy E. Larsen Sandyland Sanctuary, 51, 55
    Sam Houston Memorial Museum Complex, 56, 56, 57
    Steamboat House, 57
    Trinity River, 51, 52
    Turkey Creek Unit, 51, 53
    Village Creek, 51, 48-49
    Washington, 56, 57
    Washington-on-the-Brazos SHP, 56, 57
Three Sisters Islands (NY), 21
Tifft Nature Preserve (NY), 26, 26
Timpanogos Cave NM (UT), 73, 72, 77-78
Tongass NF (AK), 116, 117
Trail of Two Forests (WA), 97
Trinity River (TX), 51, 52

Trinity Site (NM), 133
Turkey Creek Unit (TX), 51, 53

U-V-W-X-Y-Z

Ubehebe Crater (CA), 61, 63
Umatilla NWR (OR/WA), 92, 92
Utah
    Alpine Scenic Loop, 73, 77
    Alta, 73, 77
    Antelope Island, 73, 74
    Antelope Island SP, 73, 70, 72
    Arches NP, 80, 80, 81
    Bear River Migratory Bird Refuge, 73
    Bonneville Salt Flats, 73, 72, 76
    Capitol Reef NP, 139, 139
    College of Eastern Utah Prehistoric Museum, 80, 81
    Danger Cave, 73, 76
    Eureka, 73
    Fish Springs NWR, 73, 72, 75, 76, 79
    Golden Spike NHS, 73
    Great Basin, 73, 70-79, 80-81
    Great Salt Lake, 73, 70, 76, 78
    Great Salt Lake Desert, 73, 76
    Great Salt Lake SP, 73, 70
    Little Cottonwood Canyon, 73, 77
    Little Sahara Recreation Area, 73, 72, 74
    Mount Timpanogos, 73, 79
    Newfoundland Mountains, 73, 78
    Provo Canyon, 73, 79
    Raft River Mountains, 73, 79
    Salt Lake City, 73, 80
    Snowbird, 73, 77
    Stansbury Island, 73, 74
    Stansbury Mountains, 73, 70-71
    Timpanogos Cave NM, 73, 72, 77-78
    Village Creek (TX), 51, 48-49
Waimea Canyon (HI), 125, 125
Wallowa Mountains (OR), 85, 83
Washington (state)
    Ape Cave, 97, 103
    Coldwater Lake, 97, 100
    Coldwater Ridge Visitor Center, 97, 96
    Fort Walla Walla Museum Complex, 92, 92
    Goldendale Observatory SP, 104, 105
    Hoquiam's Castle, 104, 104, 105
    Lava Canyon, 97, 103
    Mount Ranier NP, 104, 104, 105
    Mount St. Helens, 97, 94-103, 104-105
    Nisqually NWR, 104, 104
    Pioneer Farm Museum, 104, 104-105
    Spirit Lake, 97, 98
    Trail of Two Forests, 97
    Umatilla NWR, 92, 92
    Windy Ridge Viewpoint, 97
Washington (TX), 56, 57
Washington-on-the-Brazos SHP (TX), 56, 57
Whales, 10, 17, 109, 110, 113
The Whirlpool (Ontario), 21, 24
Whirlpool SP (NY), 21, 22, 24
White Bird Battlefield (ID), 92, 93
White Sands NM (NM), 133, 133
Wildflowers, 15, 52, 54, 60, 74, 84, 87, 99, 101, 103, 109, 111, 129
Wildrose Canyon (CA), 61, 60, 66
Windy Ridge Viewpoint (WA), 97
Wyoming
    Devils Tower NM, 140, 140
    Fossil Butte NM, 80, 81
    Old Faithful, 141, 141
    Yellowstone NP, 141, 141
Yellowstone NP (WY), 141, 141
Yokahu Tower (PR), 31, 35
Zalud House (CA), 68, 69

PICTURE CREDITS

Cover photograph by Fred Hirschmann
2 Jeff Gnass Photography
5 Alan Briere

THE GREAT WASS ARCHIPELAGO
8, 9 Alan Briere
10 Alan Briere
12, 13 Alan Briere
14 Rick Marsi
15 (both) Alan Briere
16 Alan Briere
17 (both) Alan Briere

NIAGARA FALLS
18, 19 Fred Hirschmann
20 (upper left) Thomas Kitchin/
    Tom Stack & Associates
20 (lower right) Mike Yamashita/Woodfin
    Camp & Associates
22 Jonathan Wallen
23 (upper) Jeff Gnass Photograph
23 (lower) Wolfgang Kaehler
24 (left) Karen Holsinger Mullen/Unicorn
    Stock Photos
24 (right) Jeff Gnass Photograph
25 (upper right) Wolfgang Kaehler
25 (lower left) Fred Hirschmann
26 Karen Holsinger Mullen/
    Unicorn Stock Photos
27 (upper) Wolfgang Kaehler
27 (lower) Courtesy of the
    George Eastman House

EL YUNQUE
28, 29 Wolfgang Kaehler
30 Wolfgang Kaehler
32 (upper) Gerry Ellis/Ellis Nature Phography
32 (lower) Tom Bean
33 Robert Frerck/Woodfin Camp
    & Associates
34 (left) Ray Pfortner
34 (left) Ray Pfortner/Peter Arnold, Inc.
35 Gerry Ellis/Ellis Nature Phography
36 Bernard Boutrit/Woodfin Camp
    & Associates
37 (upper) Jan Butchofsky/Dave G. Houser
37 (lower) Dave G. Houser

MAMMOTH CAVE
38, 39 Chip Clark
40 Jack Olson
42 (left) Chip Clark
42 (right) Tom Till Photography
43 (upper) Chip Clark

43 (lower) Connie Toops
44, 45 (all) Chip Clark
46, 47 (all) Jonathan Wallen

BIG THICKET NATIONAL PRESERVE
48, 49 John Elk III
50 (upper) Tim Thompson
50 (lower) Laurence Parent
52 (upper left) David Muench
52, 53 Tim Thompson
53 (right) David Muench
54 (left) Fred Hirschmann
54 (right) Laurence Parent
55 David Muench
56 Laurence Parent
57 (upper left) Deneve Feigh Bunde/
    Unicorn Stock Photos
57 (lower right) Laurence Parent

DEATH VALLEY
58, 59 David Muench
60 (upper left) Jeff Foott Productions
60 (upper right) Fred Hirschmann
62 (upper left) Michael Collier
62 (lower right) David Muench
63 (both) Randi Hirschmann
64 (upper left) Fred Hirschmann
64, 65 Laurence Parent
65 (upper) Jeff Foott Productions
65 (right) Gerry Ellis/Ellis Nature Phography
66 (upper) Laurence Parent
66 (lower) Randi Hirschmann
67 (left) Randi Hirschmann
67 (right) Gerry Ellis/Ellis Nature Phography
68 Spencer Swanger/Tom Stack & Associates
69 (upper) Greg Vaughn
69 (lower) Mike Yamashita/Woodfin Camp
    & Associates

THE GREAT BASIN
70, 71 David Muench
72 (upper left) Tom Bean
72 (lower right) Jim Richardson/Woodfin
    Camp & Associates
74 (upper) Tom Bean
74 (lower) David Muench
75 Jim Richardson/Woodfin Camp
    & Associates
76 (upper right) David Muench
76 (lower left) Jim Richardson/Woodfin
    Camp & Associates
77 Jim Richardson/Woodfin Camp &
    Associates

78, 79 Jeff Gnass Photograph
78 (lower left) Michael Durham/
    Ellis Nature Photography
79 Tom Bean
80 Jan Butchofsky/Dave G. Houser
81 (both) William H. Mullins/Steve Bly

HELLS CANYON
82, 83 Jeff Gnass Photography
84 (left) Jeff Gnass Photography
84 (right) Brian Parker/Tom Stack
    & Associates
86 Greg Vaughn
87 (left) Greg Vaughn/Tom Stack
    & Associates
87 (right) John Blaustein/Woodfin Camp
    & Associates
88 (left) Gerry Ellis/Ellis Nature Phography
88, 89 Ric Ergenbright Photography
89 (lower right) David Muench
90 David Jensen
91 (upper left) Dave G. Houser
91 (lower right) Jan Butchofsky/
    Dave G. Houser
92 Dave G. Houser
93 (both) David Jensen

MOUNT ST. HELENS
94, 95 Jeff Gnass Photograph
96 (both) Tim Thompson
98 (lower left) Roger Werth/Woodfin
    Camp & Associates
98, 99 Jerry Stelmack/Borland Stock Photo
99 Gary Braasch/Ellis Nature Photography
100 (upper) John Elk III
100 (lower) Wayne Aldridge/
    Borland Stock Photo
101 John Elk III
102 John Elk III
103 (upper right) Roger Werth/Woodfin
    Camp & Associates
103 (lower left) Gary Braasch/
    Ellis Nature Photography
104 Gary Crabbe
105 (upper right) Jeff Gnass Photograph
105 (lower left) David Muench

GLACIER BAY
106, 107 David Muench
108 Jeff Gnass Photograph
109 Kim Heacox
110 (upper right) Jeff Gnass Photograph
110 (lower left) Brandon D. Cole/Ellis
    Nature Photography

111 (both) Jeff Gnass Photograph
112 (lower left) Gerry Ellis/Ellis Nature
    Phography
112 (upper right) Kim Heacox
112, 113 Fred Hirschmann
113 (right) Steve Bly/Dave.G. Houser
114 Carr Clifton
115 (upper) Jeff Gnass Photography
115 (lower) Brandon D. Cole/
    Ellis Nature Photography
116 (upper left) Jeff Gnass Photograph
116, 117 (all) Carr Clifton

GAZETTEER
118 Ric Ergenbright Photography
119 (both) Fred Hirschmann
120 (left) Fred Hirschmann
120 (right) Robert Fried/Tom Stack
    & Associates
121 Laurence Parent
122 (upper right) Jeff Gnass Photography
122 (lower left) David Muench
123 Tom Stack /Tom Stack & Associates
124 (left) Tim Thompson
124 (right) David Muench
125 Tim Thompson
126 (both) Wolfgang Kaehler
127 Richard B.Dippold/
    Unicorn Stock Photos
128 (both) Jonathan Wallen
129 Laurence Parent
130 (left) Carr Clifton
130 (right) Jeff Gnass Photography
131 Stephen Kirkpatrick
132 (upper) David Muench
132 (lower) Jonathan Wallen
133 Laurence Parent
134 (both) Carr Clifton
135 Jonathan Wallen
136 (upper right) Jeff Gnass Photography
136 (lower left) Tim Thompson
137 Carr Clifton
138 Cumberland Caverns, Inc.
139 (both) David Muench
140 (upper right) Laurence Parent
140 (lower left) David Muench
141 Jeff Gnass Photography

Back cover photograph by Alan Briere

ACKNOWLEDGMENTS

Cartography: Map resource base courtesy of the USGS; shaded relief courtesy of the USGS, the National Park Service, the USDA Forest Service, and Mountain High Maps® Copyright © 1993 Digital Wisdom, Inc.

The editors would also like to thank the following: Lorraine Doré, Dominique Gagné, Pascale Hueber, and Valery Pigeon.

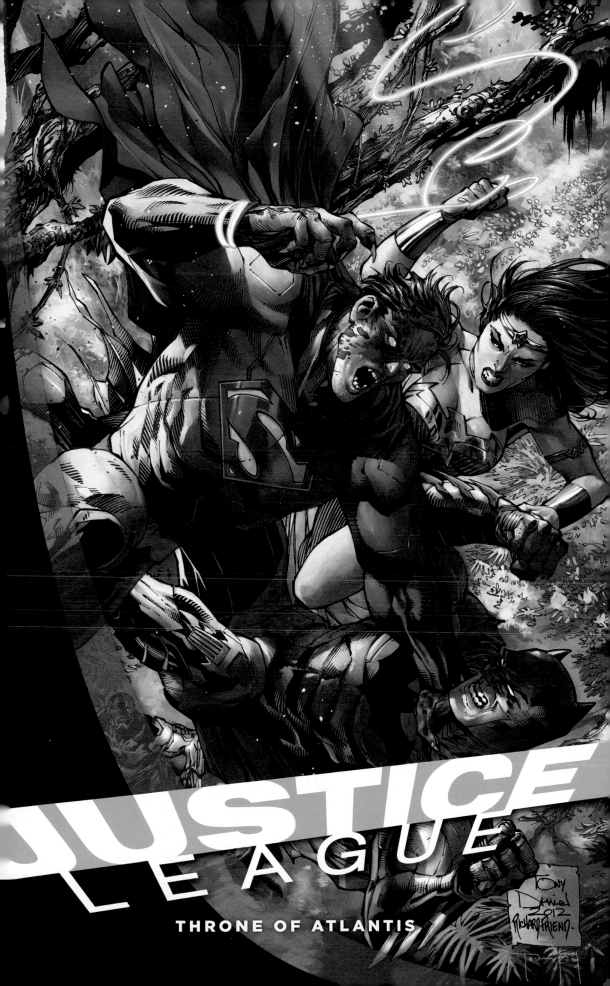

JUSTICE LEAGUE
THRONE OF ATLANTIS

GEOFF **JOHNS** writer
JEFF **LEMIRE** epilogue co-writer

IVAN **REIS** PAUL **PELLETIER** TONY S. **DANIEL**
BRAD **WALKER** pencillers

JOE **PRADO** OCLAIR **ALBERT** MATT **BANNING** SANDU **FLOREA**
RICHARD **FRIEND** DREW **HENNESSY** KARL **KESEL** SEAN **PARSONS**
IVAN **REIS** ART **THIBERT** inkers

ROD **REIS** TOMEU **MOREY** JAY DAVID **RAMOS** colorists

DAVE **SHARPE** PATRICK **BROSSEAU** NICK **NAPOLITANO** letterers

IVAN **REIS**, JOE **PRADO** AND ROD **REIS**
original series & collection cover artists

SUPERMAN created by JERRY **SIEGEL** & JOE **SHUSTER**
by special arrangement with the Jerry Siegel family

BRIAN CUNNINGHAM PAT McCALLUM Editors – Original Series KATIE KUBERT Assistant Editor – Original Series
JEB WOODARD Group Editor – Colelcted Editions PETER HAMBOUSSI Editor – Collected Edition
ROBBIE BIEDERMAN Publication Design

BOB HARRAS Senior VP – Editor-in-Chief, DC Comics

DIANE NELSON President DAN DIDIO and JIM LEE Co-Publishers GEOFF JOHNS Chief Creative Officer
AMIT DESAI Senior VP – Marketing & Global Franchise Management NAIRI GARDINER Senior VP – Finance SAM ADES VP – Digital Marketing
BOBBIE CHASE VP –Talent Development MARK CHIARELLO Senior VP – Art, Design & Collected Editions
JOHN CUNNINGHAM VP – Content Strategy ANNE DEPIES VP – Strategy Planning & Reporting
DON FALLETTI VP – Manufacturing Operations LAWRENCE GANEM VP – Editorial Administration & Talent Relations
ALISON GILL Senior VP – Manufacturing & Operations HANK KANALZ Senior VP – Editorial Strategy & Administration
JAY KOGAN VP – Legal Affairs DEREK MADDALENA Senior VP – Sales & Business Development
JACK MAHAN VP – Business Affairs DAN MIRON VP – Sales Planning & Trade Development
NICK NAPOLITANO VP – Manufacturing Administration CAROL ROEDER VP – Marketing
EDDIE SCANNELL VP – Mass Account & Digital Sales COURTNEY SIMMONS Senior VP – Publicity & Communications
JIM (SKI) SOKOLOWSKI VP – Comic Book Specialty & Newsstand Sales SANDY YI Senior VP – Global Franchise Management

JUSTICE LEAGUE: THRONE OF ATLANTIS WARNER HOME VIDEO EDITION

DC Comics, 2900 West Alameda Avenue, Burbank, CA 91505
Printed by Transcontinental Interglobe, Beauceville, QC, Canada. 12/17/15. First Printing.
ISBN: 978-1-4012-6426-0

PRINTED COVER SIZE: 6 5/8 X 10 3/16

"I CAN'T FAIL HER AGAIN."

WASHINGTON, D.C.
MEDICAL CARE UNIT OF A.R.G.U.S.

I'M SURPRISED THEY LET YOU IN HERE.

THEY DIDN'T.

SO, BATMAN, IF THE PENTAGON SEES YOU ON THE SECURITY CAMERAS, THEY CAN ADD *BREAKING AND ENTERING* TO THEIR GROWING LIST OF RIDICULOUS *COMPLAINTS.*

THE CAMERAS WON'T SHOW THEM *ANYTHING,* TREVOR.

CYBORG?

WE NEED SOME INFORMATION ON *THE CHEETAH,* COLONEL.

WHY? IS DIANA OKAY?

I'M FINE.

THE WATCHTOWER SATELLITE.
HEADQUARTERS OF THE JUSTICE LEAGUE.

WE KNOW YOU'RE *FINE.* WE'VE JUST NEVER SEEN YOU, *UH,* KNOCKED DOWN BEFORE.

WONDER WOMAN WAS OBVIOUSLY *HOLDING BACK,* FLASH.

WHY HOLD BACK?

"BECAUSE BARBARA MINERVA WAS THE FIRST FRIEND DIANA MADE."

YOU AND I HAVE OTHER RESPONSIBILITIES WE NEED TO FOCUS ON.

LIKE THE CHEETAH?

WE CAN HELP YOU FIND HER.

IT'S NOT THE CHEETAH I NEED TO FIND. IT'S THE LOST TRIBE CONNECTED TO HER.

THEY HAVE TO KNOW MORE ABOUT THE DAGGER THAT TRANSFORMED BARBARA INTO THAT MONSTER. MAYBE THEY CAN HELP.

BUT YOU CAN'T LOCATE THEM?

I HAVEN'T YET.

THEN WE CAN HELP WITH THAT, CYBORG?

I HEARD YOU, SUPERMAN.

HEARD WHAT?

I'M ALREADY SEARCHING AND MAPPING KNOWN AREAS TO COVER OFF WHERE WE DON'T NEED TO LOOK.

I'LL NARROW DOWN THE HUNT BASED ON THE RITUAL DAGGER'S LAST KNOWN LOCATION.

THEN WHEN WE BOOM DOWN I COULD DO SOME RECON. THE TERRAIN MIGHT MAKE IT A LITTLE SLOW, BUT IT SHOULDN'T TAKE ME MORE THAN AN HOUR OR TWO.

YOU DON'T NEED TO DO THIS.

IT'S NO PROBLEM.

HAPPY TO HELP.

THE SECRET OF THE CHEETAH part two

GEOFF JOHNS writer TONY S. DANIEL penciller RICHARD FRIEND & SANDU FLOREA inkers cover by TONY S. DANIEL, RICHARD FRIEND & TOMEU MOR

"FOR CENTURIES, THE SAN TRIBE HAS HUNTED ALONGSIDE THE CHEETAHS. AND EVERY GENERATION, ONE OF OUR PEOPLE WAS CHOSEN TO BECOME THE HOST OF THE GODDESS OF THE HUNT--*THE CHEETAH.*

"MY MOTHER WAS THE LAST ONE OF US TO BE SO BLESSED.

"SHE BECAME A GREAT HUNTER FOR MY PEOPLE.

"UNTIL MY MOTHER WAS MURDERED BY A MAN WIELDING THE *GODSLAYER*--A KNIFE SAID TO HAVE BEEN FORGED BY A BEING SO *EVIL,* HIS NAME MUST GO UNSPOKEN.

"THROUGHOUT TIME, THE GODSLAYER WAS USED TO KILL MANY OTHER DEITIES--THE LIONESS *PAKHET* OF EGYPT, THE FRIGID *SKADI* AND A MYSTERIOUS, ALIEN *SUN GOD* WHO ANGERED MANY OTHERS.

"MY MOTHER DIED TOO...BUT UNLIKE THE OTHER GODS, THE CHEETAH SURVIVED.

WHEN I'M THROUGH WITH YOU AND YOUR FRIENDS, I'LL GO AFTER STEVE.

"SHE SOMEHOW *POSSESSED* THE GODSLAYER, *CURSING* THE HUNTER WHO MURDERED HER.

"THE NEXT BEING THE HUNTER PURSUED WAS YA'WARA--THE CHOSEN JAGUAR GODDESS OF THE AMAZON. BUT YA'WARA BESTED THE *HUNTER* AND *FED* HIM TO HER CATS.

THIS IS *MY* TERRITORY. WE'RE IN *MY* ELEMENT.

THERE IS *NOTHING* YOU CAN DO HERE, DIANA.

"AND FOR A TIME, THE KNIFE WAS LOST.

"UNTIL IT ENDED UP IN BARBARA MINERVA'S HANDS.

"AND SHE *STOLE* THE GODSLAYER."

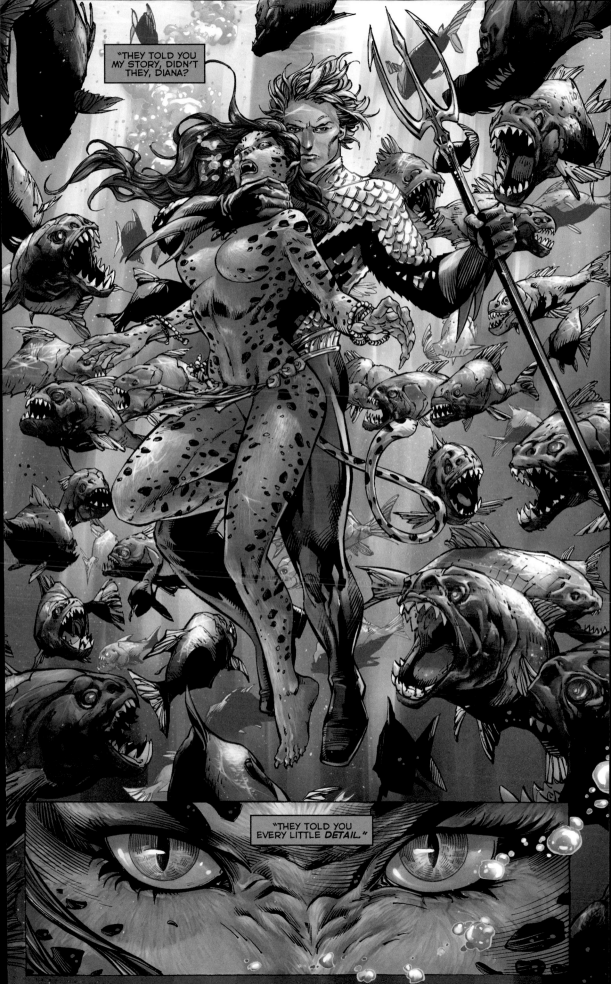

THRONE OF ATLANTIS chapter one

GEOFF JOHNS writer **IVAN REIS** penciller **JOE PRADO** inker cover by **IVAN REIS, JOE PRADO & ROD REIS**

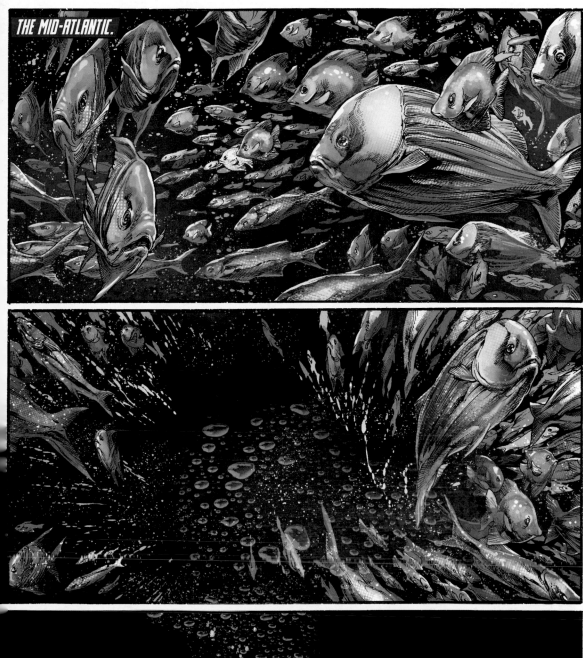

IT ALL STARTED IN SMALLVILLE.

RIGHT IN THIS ROOM, I THOUGHT ABOUT GIVING UP *CLARK KENT* COMPLETELY.

BUT I *LIKE* BEING CLARK KENT. I LIKE WHO I AM AND WHO MY PARENTS WERE. SO I CAME UP WITH THE IDEA OF A *DUAL IDENTITY.*

I THOUGHT ABOUT WEARING A *MASK* LIKE BRUCE DOES.

BUT AS CLOSE AS WE ARE, BATMAN'S GOING FOR SOMETHING *DIFFERENT* THAN I AM.

I'D RATHER *GOOD* PEOPLE TRUST ME THAN *BAD* PEOPLE FEAR ME.

I THINK THEY NEED TO SEE YOUR EYES FOR THAT.

SO CLARK KENT WEARS A MASK INSTEAD OF SUPERMAN.

HERE. TRY IT.

YOU HAVE TO BE KIDDING ME.

COME ON, DIANA...

"...YOU HAVE TO UNPLUG SOMETIME."

ADMIRAL CORBY ASKED ME TO CALL YOU PERSONALLY, VICTOR.

THE WATCHTOWER. HEADQUARTERS OF THE JUSTICE LEAGUE.

HIS DAUGHTER IS STATIONED ON THE U.S.S. MABUS.

WHY WOULD SOMEONE WANT TO SABOTAGE A MISSILE TEST AND FIRE THEM INTO EMPTY OCEAN?

I DON'T KNOW. THE NAVY LOST CONTACT WITH THE SHIP.

IF IT WAS DONE MANUALLY, I WON'T BE ABLE TO TRACK DOWN ANYTHING BEHIND THE POINT OF ACCESS, BUT SECURITY CAMERAS SHOULD GIVE US A VISUAL ONCE I DO.

I'D BOOM DOWN TO HANDLE THIS RIGHT NOW, BUT WITHOUT A DIRECT LINK TO THE CARRIER, I CAN'T PINPOINT ITS LOCATION. IF I MISS, I'LL DROWN.

WE'VE BEEN READY TO ADD THE ADDITIONAL ENVIRONMENTAL PROTECTIVE MODES TO YOU FOR MONTHS.

WHICH REQUIRES REPLACING THE ONE LUNG I HAVE LEFT. I'LL PASS.

I WOULDN'T HAVE BYPASSED A.R.G.U.S. AND CALLED YOU MYSELF IF IT WASN'T FOR ADMIRAL CORBY'S PERSONAL REQUEST.

THERE'S NOTHING A PARENT CARES MORE ABOUT THAN THEIR CHILD.

YOU KNOW THAT, DON'T YOU, SON?

WUUUMMMMMN

DAD?

MY KID SAYS AQUAMAN'S *REALLY* FROM ATLANTIS.

THAT'S THE TABLOIDS. AQUAMAN LIVES IN A LIGHTHOUSE OUTSIDE OF BOSTON WITH HIS MERMAID.

YOUR COUSIN WORK WITH HIM LIKE GORDON WORKS WITH BATMAN?

HOW DO YOU KNOW *THAT?*

MY COUSIN'S ON THE FORCE UP THERE.

OH, YEAH, *SURE.* HE'S GOT AN *AQUA-SIGNAL* THAT THROWS *FIFTY POUNDS* OF FISH FOOD INTO THE BAY WHEN-EVER A SAILBOAT CAPSIZES.

HAHAHAHAHAHA

WHAT ARE YOU DOING IN GOTHAM?

DON'T TELL ME YOU'RE UPSET THAT I HELPED STOP THESE KIDNAPPERS?

I APPRECIATE THE ASSISTANCE TAKING DOWN SCARECROW'S MEN, EVEN IF I DON'T *NEED* IT.

WELL, I NEED *YOURS.* I KNOW WE DON'T SEE EYE-TO-EYE ON HOW TO LEAD THE JUSTICE LEAGUE, AND WE NEED TO TALK ABOUT THAT, BUT FIRST, I'VE GOT A PROBLEM.

THE FISH ARE SWIMMING AWAY FROM THE ENTIRE NORTHEASTERN SEABOARD. FROM BOSTON ALL THE WAY DOWN TO GOTHAM.

THEY AREN'T RESPONDING TO MY TELEPATHIC COMMANDS, WHICH MEANS THEIR SURVIVAL INSTINCTS ARE AT FULL DRIVE.

THE LAST TIME THIS HAPPENED, IT WAS ON AN ISOLATED BEACH WHERE A GROUP OF FLESH-EATING CREATURES ROSE FROM THE OCEANS AND ATTACKED A TOWN.

I THOUGHT THEY'D BEEN...TAKEN CARE OF, BUT IF THESE THINGS ARE BACK AND IN NUMBERS GREATER THAN BEFORE, IT'S A JUSTICE LEAGUE-LEVEL PROBLEM, NOT JUST--

I'M NOT GOING TO JAIL AGAIN!

WATCH OUT! HE'S GOT MY GUN!

SPLOOSHH

CLARK?

YEAH?

THIS ACTUALLY WORKS.

I KNOW.

HOW? WHY?

WELL, I'D GUESS MOST OF THE TIME WHEN THEY *DO* GET A LOOK AT US, THEY SEE US FROM FAR AWAY OR THEY'RE LOOKING UP AT US FROM THE GROUND. MORE IMPORTANT, I DON'T THINK PEOPLE EVER *CONSIDER* THAT WE--

--HIDE AMONG THEM?

NO, NOT HIDE. I JUST DON'T THINK A LOT OF PEOPLE IMAGINE WE HAVE A LIFE *OUTSIDE* OF THE JUSTICE LEAGUE. THEY THINK IT'S SUPERMAN AND WONDER WOMAN 24/7.

IT IS FOR *ME.*

IF I HAD AN EXTENDED FAMILY LIKE YOURS, MAYBE IT'D BE FOR ME, TOO.

BUT EVEN A *GODDESS* DESERVES A DINNER OUT, DIANA.

I'VE NEVER HAD ONE. NOT LIKE THIS.

HOPEFULLY IT'S THE FIRST OF *MANY.*

HEY! WHAT HAPPENED TO THE LIGHTS?!

CLARK?

KRRRKKKKSSH-KRRRKKKKSSH

WHAT IS IT?

AND THERE ARE STILL PEOPLE *INSIDE* THE SHIP.

THERE ARE PEOPLE ON THE STREETS WHO NEED OUR *HELP*, SUPERMAN.

"DAMMIT, WE CAN'T SAVE *EVERYONE.*"

GOTHAM.

"THEY'RE LUCKY I SAW THE LIGHT."

"AND HEARD ONE OF THEM SHOUTING UNDERWATER."

"*BARBARA!*"

WHAT THE HELL JUST *HAPPENED?*

-KAFFF-

BARBARA'S *SAFE,* JIM. SHE WASN'T ANYWHERE NEAR THE EASTSIDE WHEN THE WATER HIT. ARE YOU ALL RIGHT?

I'M--KFF--I'M FINE. HARVEY AND I WERE ON THE ROOF ACTIVATING THE SIGNAL. THE SCARECROW'S THUGS KIDNAPPED A WITNESS...

WE PULLED HIM AND SOME OF YOUR OFFICERS FROM THE DOCKS. WE RESCUED EVERYONE WE COULD FROM THE WATER.

HOW MANY?

AS MANY AS WE COULD.

NO.

HOW MANY DIDN'T MAKE IT OUT?

IT LOOKS LIKE WE SHOULD BE BUILDIN' A FREAKING *ARK*. WHAT THE HELL'S GOING *ON?*

WE'RE UNDER ATTACK, BULLOCK.

BY *WHO?*

ATLANTIS.

ATLANTIS? I THOUGHT THAT WAS JUST A GIMMICK.

GIMMICK?

MAD HATTER AIN'T FROM *WONDERLAND*, IS HE?

WHOA!

SINCE WHEN DOES WATER GO *UP?*

MERA!

GOT YOU.

I...TRIED TO PUSH BACK WHAT I COULD, BUT...

YOU DID THE *IMPOSSIBLE.* YOU SAVED HUNDREDS OF LIVES.

I COULD FEEL THEM IN THE WATER AS I MOVED IT, ARTHUR.

BODIES.

THERE ARE SO MANY BODIES DOWN THERE.

IF CYBORG HADN'T ALERTED THE CITY BEFOREHAND, AND IF WE HADN'T BEEN HERE, IT COULD'VE BEEN A LOT WORSE.

IT *WILL* BE A LOT WORSE, ARTHUR.

IF YOUR BROTHER IS FOLLOWING THE *ATLANTEAN WAR PLANS*...FIRST THE FLOODS, THEN GROUND ASSAULT, AND THEN--

I KNOW, BUT WE HAVE TO KEEP THEIR END GOAL BETWEEN US RIGHT NOW.

I DON'T WANT TO PANIC THE LEAGUE.

YOU HAVE TO *TELL* THEM, ARTHUR. YOU HAVE TO WARN THE JUSTICE LEAGUE THAT IF THIS PROGRESSES, IF ATLANTIS CONTINUES THEIR ATTACK, THEY'RE GOING TO *SINK* WHATEVER CITY THEY TARGET.

AND IF IT'S NOT GOTHAM--

"--IT'LL BE SOMEPLACE ELSE."

METROPOLIS.

I DON'T SEE ANY INTERNAL INJURIES, BUT IT'S HARD TO TELL. I'M NOT EVEN SURE HE *HAS* LUNGS.

NO LUNGS? I'M GUESSING HE'S AN ATLANTEAN.

HE SAID HIS NAME WAS *VULKO.*

PLEASE KEEP YOUR DISTANCE, MISS LANE. WE DON'T KNOW WHAT WE'RE DEALING WITH.

IF HE PULLED ME FROM THE WATER, WE'RE DEALING WITH A *HERO,* WONDER WOMAN. ONE WHO LOOKS LIKE HE NEEDS HELP HIMSELF.

HEY!

WHERE IS KING ARTHUR?!

CALM DOWN.

THERE ISN'T ANY TIME!

TAKE A SWING AGAIN AND SO DO I.

I...I'M SORRY, BUT YOU HAVE TO *LISTEN.* YOU HAVE TO FIND *ARTHUR!* EVERY MOMENT WE WAIT, ATLANTIS IS ONE STEP *CLOSER!*

IF HE WERE STILL KING, THEY NEVER WOULD'VE DONE THIS.

"MERA'S CLEARING OUT THE REST OF THE STREETS. COMMISSIONER GORDON AND HIS MEN ARE GOING TO HELP RECOVER THE BODIES."

ONCE MERA'S DONE IN GOTHAM, SHE'LL HEAD TO METROPOLIS TO DO THE SAME.

THE WAVES HIT AND IT ALL GOES *QUIET?*

WHERE'S ATLANTIS?

THEY'RE WAITING.

FOR WHAT?

TO SEE WHAT CITY WAS HIT THE *HARDEST.* THAT'S WHERE THEY'LL RISE OUT OF THE OCEAN.

ACCORDING TO THESE *ATLANTEAN WAR PLANS* YOU MENTIONED?

YES... THEY PLAN TO SINK A CITY.

AND YOU KNOW THIS BECAUSE YOU *WROTE* THOSE WAR PLANS?

WITH MY BROTHER, YEARS AGO.

I WAS IN A DIFFERENT FRAME OF MIND.

SO I GATHERED.

WHY IS ATLANTIS ATTACKING? WHY NOW? I THOUGHT YOU WERE THEIR *KING*.

NOT ANYMORE. LOOK, THEY WOULDN'T DO THIS UNLESS THEY WERE *PROVOKED*.

PROVOKED?

THAT MISSILE TEST THAT SENT THOSE TOMAHAWKS STRAIGHT TO THE OCEAN FLOOR...THEY MUST'VE DETONATED ON OR NEAR ATLANTIS. THAT'S WHY--

YOU'RE *JUSTIFYING* THEIR ATTACK?

NO, I'M TRYING TO *EXPLAIN* IT.

YOU NEED TO *UNDERSTAND*, BATMAN, ATLANTIS'S INTERACTIONS WITH THE SURFACE WORLD HAVE BEEN SAILORS *SLAUGHTERING* ITS PEOPLE AND NUCLEAR TESTS AND ENVIRONMENTAL DISASTERS *POISONING* THEIR OCEANS.

THEY'RE AN EXTREMELY SUPERSTITIOUS, PROTECTIVE AND *AGGRESSIVE* PEOPLE AS IT IS. YOU COME AT THEM STRAIGHT ON AND THEY'LL COME *BACK* AT YOU *TEN TIMES HARDER*.

BUT THEY *CAN* BE REASONED WITH.

THEY'VE ALREADY *KILLED* PEOPLE, ARTHUR.

AND THEY'LL KILL *MORE* IF THEY THINK THEY'RE BEING THREATENED.

I KNOW THESE PEOPLE ARE *YOUR* PEOPLE--

THEY ARE *NOT MY* PEOPLE.

YOU'RE THE ONE THAT SAID THE LEAGUE HAS TO STOP KEEPING *SECRETS* FROM ONE ANOTHER...

...WHAT AREN'T YOU TELLING ME?

I...

I NEARLY *DIED* TRYING TO FIND ATLANTIS. WHEN I FINALLY DID, YES, THEY WELCOMED ME WITH OPEN ARMS.

EVEN MY BROTHER, WHO CHERISHES ATLANTEAN LAW, STEPPED DOWN FROM THE THRONE.

BUT WITHIN WEEKS, THERE WAS *DISSENSION.* SOME CALLED ME THE *IMPURE* KING. A HALF-HUMAN SURFACE DWELLER. THERE WAS A MOVEMENT TO *CHANGE* THE LAWS AND REINSTATE MY YOUNGER BROTHER...A *FULL* ATLANTEAN.

DURING THAT TIME, I TRIED TO BE WHAT THEY *WANTED* ME TO BE.

I TURNED MY BACK ON THE SURFACE WORLD. I SAW IT THE UGLY WAY *THEY* DO.

"UNTIL *DARKSEID* CAME AND THE JUSTICE LEAGUE WAS FOUNDED.

"IT GAVE ME A PLACE TO GO."

I'M BEGINNING TO UNDERSTAND HOW HARD THIS IS GOING TO BE FOR YOU, ARTHUR. BUT YOU'RE STILL TRYING TO RATIONALIZE THEIR ACTIONS.

AND THERE *IS* NO RATIONALIZING AN ATTACK LIKE THIS. *WHATEVER* THE CATALYST.

PROVOKED OR NOT, IF YOUR BROTHER IS BEHIND THIS, THE JUSTICE LEAGUE IS BRINGING HIM IN. THAT'S THE WAY IT HAS TO BE.

VEETVEETVEETVEET

WHAT'S THAT?

INCOMING. WE NEED TO MOVE.

BOOOOOOMM

I DON'T SEE OR HEAR ANYTHING. HAD TO BE ATLANTEAN LONG RANGE WEAPONS.

HOW DID THEY KNOW YOU WERE WITH ME?

THEY WERE AIMING FOR *YOU*, NOT *ME*. WHEN I WROTE THOSE WAR PLANS I KNEW EVEN BEFORE WE MET THAT YOU'D BE A THREAT.

I'M *FLATTERED*.

"WHO *ELSE* IS ON YOUR *HIT LIST*?"

"DR. STEPHEN SHIN."

...THE DISASTERS IN BOSTON, METROPOLIS AND GOTHAM HAVE STILL GONE *UNEXPLAINED*, THOUGH RUMORS THAT THIS WAS AN...I DON'T THINK I HAVE THIS RIGHT--AN "*ATTACK FROM ATLANTIS*"?-- ARE EMERGING OUT OF GOTHAM.

THEORETICAL MARINE BIOLOGY BY DR. STEPHEN SHIN

WHATEVER THE CAUSE, HUNDREDS HAVE ALREADY BEEN CONFIRMED DEAD.

BATMAN?

YOU OKAY? THE BATPLANE JUST WENT *OFF-LINE.*

THE BATPLANE'S DOWN, BUT WE'RE FINE.

I TRIED TO CONTACT THE FLASH, BUT HE'S NOT ANSWERING. REPORTS SAID HE WAS DEALING WITH SOME KIND OF PRIMAL ATTACK, UNRELATED.

AQUAMAN SAYS HE WON'T BE A SPECIFIC TARGET FOR THE ATLANTEANS.

YOU AND AQUAMAN NEED TO GET TO THE WATCHTOWER.

"SUPERMAN AND WONDER WOMAN HAVE AN ATLANTEAN IN CUSTODY.

"SAYS HIS NAME'S VULKO."

THE SILENCE UP HERE...IT'S LIKE HOME.

"WHO IS HE?"

ARTHUR?!

"VULKO'S THE FIRST ATLANTEAN I EVER MET. HE'D BEEN EXILED SINCE MY MOTHER'S DEATH.

"HE WAS HER *ROYAL ADVISOR.* AND THEN MINE.

"HE'S AS CLOSE TO *FAMILY* AS I HAVE LEFT."

YOUR BROTHER THINKS THIS WAS AN ATTACK FROM THE SURFACE.

IT WAS--

AN ACCIDENT, I KNOW.

ATLANTEANS DIE. THEN HUMANS DROWN. NOW WE'RE ON THE BRINK OF *WAR.*

ARTHUR, SOMEONE TARGETED ATLANTIS ON PURPOSE. SOMEONE *WANTED* TO START THIS.

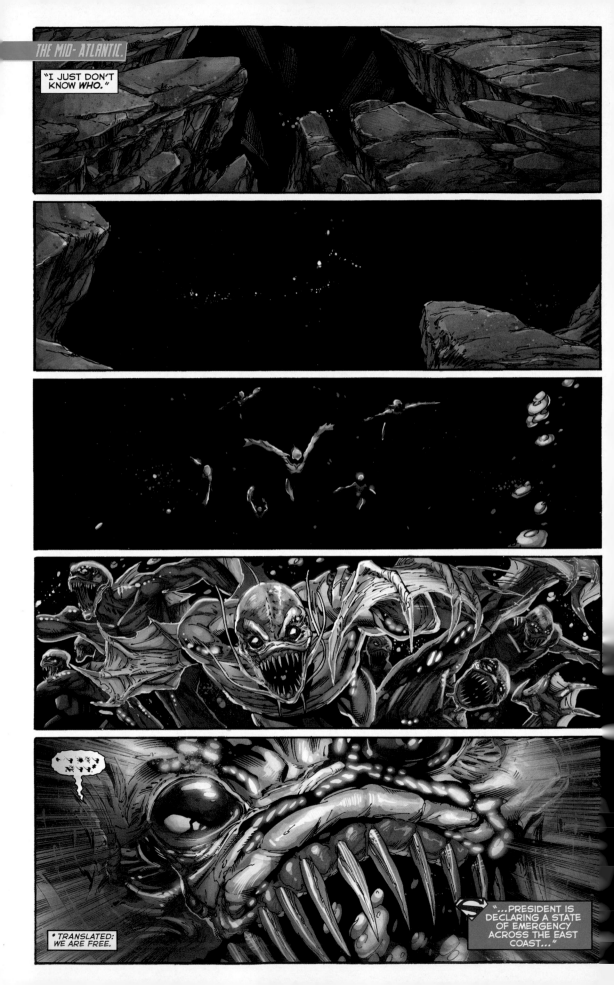

YOUR PEOPLE SEEM *CONFUSED*, BROTHER.

THEY'RE *NOT* MY PEOPLE. NOT IN THE WAY YOU THINK.

I'M *NOT* THEIR KING.

IF YOU AREN'T *RULING* THEM... THEN WHAT HAVE YOU BEEN *DOING* UP HERE?

WHERE'S THE ATLANTEAN ARMY?

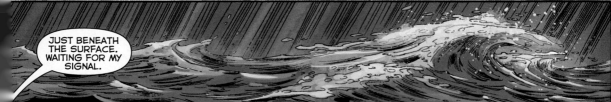

JUST BENEATH THE SURFACE. WAITING FOR MY SIGNAL.

I *SAID* I WOULD HANDLE THIS.

WE'VE BEEN *LISTENING,* ARTHUR.

AND IT DOESN'T SOUND LIKE IT'S BEING *HANDLED.*

ARE THESE *THREE* YOUR RULERS?

NO. YOU NEED TO GIVE ME *MORE TIME.*

WE'RE ALREADY TRACKING ATLANTEANS MOVING INTO EITHER SIDE OF THIS *CITY,* AQUAMAN.

THERE *IS* NO MORE TIME.

YOUR BROTHER'S COMING WITH *US.*

I'M SORRY...

I'M TRYING TO PROTECT *BOTH* WORLDS, DIANA.

IF IT WAS THE *AMAZONS* COMING ASHORE TO DESTROY THIS CITY, I'D BE FIGHTING AGAINST *THEM*--

--INSTEAD OF FIGHTING MY *FRIENDS.*

I KNOW SOMEONE HAS TO *ANSWER* FOR THIS, BUT IF ATLANTIS COMES OUT OF THE WATER, EVERY SINGLE SOLDIER-- *THOUSANDS* OF THEM--WILL FIGHT UNTIL THEIR DYING BREATH.

SO WILL *I.*

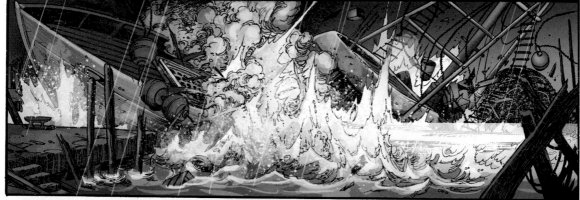

I THOUGHT YOU UNDERSTOOD, BRUCE.

AS BEST I CAN, ARTHUR, BUT IF WE WORK TOGETHER WE CAN--

AAAHHH!

KRRRZZZTT

THESE AIR-BREATHERS ARE FRAGILE, AREN'T THEY? A SECOND CHARGE SHOULD *END* HIM.

NO!

THIS SURFACE DWELLER RAISED HIS HAND TO ME--*ME,* THE *KING* OF ATLANTIS. IT IS *MY RIGHT* TO KILL HIM.

ATLANTEAN LAW DOESN'T APPLY HERE.

YOU *CONFUSE* ME, BROTHER. HAS BREATHING AIR FOR SO LONG DAMAGED YOUR MIND? FIRST YOU THREATEN ME, THEN YOU ATTACK THOSE WHO THREATEN ME, THEN YOU THREATEN ME *AGAIN?*

LISTEN TO ME, ORM. YOU'RE GOING *BACK* INTO THE WATER AND YOU'RE ORDERING THE ATLANTEANS TO *GO HOME.*

DO IT. *NOW.*

I HAD BELIEVED PERHAPS THIS COUNTERATTACK AGAINST YOUR KINGDOM WOULD BE A SATISFACTORY RETRIBUTION FOR THE WEAPONS FIRED UPON ATLANTIS, BUT THEN I COME HERE AND DISCOVER YOU ARE *NOT* THEIR LEADER.

WHY ARE YOU TRYING TO SIMPLY BE *ONE* OF THEM? YOU'RE *BETTER* THAN THEM.

MOTHER WOULD BE DISAPPOINTED. I KNOW *I* AM.

YOU'VE *ABANDONED* OUR WORLD AND JOINED ANOTHER. A WORLD THAT HAS DONE *NOTHING* BUT *ATTACK* AND *POISON* US FOR *CENTURIES.*

I DON'T WANT TO HURT YOU. SURRENDER *NOW.*

THEY *HATE* US, YOU SEE?

BUT WE ARE *DONE* FEARING THE SURFACE. WE ARE *DONE* LIVING IN *TERROR.*

"IT IS TIME TO FIGHT *BACK*."

DRIFT TWO AND THREE ENGAGING.

GO FOR HIS *JOINTS*, TULA.

VUMMMM

WHAT A *STRANGE* MACHINE.

TINK

‹GG›

C'MON, DOC!

TAKE A DEEP BREATH. THE FIRST TIME ALWAYS HURTS.

FIRST TIME--?

BOOOOOM

KRAKOOM

YOU ARE SENTENCED TO THE *DARK WATERS*, BROTHER.

BOOOOOM

WH-WHERE... WHERE ARE WE?

THE JUSTICE LEAGUE SATELLITE.

THE *WATCHTOWER*?

YOU'LL BE SAFE HERE. YOU AND VULKO CAN COMPARE NOTES. SEE IF WE--

WE HAVE TO DO SOMETHING, CYBORG.

YOU HAVE TO HELP ARTHUR AND THE OTHERS!

"THE ATLANTEANS HAVE TAKEN THE LEAGUE."

"WHERE?"

"INTO THE WATER."

MAY THEY SUFFER AS THE SURFACE WILL.

KRAK

KOOOMMM

WE SINK THIS CITY *TODAY*.

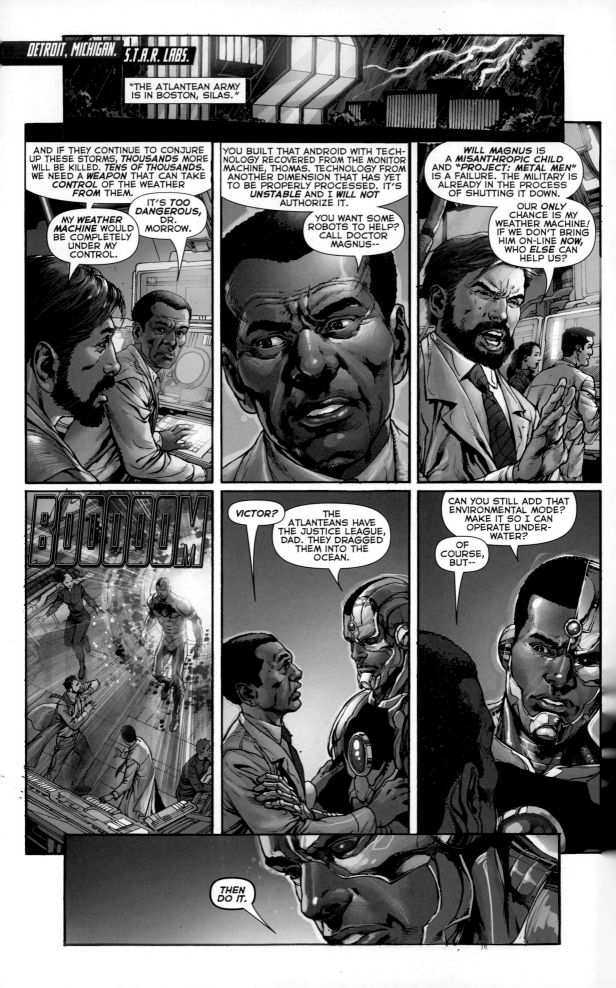

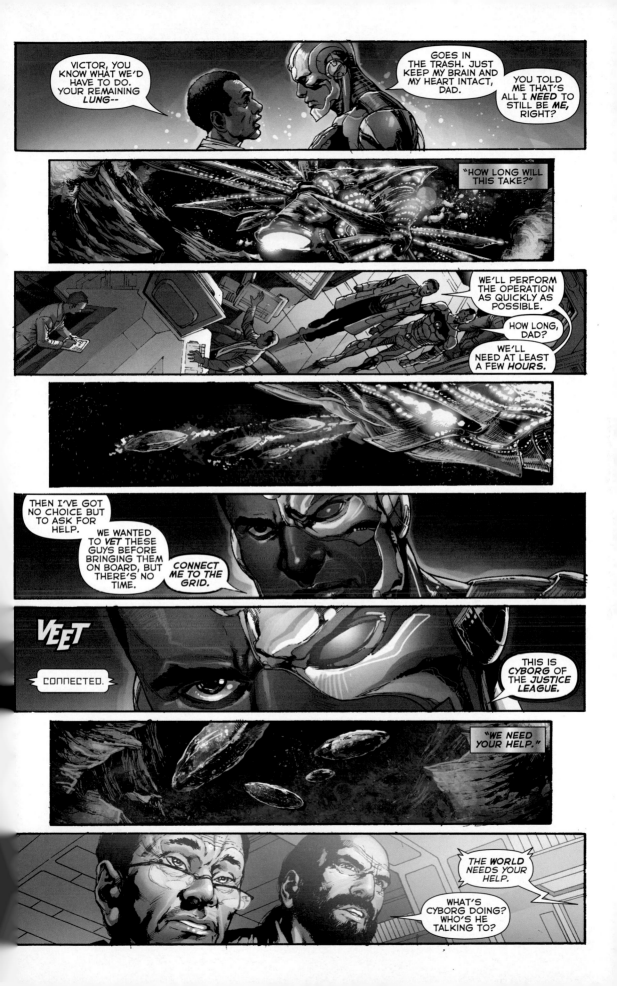

WE NEED TO MOVE QUICKLY, THOMAS.

WE WOULDN'T HAVE TO SUBJECT YOUR SON TO THIS *HORRIFIC* OPERATION IF YOU'D JUST AGREED TO LETTING ME *ACTIVATE* THE *ANDROID.*

I'M NOT HAVING THIS DISCUSSION *AGAIN,* THOMAS.

BUT THE TORNADO COULD--

WHAT IS THAT?

FILE PROCESSING.

VICTOR UPLOADED A *VIDEO SIGNAL* OF SOME KIND.

HIS MIND'S GONE DORMANT, BUT HE'S STILL RUNNING A PROGRAM.

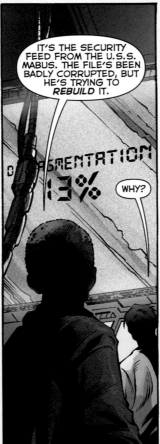

IT'S THE SECURITY FEED FROM THE U.S.S. MABUS. THE FILE'S BEEN BADLY CORRUPTED, BUT HE'S TRYING TO *REBUILD* IT.

DEFRAGMENTATION 13%

WHY?

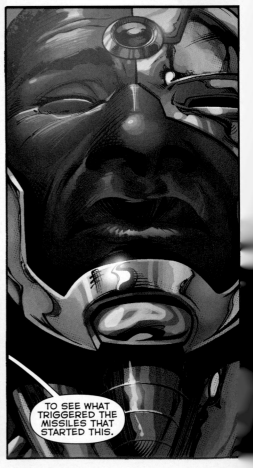

TO SEE WHAT TRIGGERED THE MISSILES THAT STARTED THIS.

--THE LEAGUE WAS LAST SEEN FIGHTING AQUAMAN BEFORE THEY *VANISHED!*

WE CAN ONLY SPECULATE AS TO WHAT'S GOING ON OUT THERE, BUT IT APPEARS AQUAMAN'S SIDING WITH *ATLANTIS* IN THIS ATTACK.

YOU ASK ME, HE WAS PROBABLY *PLANNING* THIS FROM THE BEGINNING! SINCE HE *JOINED* THE JUSTICE LEAGUE!

THEY'RE TWISTING THINGS. ARTHUR WOULD *NEVER* BETRAY US.

BUT *YOU* BETRAYED HIM BEFORE, DIDN'T YOU?

BECAUSE YOU DESPERATELY WANTED TO BE *CREDITED* FOR THE DISCOVERY OF ATLANTIS' EXISTENCE.

AND NOW YOU *WILL* BE.

YOU APPEAR TO BE A BROKEN OLD MAN, BUT LOOKS CAN BE DECEIVING, CAN'T THEY? ARTHUR TOLD ME ALL ABOUT YOU DURING THE VERY FIRST DAYS I *SERVED* HIM.

WHO *ARE* YOU?

MY NAME IS *VULKO*--FORMER ADVISOR TO THE *THRONE OF ATLANTIS* AND LOYAL TO *KING ARTHUR* UNTIL THE END.

IF YOU WERE JUDGED IN ATLANTIS FOR YOUR CRIMES AGAINST THE KING, YOU WOULD'VE BEEN EXECUTED. INSTEAD, ARTHUR SENDS CYBORG TO *SAVE* YOU FROM DEATH.

EVEN AFTER EVERYTHING YOU'VE DONE, HE STILL PROTECTS YOU. THAT IS *TRUE* HEROISM. *TRUE* VALOR.

YOU HAVE NONE OF THAT, DO YOU?

KEEP YOUR DISTANCE.

ARTHUR AND HIS LEAGUE ARE *LOST!* THE ATLANTEANS PULLED THEM INTO THE WATER!

WHERE DID THEY TAKE THEM?

ORM HAS GIVEN THEM A *DEATH SENTENCE.*

"HE'S BANISHED THEM TO THE DARK WATERS."

AQUAMAN?

BATMAN?

YOU OKAY?

MY REGULATOR IS ADJUSTING THE OXYGEN LEVELS TO *AVOID* TOXICITY, AND I'VE ACTIVATED A *BEACON* TO ALERT CYBORG, THOUGH *VOICE COMMUNICATION* ISN'T GETTING THROUGH. WE MUST BE ON THE OTHER SIDE OF THE THERMOCLINE.

MY SUIT CAN HANDLE EXTREME PRESSURES.

NOT THIS EXTREME, BRUCE.

LASER CUTTER SHOULD GET ME OUT--

I'D RECOMMEND SITTING TIGHT. THE PODS ARE DESIGNED TO KEEP THE IMPRISONED *ALIVE* SO THEY'RE MAINTAINING PRESSURE.

HOW DEEP ARE WE?

BOTTOM OF THE OCEAN. MAYBE FURTHER. I'M GOING TO GATHER WHAT BIOLUMINESCENT FISH I CAN TO LIGHT UP THE AREA.

WE DON'T NEED LIGHT TO SEE WHERE WE ARE.

YOU HAVE A *POWER* I DON'T KNOW ABOUT?

THIS ISN'T THE FIRST TIME I'VE BEEN TRAPPED IN A CONFINED SPACE.

VUU VUUVUU VUU VUU

SUBSONIC EMITTERS WILL HELP MAP THE AREA. OUR JUSTICE LEAGUE COMMUNICATORS CAN CONSTRUCT A THREE-DIMENSIONAL HOLOGRAM OF IT.

SONAR?

NEVER LEAVE HOME WITHOUT IT.

WE'RE IN THE MID-ATLANTIC TRENCH.

THIS IS WHERE THE MAN-EATING CREATURES I TOLD YOU ABOUT CAME FROM.

THAT'S WHY THEY WANT US IN THESE PODS ALIVE?

EATEN ALIVE. ANCIENT ATLANTEAN PUNISHMENT. THOUGH USUALLY BY SHARKS.

ANY SIGN OF SUPERMAN OR WONDER WOMAN?

BELOW US, I THINK.

I THOUGHT WE WERE AT THE BOTTOM OF THE TRENCH.

THERE'S SOMETHING ELSE CARVED DOWN INTO THE ROCK. IT LOOKS LIKE A TEMPLE OF SOME KIND.

IS IT ATLANTEAN?

POSSIBLY. I FOUND AN ANCIENT ATLANTEAN CRAFT DOWN HERE, BUT IT WAS CLEARLY LOST WHEN IT CRASHED.

SONAR'S PICKING UP SOMETHING APPROACH-ING.

FISH ARE HERE--

AQUAMAN?

HAWKMAN JUST SPLIT THAT GUY'S HEAD OPEN!

DON'T WORRY ABOUT HAWKMAN, RONNIE. CONCENTRATE ON TURNING THE WATER AROUND THESE ATLANTEANS INTO HELIUM.

TO MAKE THEM *TALK* FUNNY?

TO *DRY* THEM OUT. I READ THAT WAS AQUAMAN'S *KRYPTONITE.*

I WOULDN'T BELIEVE *ANYTHING* YOU READ ABOUT HIM NOW, JASON.

WATCH WHERE YOU'RE *FLYING* FIRESTORM!

WE NEED TO GET *ORGANIZED,* BLACK CANARY. WHERE'S BATMAN?

I DON'T KNOW, VIXEN. CAN'T YOU GET A *SCENT* ON HIM?

ALL I SMELL IS *SEAWATER.*

YOU ALL KEEP HOLDING BACK LIKE *CHILDREN* AND PEOPLE ARE GOING TO *DIE.*

WHO MADE *YOU* BOSS?

I, UH, I DON'T THINK WE'VE MET, BLACK LIGHTNING. I'M *ELEMENT WOMAN!* CAN YOU BELIEVE CYBORG CALLED US? THIS IS *SO EXCITING!*

REFUSE TO SPILL BLOOD IN A WAR AND YOU'RE GOING TO GET YOURSELVES *KILLED.*

GET DOWN, HAWKMAN!

BOOOOOMMMMM

SET *DETONATOR TWO* HERE.

HAWKMAN? HAWKMAN, *GET UP!*

MY BROTHER'S ALLIES WILL NOT STOP US FROM RETRIBUTION.

WHY DID I LEAVE MY GUILD FOR *THIS?*

RETRIBUTION FOR ALL THOSE *TORTURED,* *POISONED* AND *MURDERED* OVER THE CENTURIES BY THE SURFACE DWELLERS.

"THEY WILL KNOW THE *POWER OF ATLANTIS.*"

"AND THEY WILL FEAR *US* AS WE ONCE DID THEM."

I'M SORRY ABOUT MY PARENTS.

THEY WANT TO KNOW MORE ABOUT WHO THEIR DAUGHTER'S SPENDING TIME WITH. I *EXPECTED* THE THIRD DEGREE, SARAH.

BUT NOT *ADVICE* ON HOW TO TAKE THE LIONS TO THE PLAY-OFFS.

HE'S A FAN. AND AT LEAST *ONE* OF OUR FATHERS HAS *SOME* INTEREST IN WHAT I DO.

VICTOR?

IT'S TIME TO WAKE UP.

NO. PLEASE.

JUST A LITTLE LONG--

VICTOR?

I'M BACK ONLINE.

YOUR SYSTEM WILL SUPPLY THE OXYGEN YOUR BRAIN NEEDS NOW. YOU CAN SURVIVE IN WATER OR IN SPACE. NOTHING CAN HURT YOU.

YEAH.

THE RESERVES YOU CALLED IN TO HELP ARE SLOWING ATLANTIS DOWN.

THAT'S ALL I NEED THEM TO DO. GRID, KEEP ME UPDATED ON THEIR PROGRESS.

AFFIRMITIVE.

VICTOR? THE FILE YOU'RE WORKING ON--

THANKS FOR THE HELP, DAD. TELL SARAH HELLO FOR ME.

I'VE GOT A LOCK ON BATMAN'S BEACON.

THEN LET'S GO GET THEM.

CAN YOU SEE THE WALLS OF THIS TUNNEL?

NOT VERY WELL, WHY?

THERE'S SOMETHING ON THEM.

FEELS LIKE AN ENGRAVING.

GET ME CLOSER AND I CAN PROBABLY GET AN IMAGE.

SOME KIND OF HIEROGLYPHICS. A LANGUAGE I DON'T RECOGNIZE--

MOST LIKELY ANCIENT ATLANTEAN. NO ONE EVER THOUGHT THEY'D JOURNEYED THIS DEEP.

THERE'S AN IMAGE OF A *MAN* HOLDING A *SCEPTER.* HE'S WEARING A CROWN.

A KING?

AND HE'S STRIKING THE GROUND, TRIGGERING SOME KIND OF EARTHQUAKE.

I TAKE IT THIS IS THE SCEPTER YOU WERE TALKING ABOUT.

YES. I CAN FEEL THE OUTLINE OF IT. AND THERE'S SOMETHING ELSE.

AN IMAGE OF THIS KING... AND THOSE CREATURES.

FIGHTING THEM?

NO.

HE'S *LEADING* THEM, AQUAMAN.

WHAT COULD THE TRENCH HAVE TO DO WITH AN *ATLANTEAN* KING?

THE REST LOOKS LIKE IT'S SCRATCHED OFF... BROKEN OPEN AND LEADING INTO...

THE CHAMBER...

BOOODOOM

WHAT THE HELL *ARE* THOSE THINGS?

UNFRIENDLY.

VUMMMMMM

THEY DON'T LIKE *LOUD NOISE.*

KROOOMMM

MERA? HOW DID YOU FIND US?

CYBORG LOCKED ONTO BATMAN'S SIGNAL. IT WAS FAINT, BUT IT WAS ACTIVE.

HELP ME OPEN THESE PODS, MERA. VIC, MAKE SURE BATMAN'S STAYS *SHUT*.

YOU'RE DOWN HERE, VIC? YOU ACTUALLY WENT *THROUGH* WITH IT?

YOU NEEDED ME.

A-ARTHUR?

THE PRESSURE COMBINED WITH THAT SLIME IS GOING TO BE A SHOCK TO BOTH OF YOUR SYSTEMS.

YOU SHOULD RETURN TO NORMAL MOMENTARILY, SUPERMAN.

WE NEED TO SWIM UP SO I CAN CONNECT WITH THE SATELLITE. WITHOUT A LINK, I CAN'T JUMP US BACK TO BOSTON.

YOU SHOULD'VE STAYED... FOUGHT THEM...

I CALLED IN SOME *RESERVES* TO HELP.

RESERVES?

WE WERE SUPPOSED TO CLEAR THOSE WITH THE REST OF THE TEAM, VIC. WITH ME. HAWKMAN, ESPECIALLY--

NO TIME, BATMAN.

"I HAD TO GET WHO I *COULD*."

THOSE CREATURES MIGHT HAVE BEEN FRIGHTENED OFF, BUT THEY'LL BE BACK. AND THERE WILL BE *MORE*.

THERE SHOULD BE, MERA, BUT I DON'T SENSE ANY.

BUT ARUTHUR--

MY KING?

WHAT IS IT?

"--IF YOU CAN'T SENSE THEM--"

THERE'S SOMETHING COMING OUT OF THE WATER BEHIND US.

IF THEY AREN'T HERE...

MY BROTHER MUST BE *CONTROLLING* THOSE MONSTERS.

"HOW COULD ORM DO THAT?"

AAIIEE!

KRAKK-ZTTT

WHAT *CREATURES* ARE THESE?

"WITH THE ATLANTEAN RELIC--THE SCEPTER. BATMAN AND I FOUND SOME IMAGES DOWN THERE THAT SUGGEST IT NOT ONLY HAS THE POWER TO *SINK* CONTINENTS BUT TO *COMMAND* THOSE CREATURES."

...SIGHTINGS NOW OF *ANOTHER* ARMY COMING OUT OF THE WATER...

THE TRENCH.

IF ORM HAS A *SCEPTER* THAT CAN *SINK* LAND, WHY IS HE PLANTING DETONATION DEVICES IN BOSTON TO DO IT?

WHY NOT USE THE SCEPTER HIMSELF?

DEFRAGMENTATION COMPLETE.

VOET

DEFRAGMENTATION COMPLETE

SILAS?

"WHO *IS* THAT?"

DR. SHIN.

ARTHUR, THE SECURITY VIDEO FROM THE U.S.S. MABUS...I'VE GOT IT.

I BLAME *YOU* FOR THIS.

WHAT ARE YOU DOING?

YOU *ENTANGLED* ARTHUR IN A GAME OF *REVENGE* AGAINST BLACK MANTA. YOU TURNED THE WORLD *AGAINST* HIM.

ORM ISN'T USING THE SCEPTER, BECAUSE HE DOESN'T HAVE IT.

AND WHEN HE LEFT ATLANTIS, THEY TURNED AGAINST *ME.*

SOMEONE ELSE STARTED THIS WAR.

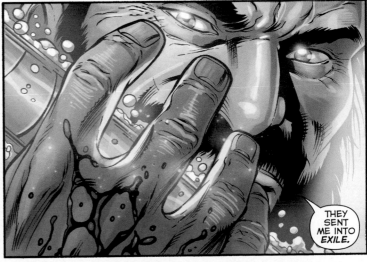

THEY SENT ME INTO *EXILE.*

THRONE OF ATLANTIS chapter five
GEOFF JOHNS writer IVAN REIS & PAUL PELLETIER pencillers JOE PRADO, OCLAIR ALBERT & SEAN PARSONS inkers cover by IVAN REIS, JOE PRADO & ROD REIS
EPILOGUE
GEOFF JOHNS & JEFF LEMIRE writers BRAD WALKER penciller DREW HENNESSY inker

BUT IT'S TOO LATE FOR WARNINGS.

DOCTOR SHIN?

FAR TOO LATE.

CYBORG-- WHERE'S VULKO?

NOT HERE. AND THE TELEPORTER'S HISTORY HAS BEEN WIPED.

WE CAN ONLY WONDER WHAT ROLE AQUAMAN PLAYED IN ALL OF THIS!

THIS WAR IS *MY* FAULT.

WHY WOULD ARTHUR'S *FRIEND* WANT TO START A WAR WITH ATLANTIS?

BECAUSE VULKO WAS *EXILED* AFTER ARTHUR LEFT THE THRONE, SUPERMAN. I'D GUESS HE'S LOOKING FOR REVENGE-- THOUGH I *ADMIT* I MAY BE *PROJECTING.*

WHAT DID THEY DO TO *YOU*, MERA?

IT'S WHAT THEY DID TO MY ANCESTORS.

MY GOD!

SOMETHING ELSE IS EMERGING FROM THE WATER!

VULKO'S GOTTEN ATLANTIS WHERE THEY'RE MOST VULNERABLE AND HE'S USING THE DEAD KING'S SCEPTER TO SEND *THE TRENCH* AFTER THEM.

ARE YOU ALL RIGHT?

IT WAS *VULKO*, ARTHUR. HE SABOTAGED THE WARSHIP. *HE* SENT THOSE MISSLES TO ATLANTIS.

HE *STARTED* THIS *WAR*.

YOU DIDN'T *ATTACK* ATLANTIS, ARTHUR.

AND YOU DIDN'T *DROWN* HUNDREDS OF PEOPLE.

I LEFT ATLANTIS IN MY BROTHER *ORM'S* HANDS, WONDER WOMAN, KNOWING FULL WELL HOW HE FELT ABOUT THE SURFACE WORLD--AND WHAT THE PLAN WAS IF WE EVER WENT TO WAR.

ATLANTIS WAS *MY* RESPONSIBILITY.

BUT A WAR WITH ATLANTIS *ISN'T*.

IT'S THE RESPONSIBILITY OF *ALL* OF US.

"THIS IS WHY THE JUSTICE LEAGUE EXISTS."

IF WE WORK TOGETHER, WE CAN PUSH THE TRENCH *BACK* INTO THE OCEAN. YOU CAN STILL MAKE THE *RIGHT* DECISION. YOU CAN STILL BE THE *KING* WE *NEED* RIGHT NOW.

TELL THE ATLANTEANS TO STAND DOWN AND--

WAMMM

STOP *TREATING* ME LIKE A *FOOL.*

KRRKKZZTT

AAAHH!

COME ON, ARTHUR.

WHAT ARE YOU WAITING FOR?

"EVEN IF VULKO *WAS* RESPONSIBLE FOR THIS, HIS ACTIONS WOULD ONLY *CONFIRM* THE POISONOUS NATURE OF THE SURFACE WORLD."

KRZKKKKTTT

YOUR LOYALTY LIES WITH THE SURFACE NOW--YOU CHOSE *THIS* WORLD OVER YOUR *OWN*--AND THEREFORE YOU'VE *BETRAYED* YOUR BROTHER, YOUR MOTHER AND ALL OF ATLANTIS.

ON MY COMMAND--

"--DETONATE!"

SOMETHING'S *WRONG.* IT'S NOT RESPONDING.

WHAT DID YOU DO, VICTOR?

IT WASN'T *ME,* MERA. SOMEONE ELSE SHUT IT DOWN.

YOU'RE WELCOME.

WONDER WOMAN, THERE'S A *SECOND* BOMB--

SUPERMAN AND I HAVE IT, CYBORG.

KKRAKKOOOMM

THAT *CONVICT* CAN'T HOLD THE *WATER* UP FOREVER.

RETAW OT ECI.

"SHE WON'T HAVE TO."

I WAS AS *HAPPY* AS YOU TO DISCOVER I HAD A BROTHER, ORM.

TO FEEL LIKE I WASN'T SO *ALONE.*

"BUT I *AM* ALONE."

THAT'S THE LIFE OF A *TRUE* LEADER.

"...I TRULY AM."

...CLEAN-UP IN BOSTON, METROPOLIS AND GOTHAM AS FUNERALS FOR THE PEOPLE LOST CONTINUE.

THE *TERRORIST* BEHIND THIS, THE *MONSTROUS "OCEAN MASTER,"* IS BEING HELD IN BELLE REVE PRISON AWAITING TRIAL.

HELLO? HELLO, ARE YOU STILL *THERE?* I'M THIRSTY AGAIN.

AND I WANT TO TALK TO MY *BROTHER.*

PLEASE. PLEASE LET ME TALK TO HIM.

I DON'T BELONG HERE.

BUT I HAVE TO GO.

THE LAST TIME YOU TOOK THE CROWN, THE ATLANTEANS NEARLY *KILLED* YOU FOR IT.

IF I REFUSE TO TAKE THE THRONE NOW, WHAT DOES ATLANTIS DO *NEXT?* DO THEY *STORM* THE BEACHES *AGAIN* TO BREAK OUT MY BROTHER?

MY BROTHER WHO IS *CONFUSED* AND *FRIGHTENED* AND--

AND *UNREMORSEFUL* ABOUT THE PEOPLE WHO *DIED,* ARTHUR. DON'T MAKE HIM A *MARTYR* LIKE MOST OF THE OTHER ATLANTEANS WILL. AND DON'T MAKE *YOURSELF* A MARTYR, EITHER.

DON'T GO. PLEASE, DON'T GO.

IT'S THE *LAST* THING I WANT TO DO... BUT I CAN'T RISK THIS HAPPENING AGAIN. I'VE BEEN PUSHING THESE TWO WORLDS APART MY ENTIRE LIFE, BUT I NEED TO BRING THEM *TOGETHER* SOMEHOW.

COME *WITH* ME.

YOU KNOW WHY I CAN'T.

"CAN YOU TELL US WHAT THE *FUTURE* HOLDS FOR ATLANTIS?"

ARE THEY OUR **ENEMIES**, DOCTOR SHIN? WILL THEY ATTACK AGAIN?

HOW LONG HAVE YOU **KNOWN** ABOUT THEIR EXISTENCE?

PEOPLE CALLED YOU **CRAZY**. DO YOU FEEL VINDICATED?

NO.

YOU SAW HOW HE **HIT** SUPERMAN. HE WAS **OUT OF CONTROL**.

MY KIDS WON'T GO IN THE **WATER**. **NO ONE** WILL.

I NEVER THOUGHT I'D SAY THIS, BUT...

...HE'S **DANGEROUS**.

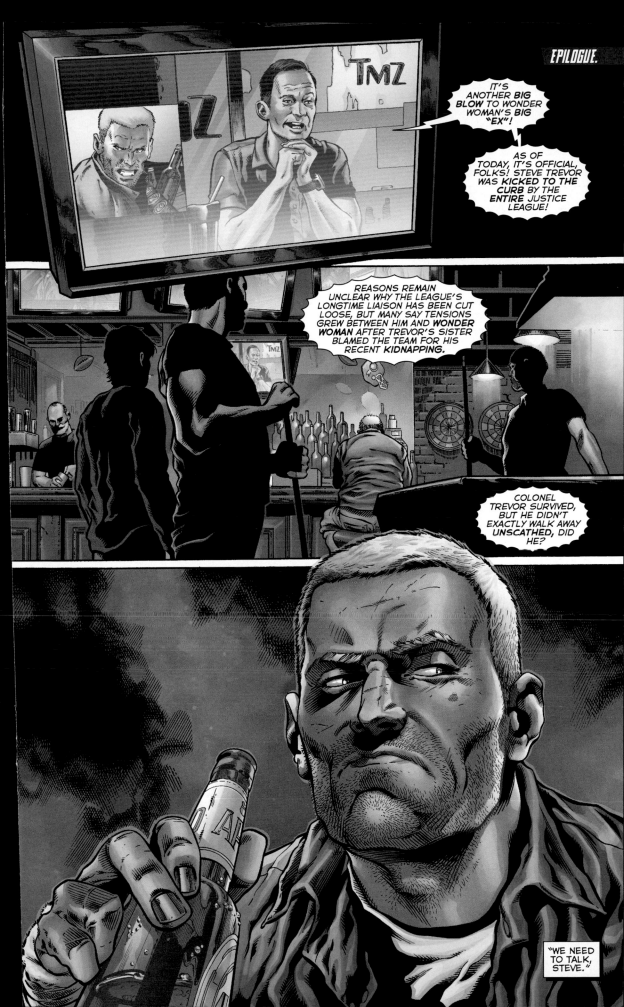

IT'S ANOTHER *BIG BLOW* TO WONDER WOMAN'S BIG "EX"!

AS OF TODAY, IT'S OFFICIAL, FOLKS! STEVE TREVOR WAS *KICKED TO THE CURB* BY THE *ENTIRE JUSTICE LEAGUE!*

REASONS REMAIN UNCLEAR WHY THE LEAGUE'S LONGTIME LIAISON HAS BEEN CUT LOOSE, BUT MANY SAY TENSIONS GREW BETWEEN HIM AND *WONDER WOMAN* AFTER TREVOR'S SISTER BLAMED THE TEAM FOR HIS RECENT *KIDNAPPING.*

COLONEL TREVOR SURVIVED, BUT HE DIDN'T EXACTLY WALK AWAY UNSCATHED, DID HE?

"WE NEED TO TALK, STEVE."

VARIANT COVER GALLERY

JUSTICE LEAGUE 13
By Alex Garner

JUSTICE LEAGUE 14
By Jason Fabok & Alex Sinclair

JUSTICE LEAGUE 15
By Jim Lee, Scott Williams & Alex Sinclair

AQUAMAN 15
By Jim Lee, Scott Williams & Alex Sinclair

JUSTICE LEAGUE 15
By Billy Tucci & Hi-Fi

JUSTICE LEAGUE 16
By Langdon Foss & Jose Villarrubia

JUSTICE LEAGUE 17
By Steve Skroce & Alex Sinclair

DC COMICS™

"Welcoming to new fans looking to get into superhero comics for the first time and old fans who gave up on the funny-books long ago."
—SCRIPPS HOWARD NEWS SERVICE

START AT THE BEGINNING!

JUSTICE LEAGUE VOLUME 1:ORIGIN

AQUAMAN
VOLUME 1:
THE TRENCH

THE SAVAGE
HAWKMAN VOLUME 1:
DARKNESS RISING

GREEN ARROW
VOLUME 1:
THE MIDAS TOUCH

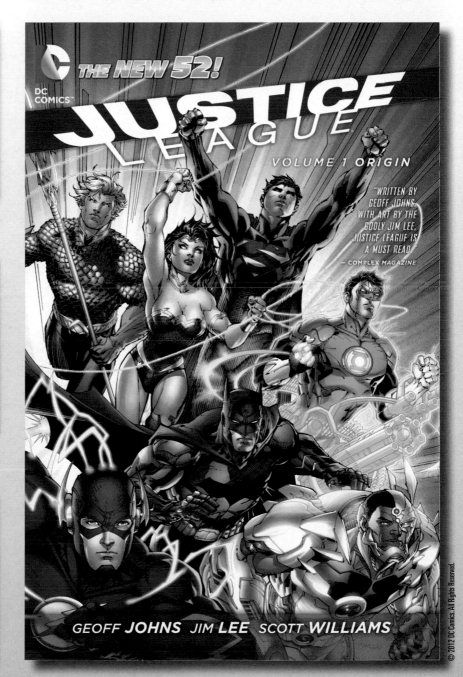

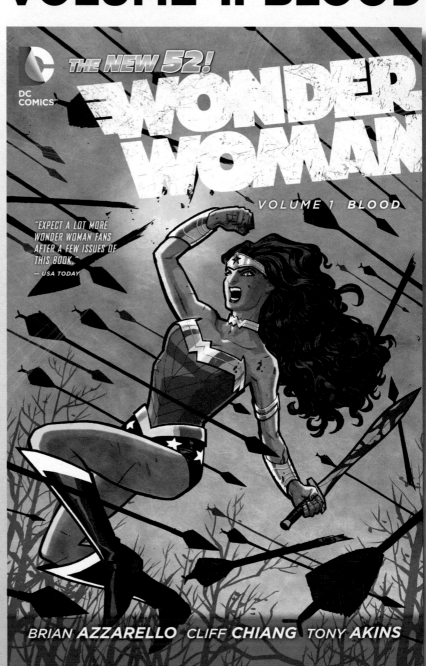

"This is the perfect place for people wary of the Green Lantern to start reading his adventures in order to see just how dynamic his world really is."
—COMPLEX MAGAZINE

START AT THE BEGINNING!
GREEN LANTERN
VOLUME 1: SINESTRO

GREEN LANTERN CORPS VOLUME 1: FEARSOME

RED LANTERNS VOLUME 1: BLOOD AND RAGE

GREEN LANTERN: NEW GUARDIANS VOLUME 1: THE RING BEARER

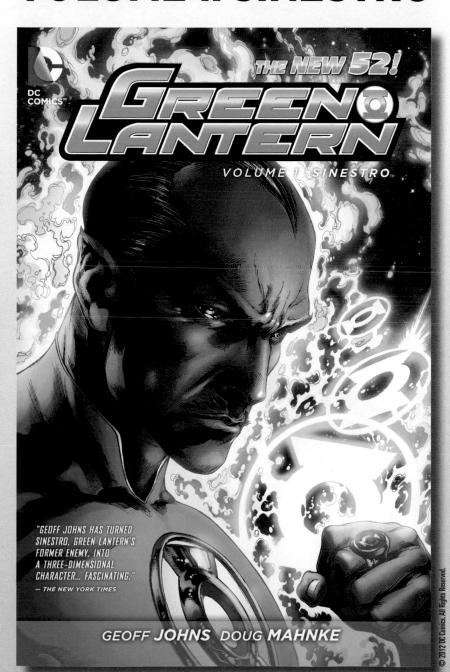

"GEOFF JOHNS HAS TURNED SINESTRO, GREEN LANTERN'S FORMER ENEMY, INTO A THREE-DIMENSIONAL CHARACTER... FASCINATING."
— THE NEW YORK TIMES

GEOFF **JOHNS** DOUG **MAHNKE**

DC COMICS™

START AT THE BEGINNING!
THE FLASH
VOLUME 1: MOVE FORWARD

JUSTICE LEAGUE INTERNATIONAL VOLUME 1: THE SIGNAL MASTERS

O.M.A.C. VOLUME 1: OMACTIVATE!

CAPTAIN ATOM VOLUME 1: EVOLUTION

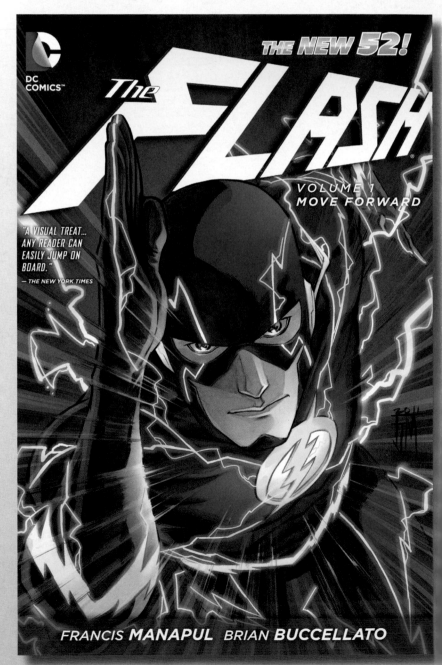

FRANCIS **MANAPUL** BRIAN **BUCCELLATO**